CONTENTS

ACKNOWLEDGMENTS

The assistance given by A. C. Miller and R. Hendrie in the preparation of data, computer programming and data processing is gratefully acknowledged.

FORESTRY COMMISSION BULLETIN
No. 52

ASANAETH LLYFRGELL A. WYDDOR GTH

Influence of Spacing on
Crop Characteristics & Yield

By
G. J. HAMILTON, M. Sc. and J. M. CHRISTIE

LONDON: HER MAJESTY'S STATIONERY OFFICE
1974

A

© Crown copyright 1974

ISBN 0 11 710144 3

I. INTRODUCTION

The early recognition of the importance to the Forestry Commission of plant spacing was reflected in the establishment of a small number of spacing experiments during the period 1921–24. Subsequent experiments in spacing, with few exceptions, originated in the years 1935–36 when a large number of experiments were established throughout Britain, covering the major commercial species. Although the main effects of spacing have been generally appreciated, the experiments have never been satisfactorily analysed.

The analysis described in this paper was designed to provide quantitative information on the effects of spacing on yield and the components of yield. It is preceded by a brief review of the more important features of the history of these spacing experiments.

II. HISTORY OF FORESTRY COMMISSION SPACING EXPERIMENTS

The earlier experiments established in the period 1921–24 ranged from 1·07 x 1·07 m (3½ x 3½ ft) to 2·7 x 2·7 m (9 x 9 ft) spacings. Each experiment consisted of an unreplicated series of three or four plots of varying spacings. The actual spacings employed usually differed between series. In total there were eleven series, all of which were the responsibility of Research Branch.

The more important 1935–36 series were laid down by the territorial Divisions (now Conservancies) at the request of the Research Branch. In some cases two or three replications were established at the same site but single series predominate. The most useful feature of these experiments is that, with very few exceptions, common spacings were used.

The four spacings comprising a series were:

> 0·91 m x 0·91 m – (3 ft x 3 ft)
> 1·37 m x 1·37 m – (4½ ft x 4½ ft)
> 1·83 m x 1·83 m – (6 ft x 6 ft)
> 2·44 m x 2·44 m – (8 ft x 8 ft)

(Henceforth the metric equivalents used are 0·9, 1·4, 1·8 and 2·4.)

In the larch and Douglas fir series in the south, the two closer spacings were usually replaced by one spacing of 1·22 m x 1·22 m (4 ft x 4 ft). The allocation of spacings within a series was rarely randomised, and this has proved a deficiency. In total some 134 series were known to have been established in this period.

A survey of the spacing experiments was carried out in 1949 by the Research Branch (Rowan and Skinner, 1949) and this revealed that a substantial number of the experiments had been destroyed by fire, lack of weeding, deer damage, etc., or were in other ways so unsatisfactory that they were discontinued as experiments.

In 1953 approximately 100 series were recorded as being viable. At this time a plan was prepared for the subsequent treatment of the series. Three distinct treatments were proposed, denoted by the letters P, Q and R. These are described below.

'P' Treatments

Each of the four (or three) spacings in each series were to be thinned to a common stand density index (SDI) which would be similar to that achieved by 'C/D' grade thinnings (Hummel, 1954) in conventionally spaced crops. The original schedule (in Imperial units) is given in Table 1. This plan has broadly been adhered to, except for minor modifications.

'Q' Treatment

The object of the Q treatments was to maintain the growth differences apparent at the time of first thinning. In effect this meant a B grade thinning (removal of dead and dying trees only) in the 0·9 x 0·9 m spacing, a moderate C/D grade in the 1·4 x 1·4 m spacing, a heavy 'D' grade thinning in the 1·8 x 1·8 m spacing and a very heavy 'E' grade thinning in the 2·4 x 2·4 m spacing.

Pruning treatments were also incorporated, except in the 0·9 m spacings. Two hundred selected trees per acre were to be pruned in the 1·4 m and 1·8 m spacings, and one hundred and fifty per acre in the 2·4 m spacing.

'R' Treatment

In these plots no thinning or minimal 'A' grade thinning (dead trees only) was proposed.

Where two or three series had been established at the same location it was usually the case that a different treatment was applied to each series. The

TABLE 1

THINNING SCHEDULE FOR SPACING EXPERIMENTS – 'P' TREATMENTS
Number of stems or stand density after thinning at top heights specified:

Spacing ft.	Initial No. per acre	20 ft. all Species	25 ft.		30ft.			40 ft.	40 ft. + Stand Density Index	50 ft. + Stand Density Index
			Larch	Other	Larch	Pine	Douglas fir, Spruce	Douglas fir, Spruce		
3	4840	2500	1200	1800	500	1400	1500	1100	All spacings	All spacings
4½	2150	—	1000	1500	750	1200	1300	1000	Larch 0.4	
6	1210	—	—	—	600	1000	1100	900	Scots pine 0.55	Spruce & Douglas fir 0.75
8	680	—	—	—	450	—	—	—	Corsican pine 0.65	

Stand Density Index is obtained as follows:
(No. of trees per acre × mean b.h.g. (true measure in inches) × top height (ft.)) ÷ 1,000,000

allocation of treatments to the series resulted in about half of the total being 'P' series. About 30% were designated 'Q' series and less than 10% were 'R' series. The remainder were excluded from the general scheme for various reasons.

The result of these treatments has been to produce widely differing crop types. Since the 1953 plan was prepared, and in a few cases before that time, most of the series in the southern half of England and in Wales were taken over and managed as permanent sample plots by the Mensuration Section, whereas the series in the north of England and Scotland, with a few more recent exceptions, have remained the responsibility of the Silviculture (North) Section. As a result there has been different emphasis on certain features of assessment, and this fact has a bearing on the method of analysis which has been used.

Until now no complete analysis of the yield aspects of the experimental data has been available. The Rowan and Skinner report of 1949 was of necessity confined to the early effects of spacing, e.g. survival, early height growth, canopy closure, suppression of vegetation and branch suppression.

From time to time, some raw data has been extracted from some of the Mensuration Section series to meet specific needs. A number of 'P' series in spruce in the north of England and in Scotland were analysed by Hamilton (1964) but the results were not published.

The only spacing experiments other than respacing experiments (Hamilton, 1972) – laid down since the 1935/6 series, have been in poplar. These are considered separately on page 42. The main analysis described here concerns six species; Scots pine, Sitka spruce, Norway spruce, European larch, Japanese larch and Douglas fir.

III. ANALYSES

1. General

Only data from the 1935/36 experiments have been used in the analyses. Data from earlier spacing experiments has inevitably been excluded because the spacings used in these experiments differed between series and were therefore not comparable.

The effects of spacing on individual parameters have been analysed independently. The overall picture of the effect of spacing has been subsequently derived by synthesising the results of the individual analyses. The data used in the analysis of any one component has been confined to those plots providing reliable information on that component. Since there are many plots which have not produced data on one or more particular aspects of yield, the weight of information varies appreciably from one parameter to another.

The following aspects of spacing have been separately analysed:

- a. Mortality
- b. Height growth
- c. Basal area production
- d. Volume production
- e. Mean diameter at breast height (dbh)
- f. Form and taper
- g. Assortments.

These aspects have then been combined in yield models, depicting the overall effect of spacing. A 'master table' technique has been used in preparing these models, which means that all parameters have in the first instance been related to top height. Rate of growth (yield class) has subsequently been superimposed.

Some difficulty has been experienced in separating the effects of spacing from that of subsequent thinning. This is particularly true of the 'Q' treatments where not only are these treatments extreme, but the yield aspects are further confounded by the green pruning incorporated in the treatments. For this reason the post-thinning data of the 'Q' treatment series has largely been discounted. A further difficulty arises from the fact that relatively few measurements (frequently only one) were made before thinning was carried out.

Site differences are evident in many of the series. This problem has been overcome to some extent by relating parameters to height in the first instance. The error thus attached to the comparison of various parameters is dependent on the reliability of establishing the effects of spacing on height. Fortunately, reliable data on height are available from all the series, and the number of experiments for any one species is generally almost sufficient to nullify the effects of site in the case of Scots pine, Sitka spruce, Norway spruce and Japanese larch. This is not the case in Douglas fir and European larch and the analysis of these species has inevitably been limited. No yield models are presented for European larch and Douglas fir.

All records are in Imperial units and the analyses have been completed mostly in these units. The final presentation, however, is in metric units.

The experiments used in the analyses are listed in Appendix I, page 46.

2. Mortality

Rowan and Skinner (1949) reported on survival in the 1935/6 series in the thicket and pre-thicket stages of growth, and concluded that prior to canopy closure survival was independent of spacing. Thereafter it was recognised that competition, which set in earlier in the closer spacings, resulted in a higher number of deaths in these plots. That this situation continues to the time of first thinning can be seen from Table 2 below. This shows the percentage survival at an average top height of 10 m.

TABLE 2

SURVIVAL (AT 10 m TOP HT) AS PERCENTAGE OF ORIGINAL STOCKINGS

Species	Spacing				
	0·9 m	1·4 m	1·8 m	2·4 m	Number of Series
Scots pine	48	66	79	84	13
Sitka spruce	57	74	88	94	14
Norway spruce	54	72	85	93	19
European larch	—	62*	80	88	6
Japanese larch	48	65*	85	90	13
Douglas fir	53	71*	88	94	5
Original stocking (stems/ha)	11960	5315 (6726)*	2990	1682	

*1·2 m spacing (4 ft)

To produce a more complete picture of mortality patterns and rates, periodic information is required from unthinned spacing experiments. The main difficulty here is that relatively few measurements are recorded for the unthinned 'R' treatment experiments, which are in any case few in number.

The slender information which is available for Scots pine, Sitka spruce and Norway spruce has been used to prepare Figure 1 which shows the pattern of mortality over an extended top height range. The curves have inevitably been drawn free-hand and the element of error is considerable. Reference has been made, however, to mortality patterns in other unthinned permanent sample plots of known spacings in assessing the pattern of these curves.

3. Height

Top height, defined as the mean height of the 250 trees of largest diameter at breast height (dbh) per hectare (the current convention is the mean height of the 100 trees of largest dbh per hectare) has been measured in virtually all the spacing series and frequently at two or three assessments. The body of information available on this parameter is therefore substantial, and exceeds that on any other.

The height range, over which each plot has been measured, tends to be variable and this has created problems in analysis. Figure 2 has been prepared by first calculating, at the common ages of each assessment, the average top height of the four spacings in each Scots pine series. The difference between the actual top height in each plot and the average of the series, of which it is part, has been plotted at each assessment and for each spacing. It is clear from this diagram that differences exist between spacings but the magnitude of these differences is somewhat obscure in such an illustration. It is also difficult to detect trends in these differences over the height range represented.

In order to establish these differences more precisely, a common mean top height of each series has been selected for each species at a point where the largest amount of information is available. In

Scots pine, for example, this was at 9·14 m (30 ft). In the few cases where a series had not been assessed at the common mean top height, the available data was extrapolated to cross this point.

Then, for each series, the top height deviation of each spacing from the mean top height of the series was calculated. The average deviation of each spacing was then calculated from the pooled data, and these are given in Table 3, together with the calculated average top heights for each spacing.

The closest spacing (0·9 m) plot is absent from most of the European larch, Japanese larch and Douglas fir series. Data from the few 1·4 m (4½ ft) spacings have been combined with that of the 1·2 m (4 ft) spacings and the mean top height calculated from three spacings only. The 0·9 m plot data has been related to the mean top height thus calculated, but is shown in brackets since it is from fewer plots.

Having established top height differences for each species at a common mean top height, the next stage required was to examine how these differences varied over an extended top height range. This was done in successive 1·52 m (5 ft) intervals of mean top height. For example, in Scots pine the common mean top height was 9·14 m. The next point considered was therefore 9·14 + 1·52 m = 10·66 m. The height difference of each plot, relative to the mean top height of the series, was then calculated at a mean top height of 10·66 m, extrapolating to this point if necessary but not beyond it. The slope of the line (regression coefficient) joining the height differences established at 9·14 and 10·66 m mean top height was established for each plot. By combining the regression coefficients of individual plots of a given spacing, an average slope was obtained over this top height interval.

Starting from the top height difference at the common height, these successive segments were simply joined together to form an extended regression of top height difference on mean top height – both

TABLE 3
DIFFERENCES IN TOP HEIGHT BETWEEN SPACINGS

Species	Common mean top ht (250) (m)	Deviations (m)				Mean Top Height (m)				No. of Series
		0·9 m	1·4 m	1·8 m	2·4 m	0·9 m	1·4 m	1·8 m	2·4 m	
Scots pine	9·1	+0·35	+0·14	+0·01	—0·51	9·45	9·24	9·11	8·59	16
Sitka spruce	12·2	+0·35	+0·12	+0·05	—0·48	12·55	12·32	12·25	11·72	12
Norway spruce	12·2	—0·04	+0·12	+0·10	—0·18	12·16	12·32	12·30	12·02	19
European larch	12·2	(—0·21)	—0·17*	+0·10	+0·14	(11·99)	12·03*	12·30	12·34	6
Japanese larch	13·7	(+0·13)	0·0*	+0·07	—0·14	(13·83)	13·70*	13·77	13·56	13
Douglas fir	15·2	(+0·09)	+0·79*	—0·43	—0·45	(15·11)	15·99*	14·77	14·75	4

*1·2/1·4 m combined

TABLE 4
TOP HEIGHT (100) RELATIVE TO COMMON MEAN TOP HEIGHT (250)

Species	Common mean top ht (250) (m)	Top height (100) (m)				No. of series
		0·9 m	1·4 m	1·8 m	2·4 m	
Scots pine	9·1	9·65	9·44	9·31	8·79	6
Sitka spruce	12·2	12·85	12·62	12·55	12·02	6
Norway spruce	12·2	12·51	12·67	12·65	12·37	5
European larch	12·2	(12·34)	12·38*	12·65	12·69	5
Japanese larch	13·7	(14·03)	13·90*	13·97	13·76	10
Douglas fir	15·2	(15·61)	16·49*	15·27	15·25	3

*1·2/1·4 m combined

below and above the common mean top height. An element of smoothing was introduced by averaging the slopes of each pair of successive segments, but always keeping the height difference established at the common mean top height constant. The results of this process are shown in Fig. 3. In the case of Scots pine a useful demonstration of the technique can be seen by comparing Fig. 2 and Fig. 3.

Two other expressions of height were considered. The expression of top height currently used in crop assessment in the Forestry Commission and in yield table construction is the mean height of the 100 largest (by dbh) trees per hectare, as compared with that of the 250 largest per hectare already discussed. Not all series contain direct information on the top height (100). Table 4 has been derived largely from the southern series, firstly by determining average differences between the top height (100) and top height (250) and applying these differences to the data in Table 3.

As in the case of top height (100), mean height data could only be obtained from the southern series. Table 5 shows mean height, again tabulated for each spacing against a common mean top height of all series for a given species.

The first comment that must be made about the results concerns their consistency. Clearly, from Fig. 3, it is apparent that reasonably consistent results are obtained from the Scots pine, Sitka spruce, Norway spruce and Japanese larch series, while the Douglas fir and European larch results give less indication of an identifiable relationship between spacing and height growth.

The fact that site differences plague many of the series has already been mentioned. This drawback can only be countered by an adequate number of replications, and it is no coincidence that in this respect both Douglas fir and European larch fall well short of the other species.

Of the remaining four species the general trend emerging is one showing greater top height with closer spacing. The 0·9 m spacing in Norway spruce is a notable exception to this trend, but is accountable by the fact that a significant number of the plots of this spacing have fallen on different site qualities

TABLE 5
MEAN HEIGHT RELATIVE TO COMMON MEAN TOP HEIGHT (250)

Species	Common mean top ht (250) (m)	Mean height (m)				No of Series
		0·9 m	1·4 m	1·8 m	2·4 m	
Scots pine	9·1	8·55	8·44	8·41	7·99	6
Sitka spruce	12·2	10·95	11·22	11·05	10·82	6
Norway spruce	12·2	10·46	10·92	11·10	11·12	5
European larch	12·2	(10·59)	10·83*	11·20	11·44	5
Japanese larch	13·7	(13·08)	13·00*	13·12	12·96	10
Douglas fir	15·2	(13·31)	14·39*	13·47	13·85	3

*1·2/1·4 m combined

from the other spacings in the series. The smoothed height differences are shown in Figure 4.

Regarding the question of whether these differences change with time, one must consider first the experimental error in assessing top height (demonstrated in Fig. 2) and secondly the fact that the extremities of the regressions carry least weight. The conclusion reached is that the differences are established by the time of the first assessment (6–8 m top height) and tend to remain constant thereafter.

There are two possible explanations for the top height differences. In the first place the planting stock could be expected to consist of varied genotypes and with a larger population on a given area in the closer spacings, the absolute number of better genotypes would naturally be higher. In this case, if one selected the best 5 genotypes per hectare from each spacing one would hardly expect the same order of average height differences as one could reasonably expect by comparing the average heights of the best 500 genotypes per hectare in each spacing. It was, nonetheless, found that the height differences remain of the same magnitude whether comparisons between spacings are made using top height (100) or top height (250). Another feature tending to cast doubt on the validity of this explanation is that the top height differences remain more or less constant beyond 6–8 m top height, whereas it might be expected that the inherent vigour of the better genotypes would, in time, accentuate the differences.

The second explanation concerns the early development of the crops where it has occasionally been observed that the closer spacings have been marginally more successful in suppressing competing vegetation.

It seems unlikely, and this is confirmed by experience with thinning experiments, that stand density in itself promotes greater height growth in dominants.

With greater stand densities at any given height it is well established that the proportion of the tree population occupying positions in the lower canopy is greater. Hence the differences between top height and mean height tend to be greater with closer spacings. This is confirmed by this analysis, and the data in Table 5 indicate that these differences offset the top height differences at about the normal time of first thinning. Lack of data and confounding thinning treatments deny adequate analysis of mean height beyond this point, where it would normally be expected that mean heights would eventually be greater in the wider spacings.

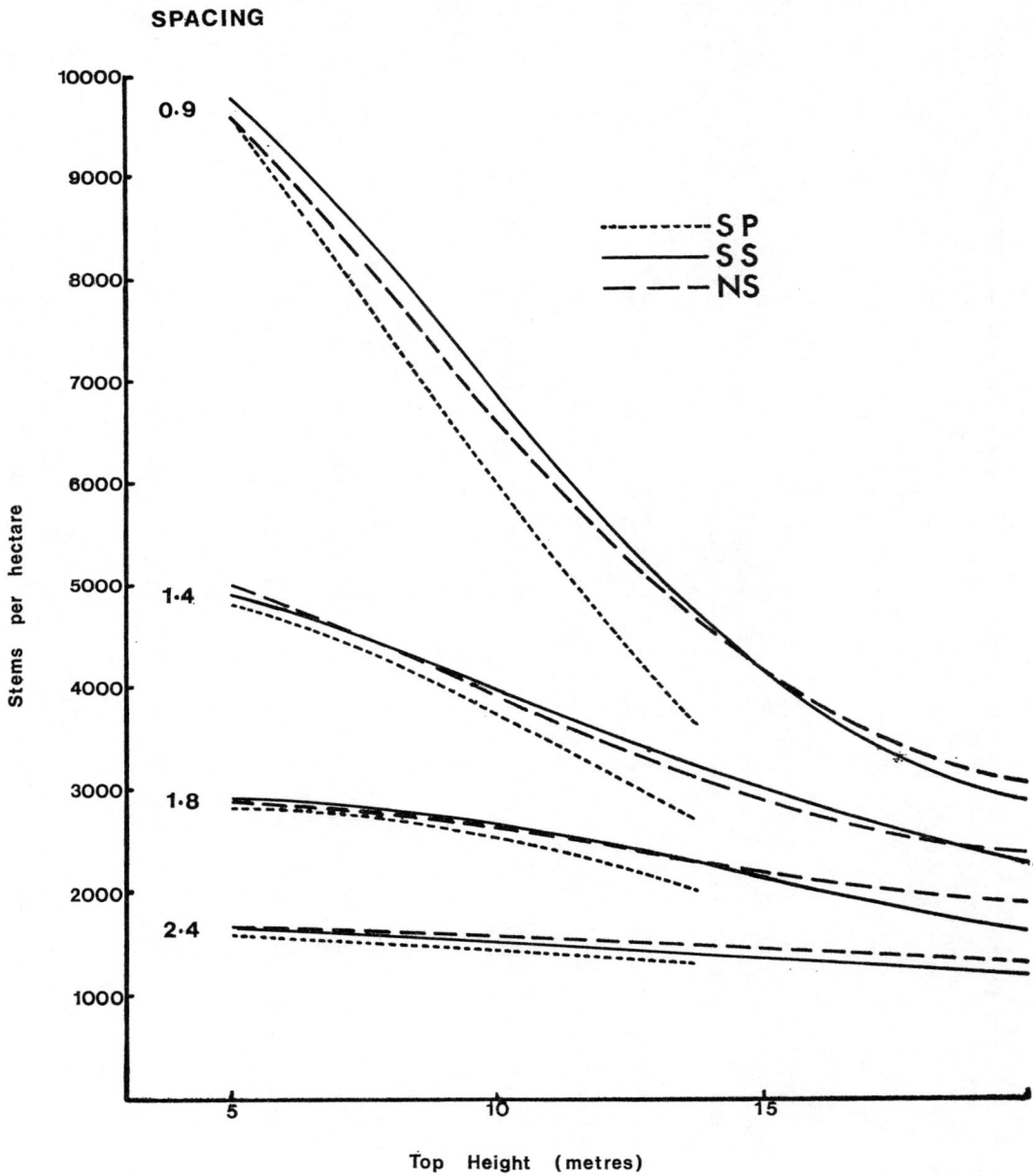

Figure 1. Surviving stem numbers in unthinned Scots pine, Sitka spruce and Norway spruce for different initial spacings.

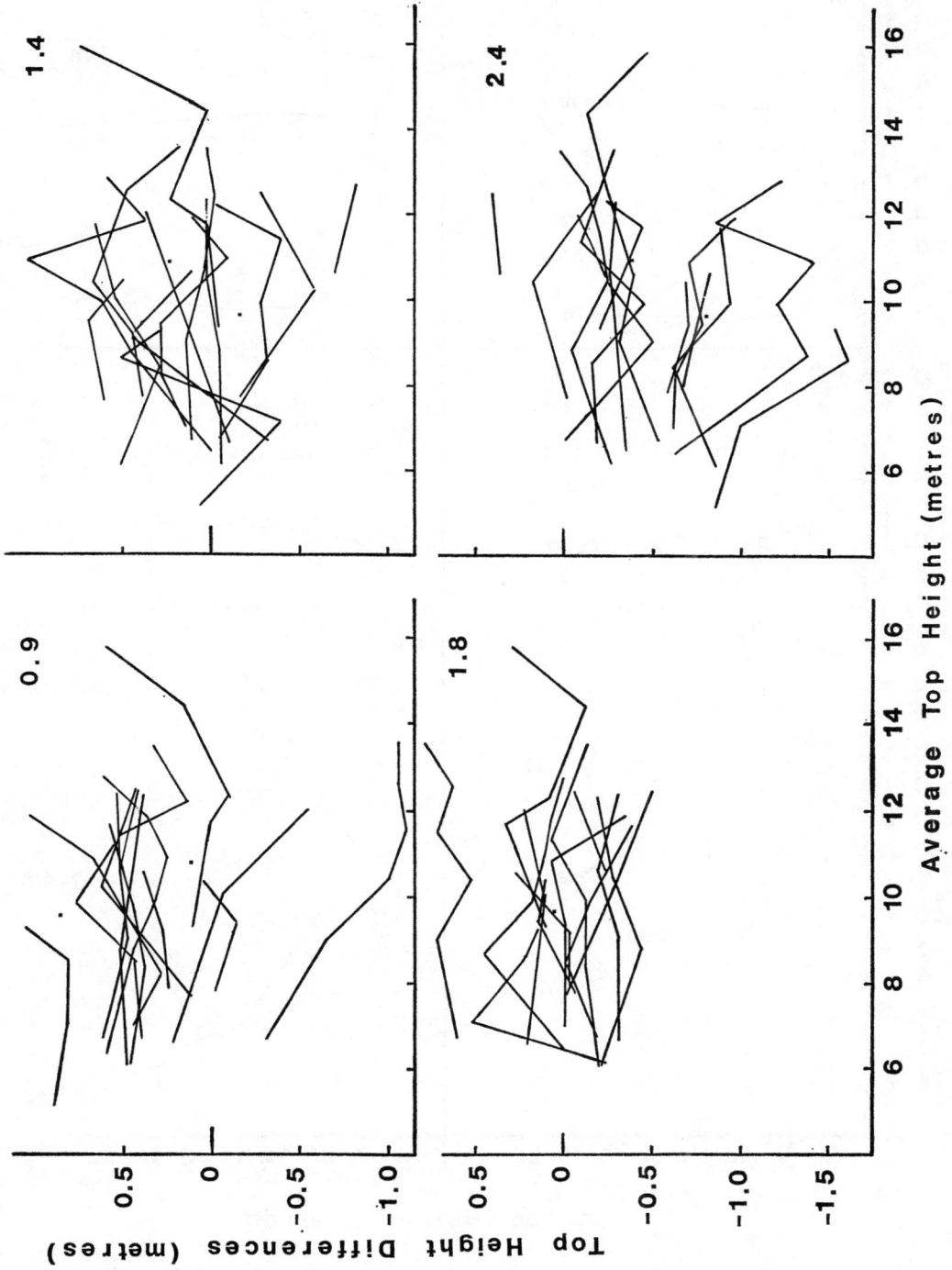

Figure 2. Top height of individual Scots pine plots of each spacing, expressed in terms of deviation from the mean top height of their series, and shown relative to the mean top height of their series.

9

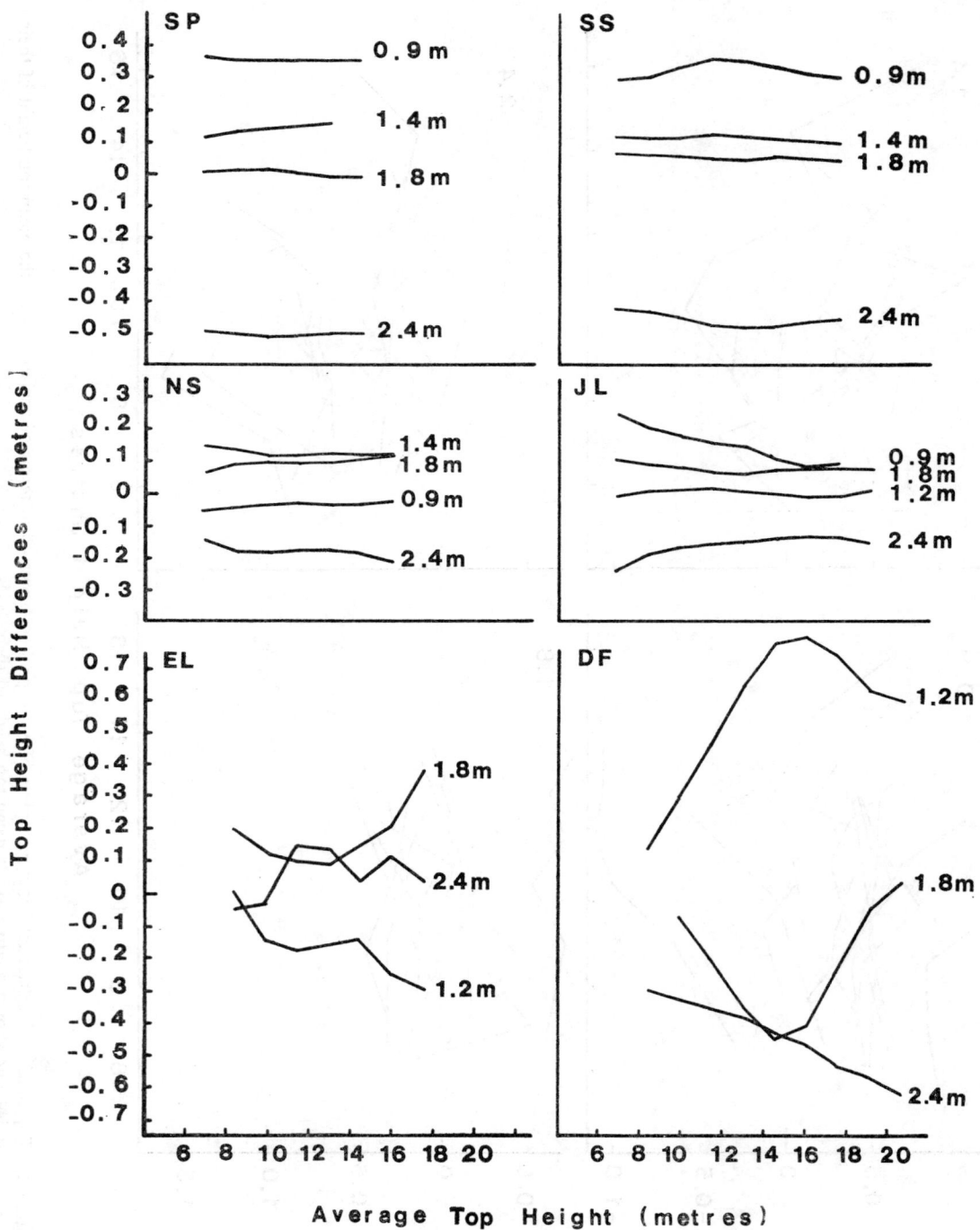

Figure 3. Relative top heights of different spacings in relation to mean top height of all spacings.

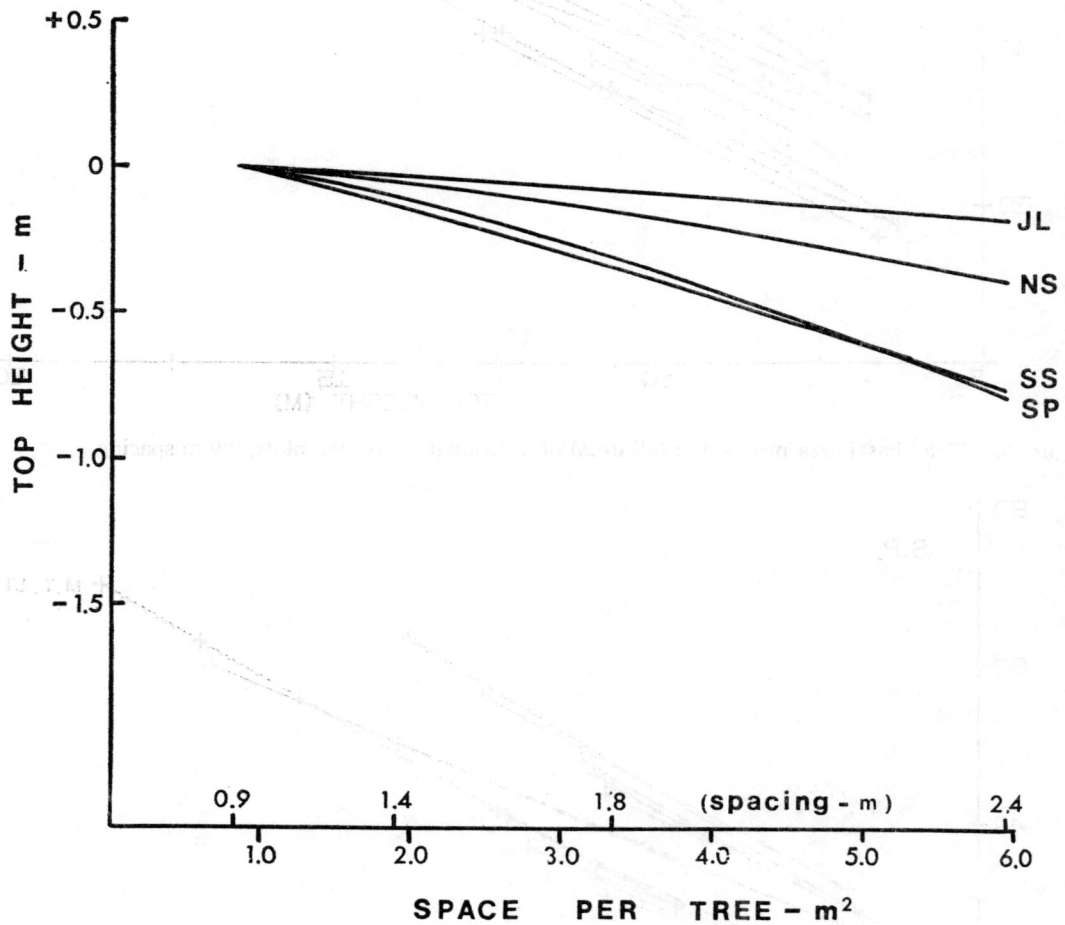

Figure 4.   Top heights (smoothed) of different spacings shown relative to that of 0·9 m spacing.

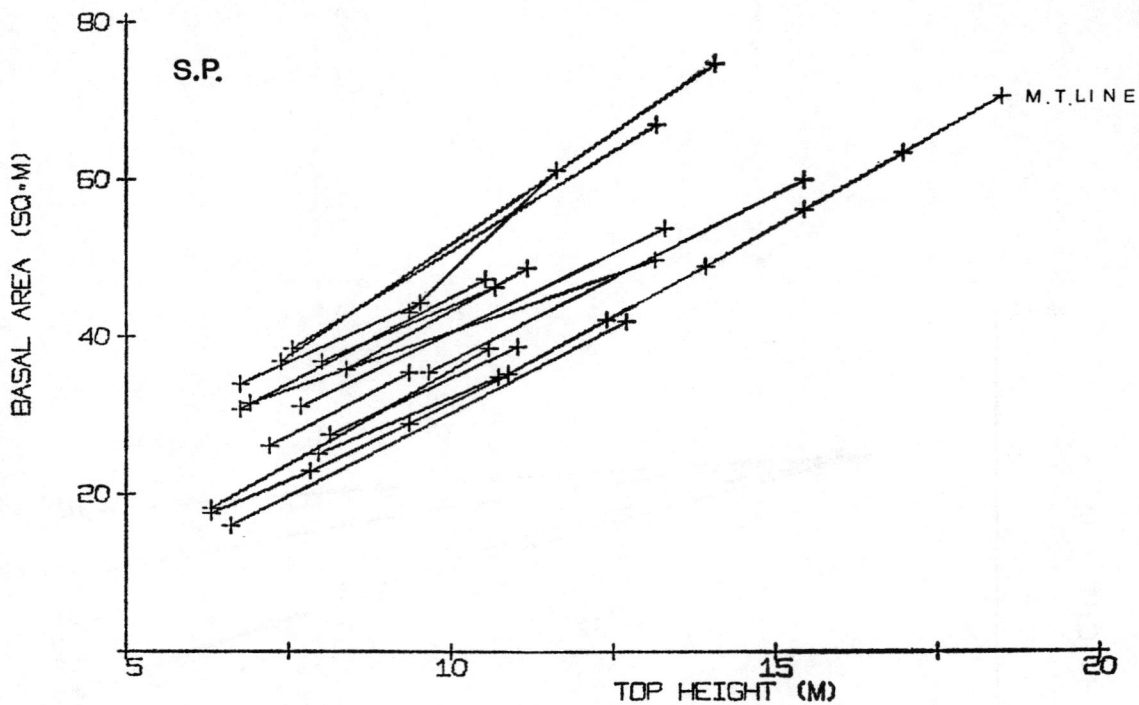

Figure 5.   Total basal area production (all trees) of individual Scots pine plots, 0·9 m spacing

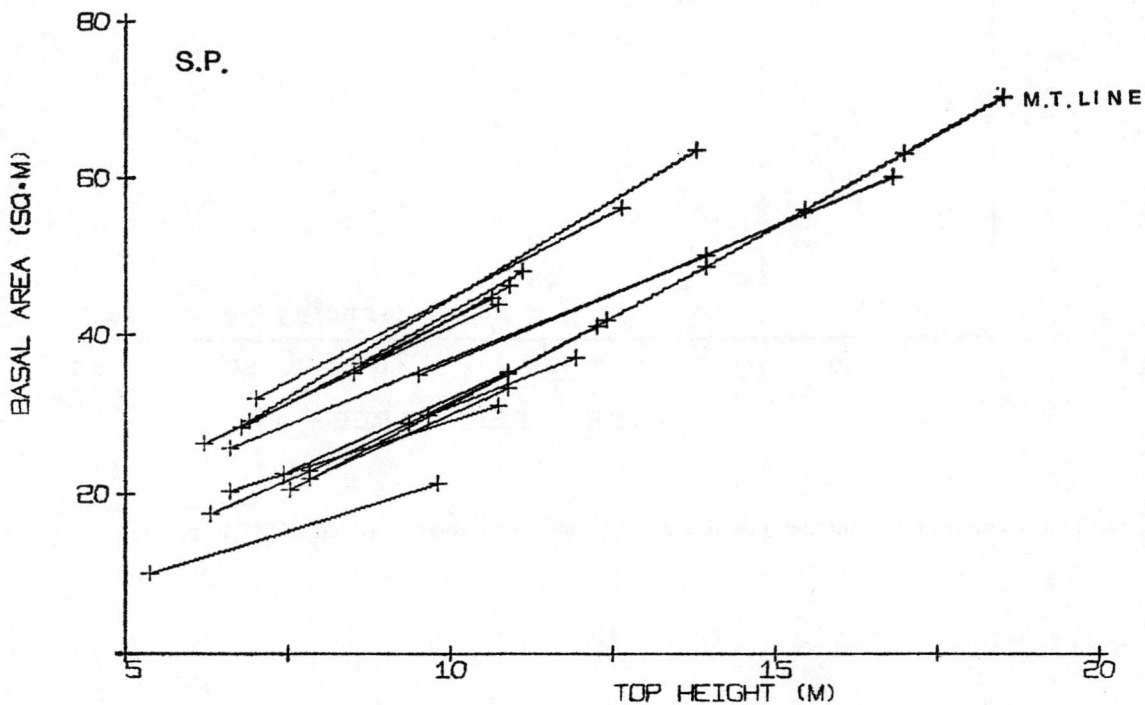

Figure 6.   Total basal area production (all trees) of individual Scots pine plots, 1·4 m spacing.

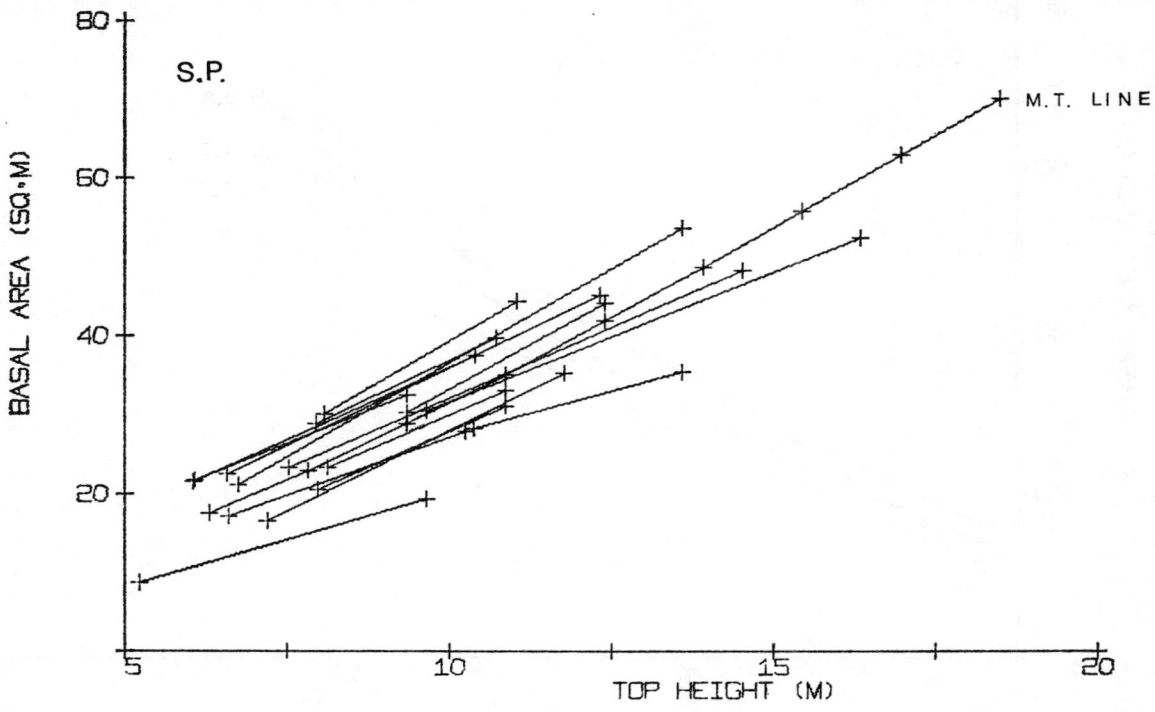

Figure 7. Total basal area production (all trees) of individual Scots pine plots, 1·8 m spacing

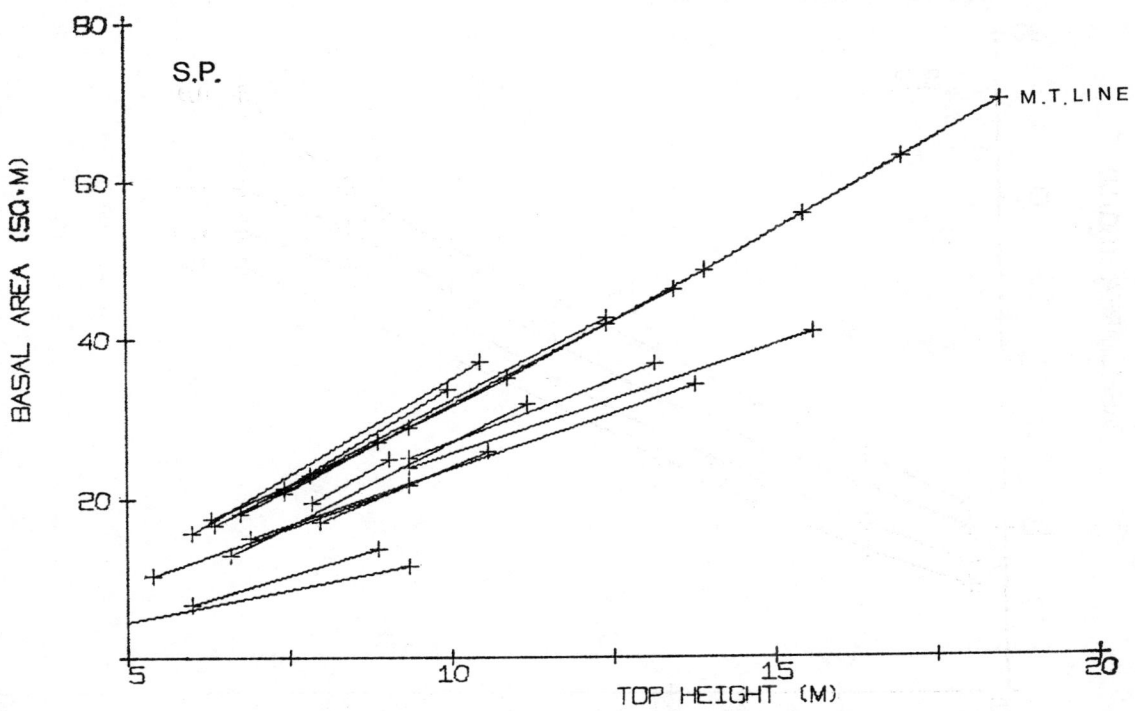

Figure 8. Total basal area production (all trees) of individual Scots pine plots, 2·4 m spacing.

13

B

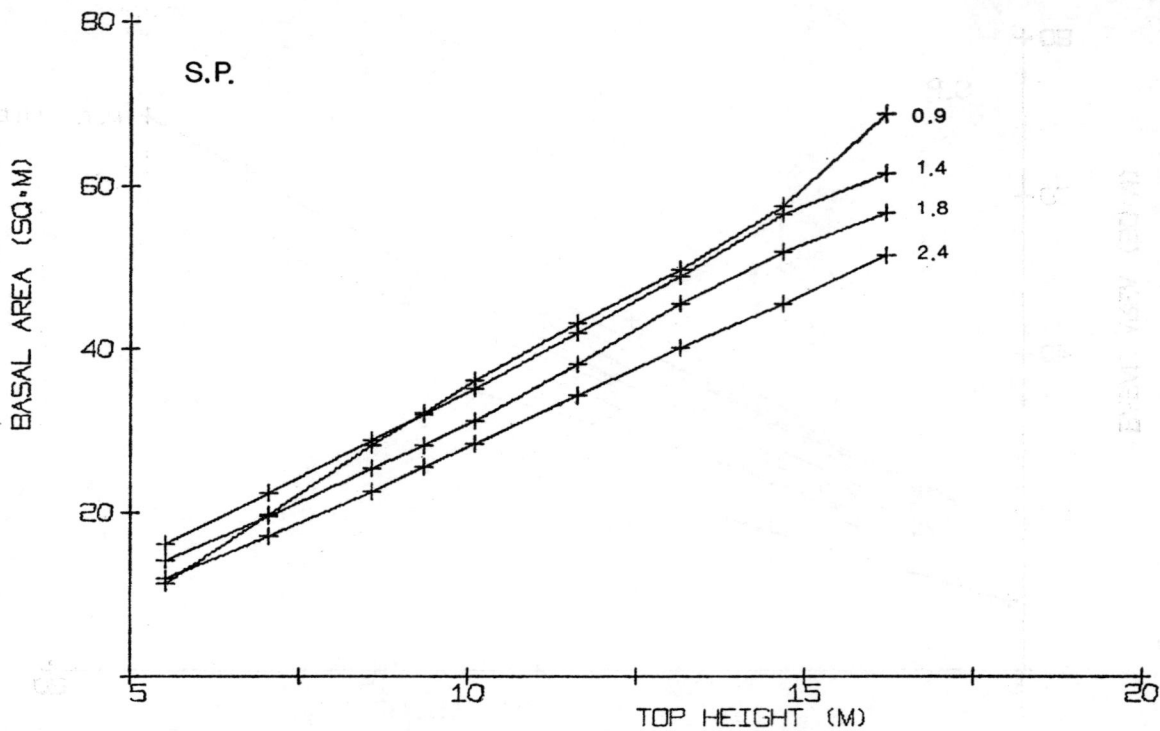

Figure 9. Relationship between total basal area production (trees of dbh 7 cm +) and top height for different spacings in Scots pine.

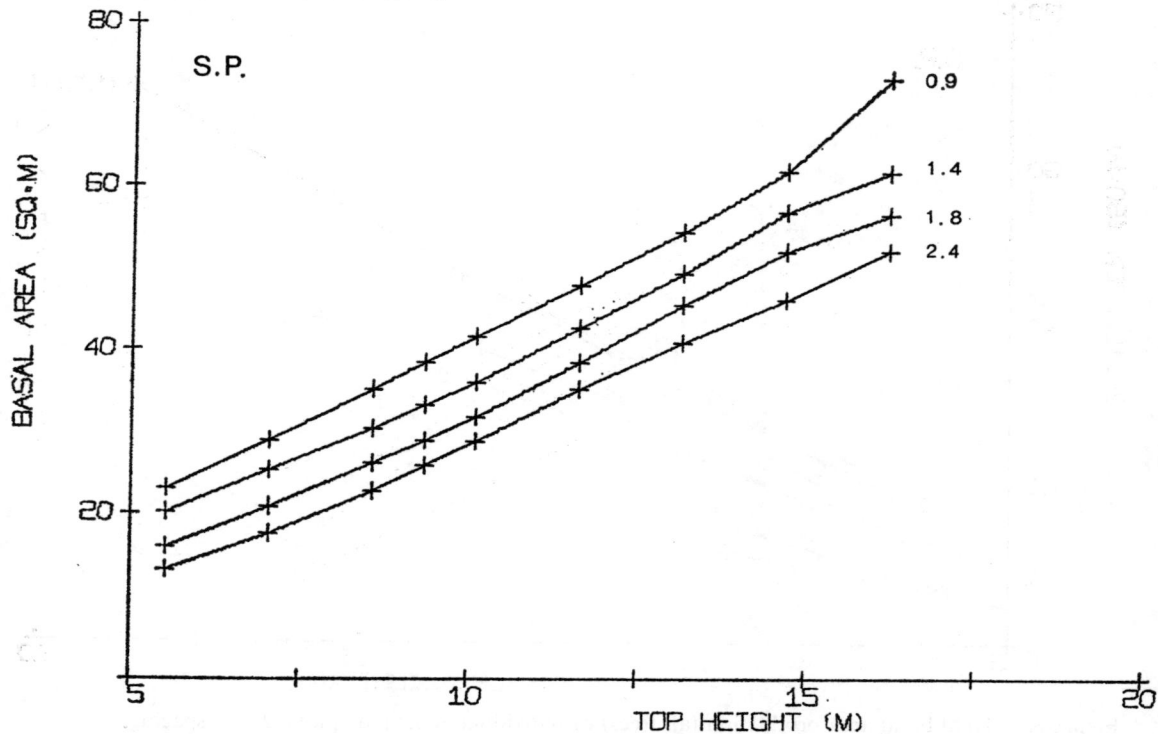

Figure 10. Relationship between total basal area production (all trees) and top height for different spacings in Scots pine.

14

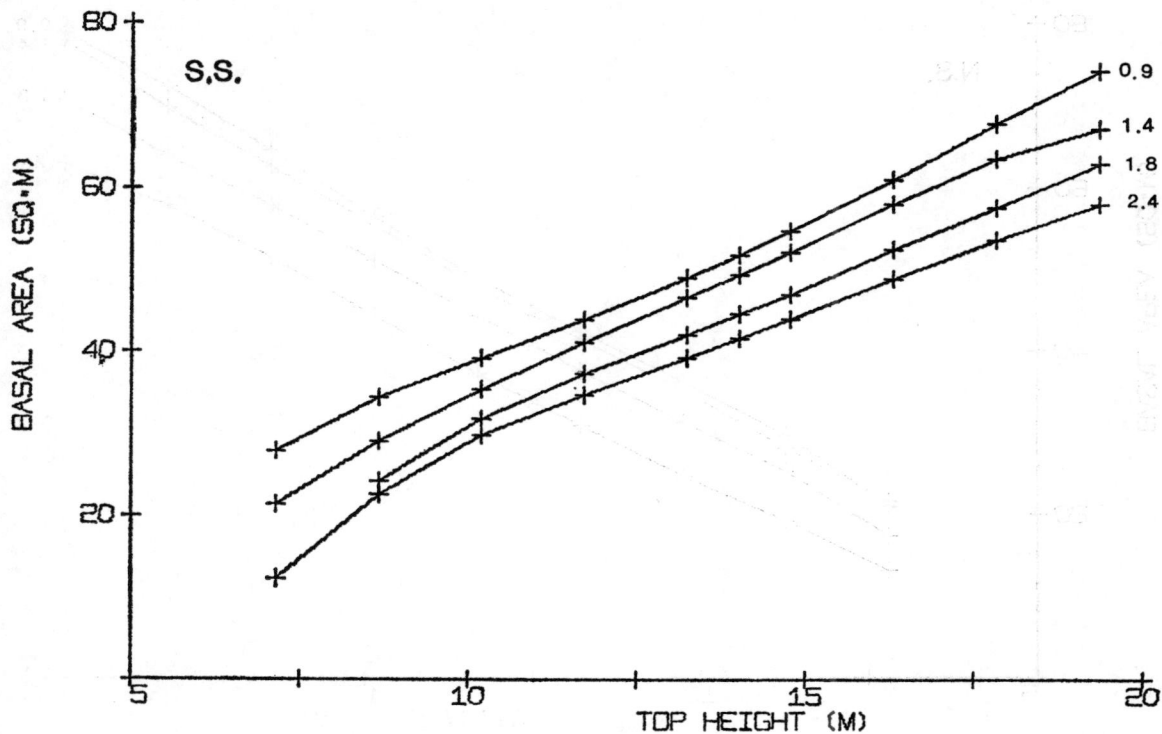

Figure 11.   Relationship between total basal area production (trees of dbh 7 cm +) and top height for different spacings in Sitka spruce.

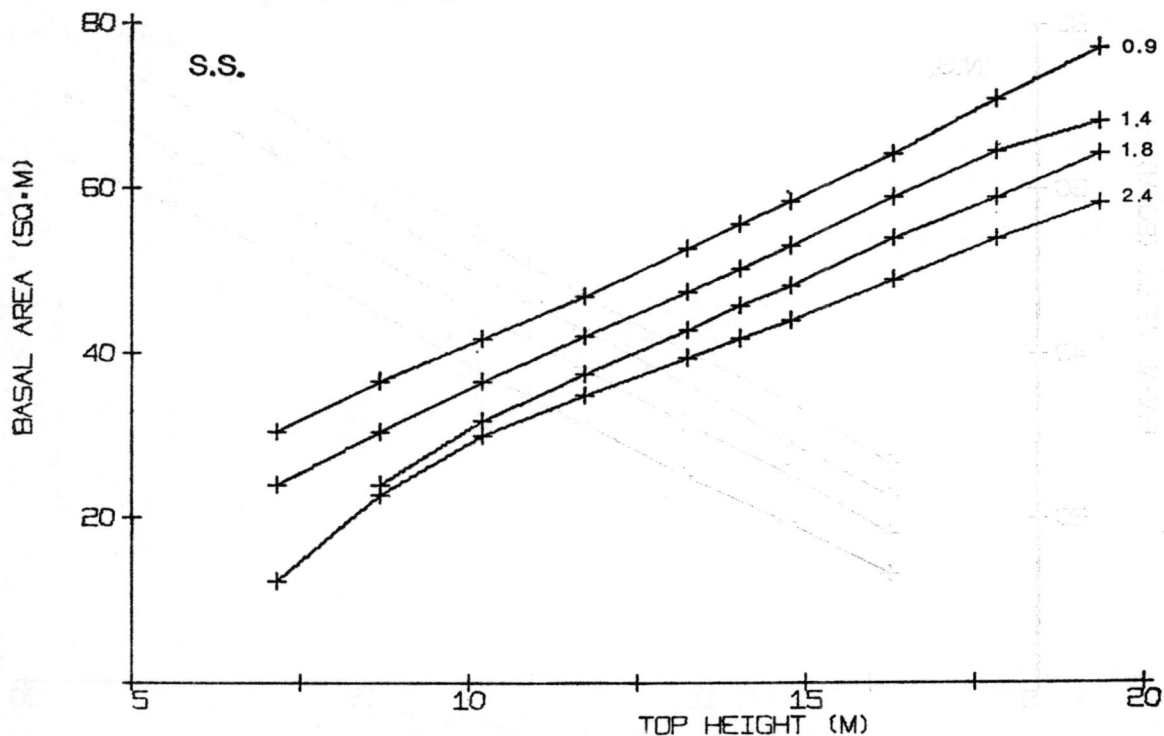

Figure 12.   Relationship between total basal area production (all trees) and top height for different spacings in Sitka spruce.

15

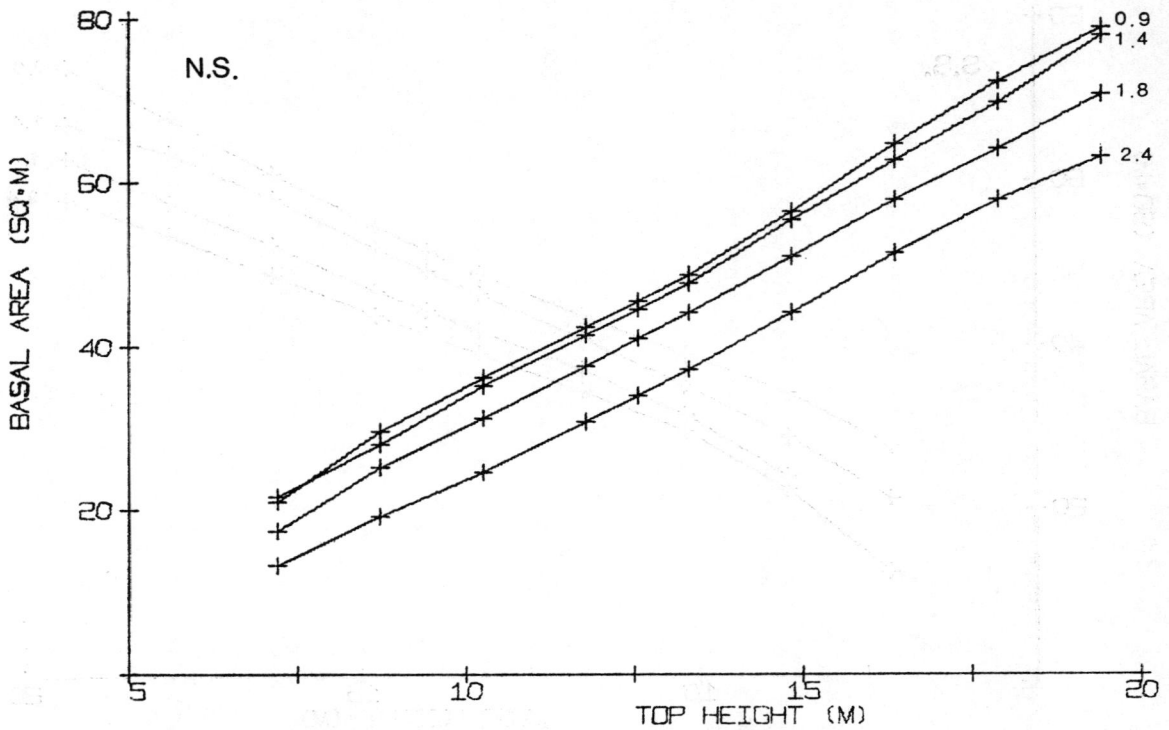

Figure 13.   Relationship between total basal area production (trees of dbh 7 cm+) and top height for different spacings in Norway spruce.

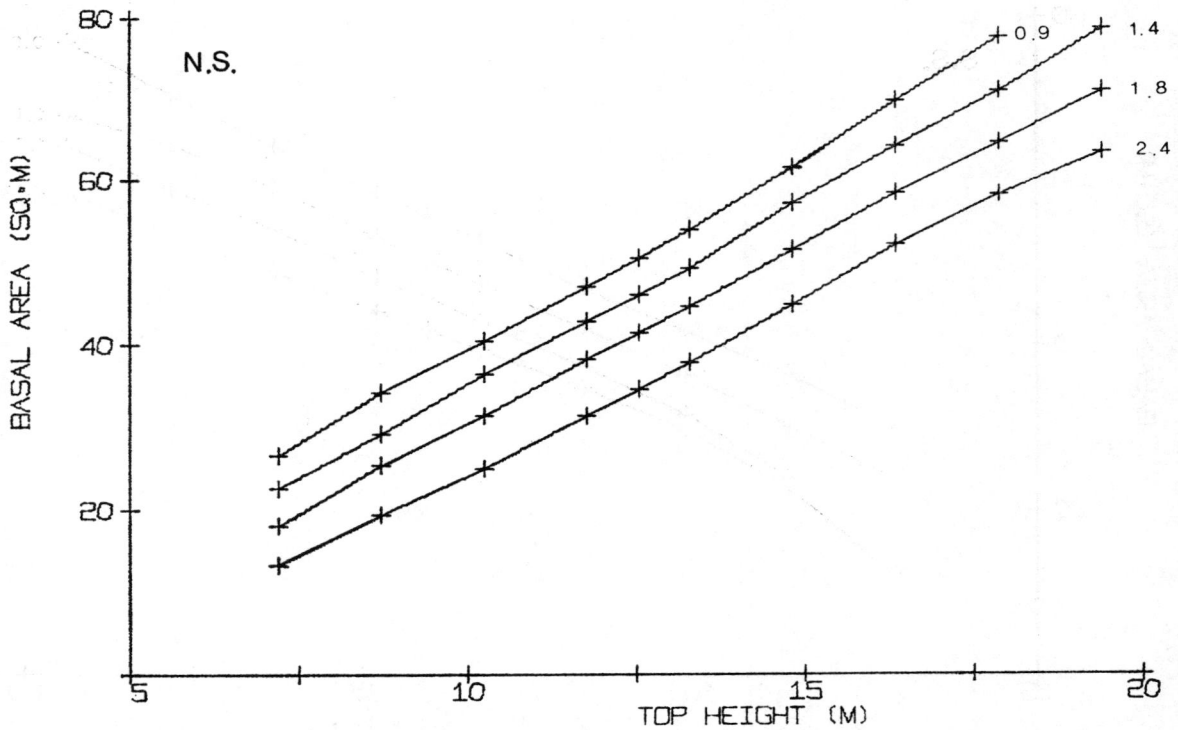

Figure 14.   Relationship between total basal area production (all trees) and top height for different spacings in Norway spruce.

16

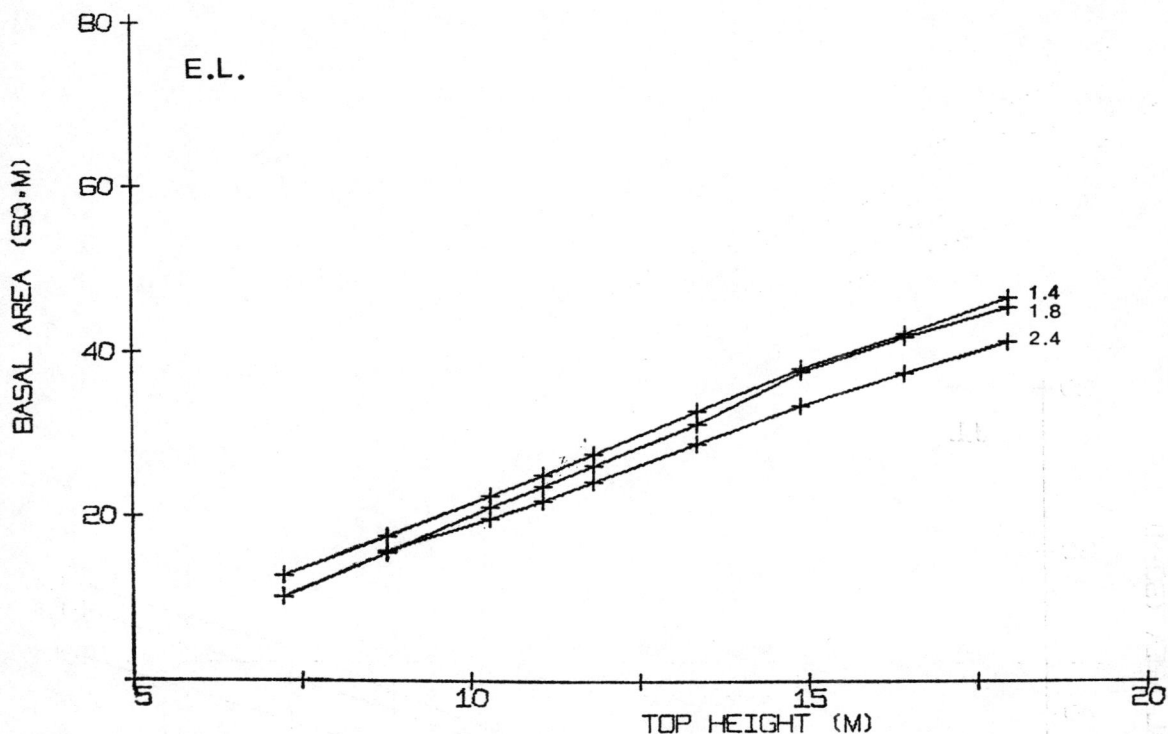

Figure 15.   Relationship between total basal area production (trees of dbh 7 cm +) and top height for different spacings in European larch.

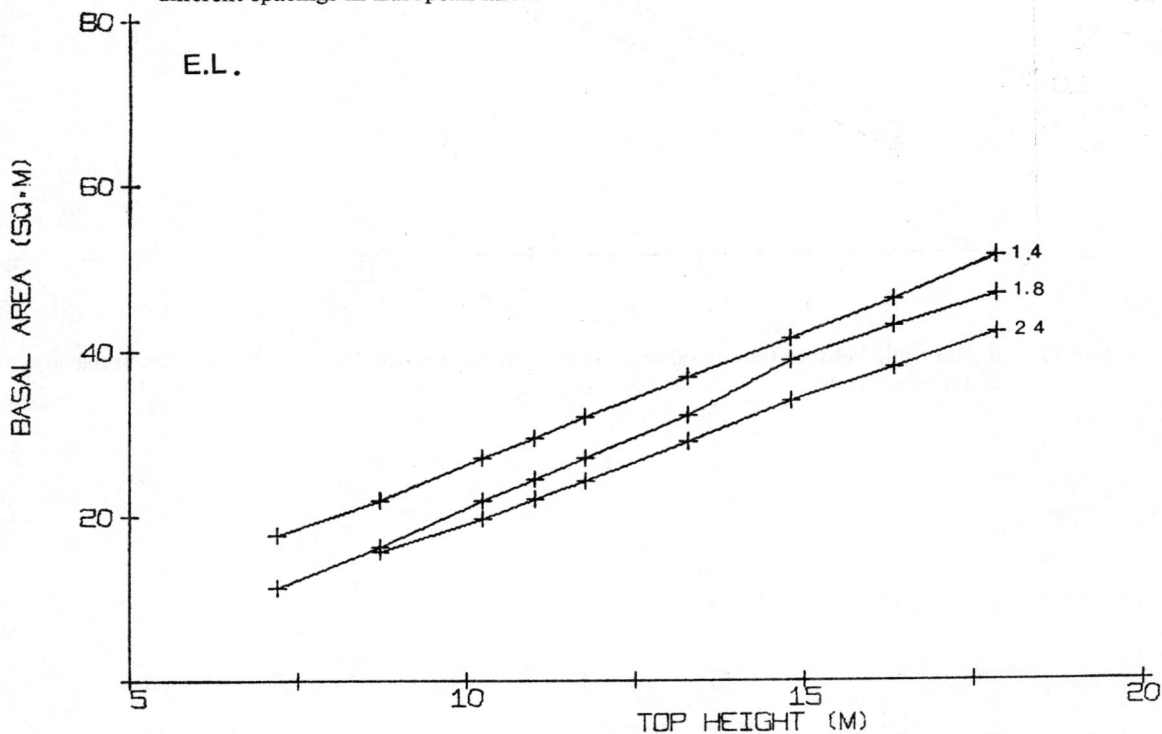

Figure 16.   Relationship between total basal area production (all trees) and top height for different spacings of European larch.

17

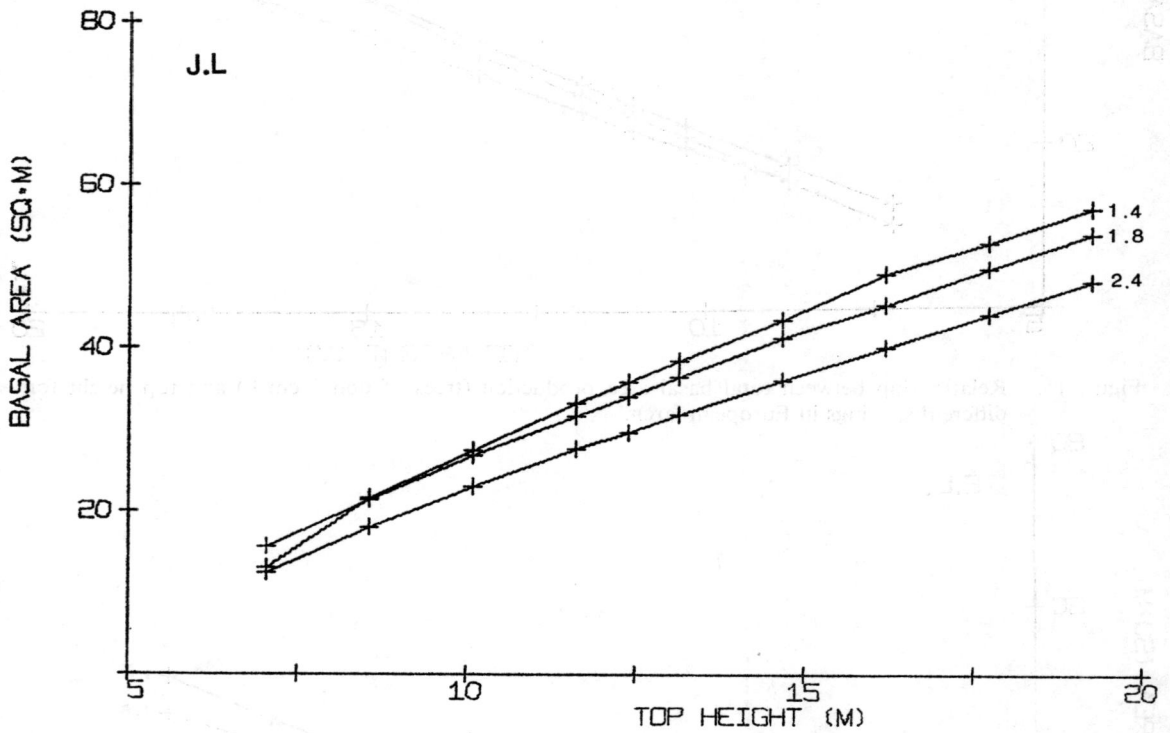

Figure 17. Relationship between total basal area production (all trees) and top height for different spacings of Japanese larch.

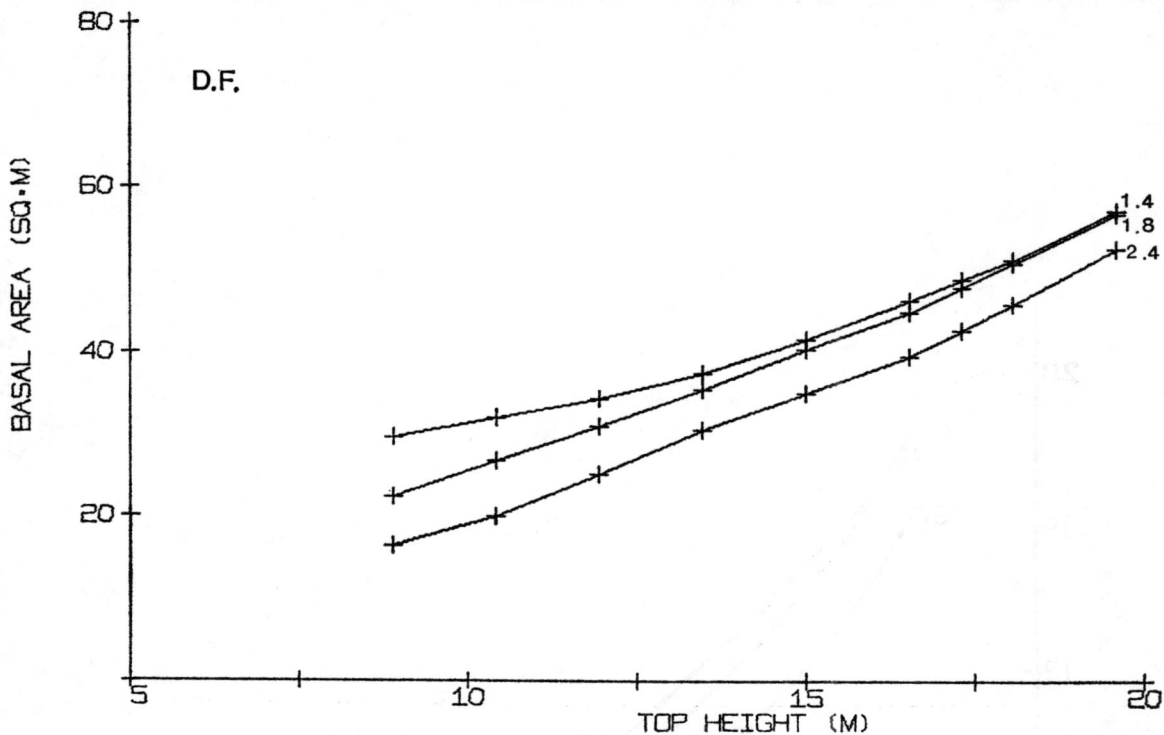

Figure 18.   Relationship between total basal area production (trees of dbh 7 cm +) and top height for different spacings of Douglas fir.

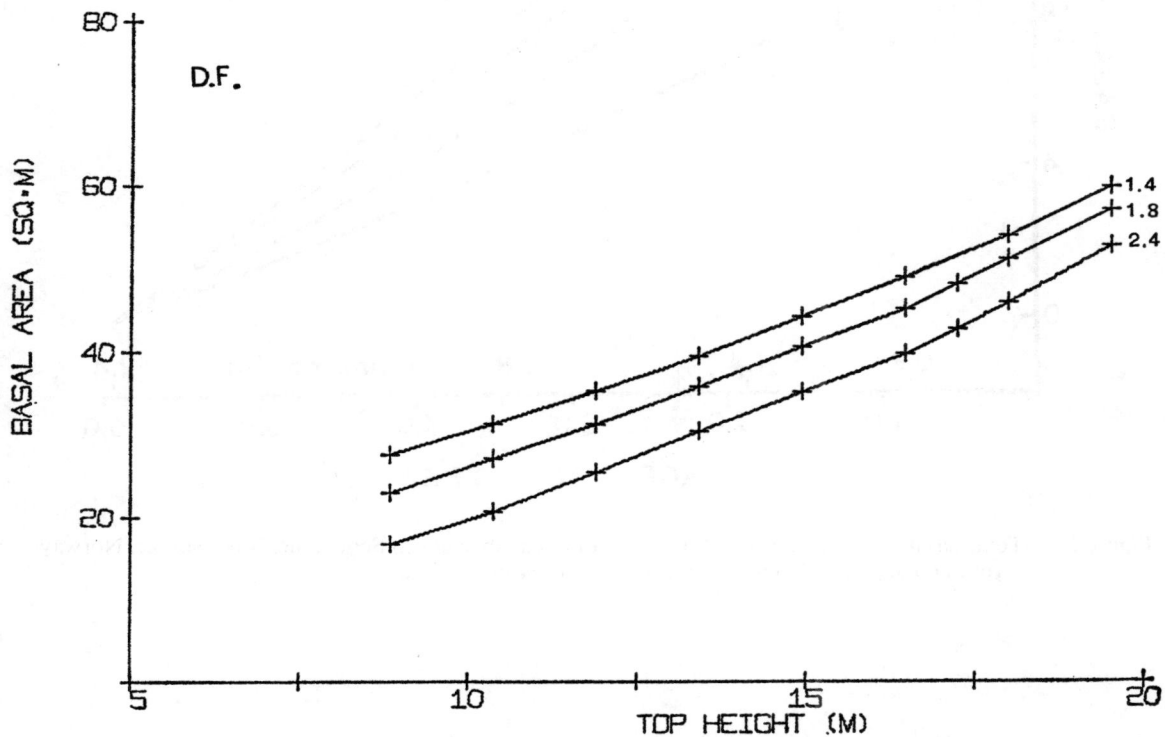

Figure 19.   Relationship between total basal area production (all trees) and top height for different spacings of Douglas fir.

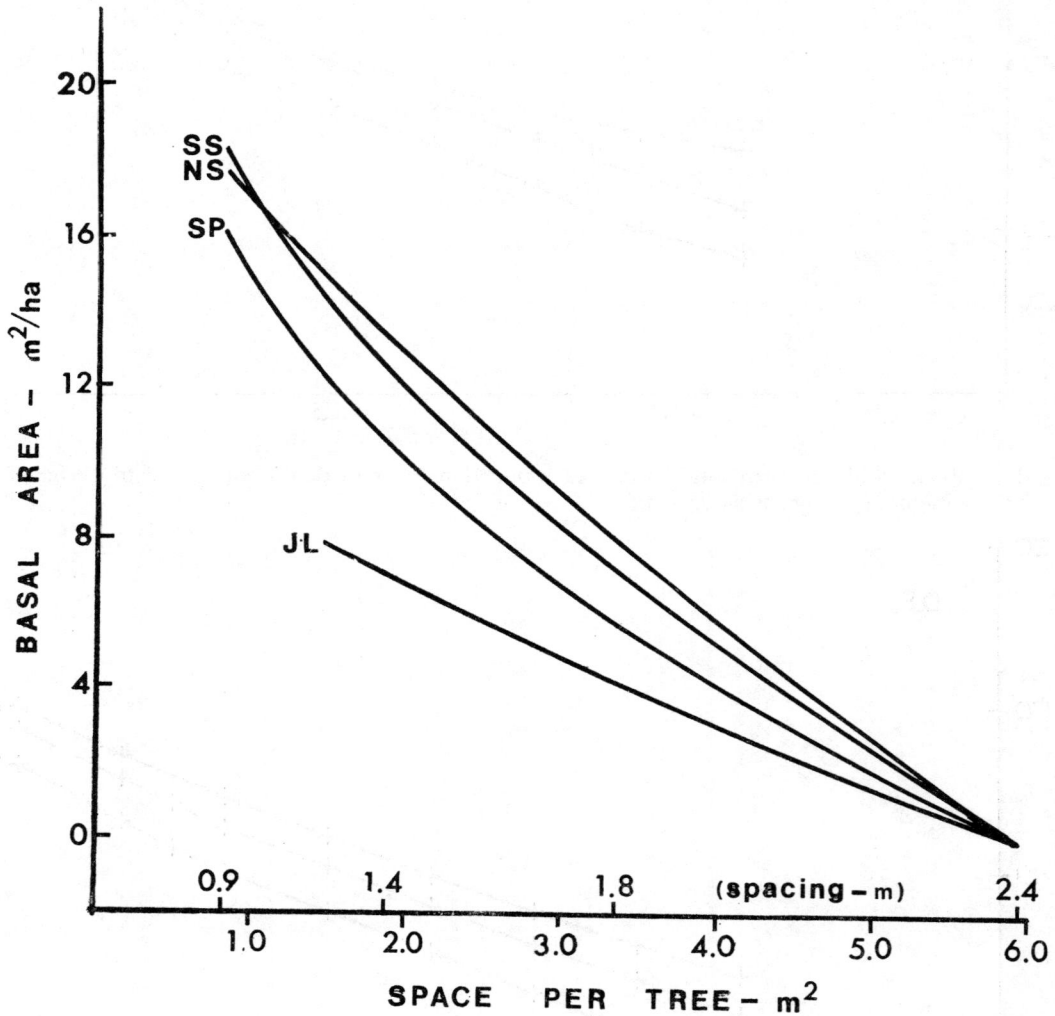

Figure 20. Total basal area production (all trees) of different spacings in Scots pine, Sitka spruce, Norway spruce and Japanese larch, relative to that of 2·4 m spacing.

4. Basal Area Production

There are two aspects of basal area production which are of interest. The first is the effect of spacing on basal area of all trees irrespective of diameter. Secondly, for subsequent volume production estimates it is necessary to quantify spacing effects on the basal area of conventionally measurable trees only, that is, trees of 7 cm dbh and above.

Since dbh has been measured in all series, information on basal area production is more reliable than all other parameters bar height. Limitations have been imposed, however, by the paucity of assessments in some series, and by the occasional omission of dbh measurements on unmeasurable trees, i.e. trees of less than 7 cm dbh.

It is acknowledged that over an extended height range, regressions of basal area on height tend to be curvilinear. However, over the limited height range available for any one plot, plotting basal area against height invariably produced a regression so nearly linear – most correlation coefficients greater than 0·985 – as to make a standard assumption on linearity wholly justifiable. Linear regressions of basal area on height were therefore calculated for each plot using data:

    a. from all trees up to and including first thinning.

    b. from all trees up to and including first thinning together with data from 'P' treatment series beyond first thinning, and 'Q' treatment series up to the time of thinning of the 2·4 m plot.

    c. as (a) but excluding trees < 7 cm dbh.

    d. as (b) but excluding trees < 7 cm dbh.

The 1·2 and 1·4 m spacings of European larch, Japanese larch and Douglas fir were combined and the 0·9 spacings omitted.

An example of the linear regressions of individual Scots pine plots for the four spacings (Category (b) above) is shown in Figures 5–8.

The normal total basal area/top height regression derived from the Forestry Commission Normal Yield Tables (Hamilton & Christie, 1971) is shown for comparison. (M. T. Line).

A method of combining these regressions was designed such that from the individual regressions the combined regressions could be calculated and graphed entirely by computer. This method is essentially similar to that used in analysing height growth.

For each species a modal height was calculated for each spacing. The modal height is the height through which the greatest number of individual regression lines passed. In Scots pine, for example, the modal height of the 0·9 m spacing plots was 9·14 m. Since each regression line terminated at the first and last assessment of the particular plot, a few cases arose where regression lines fell short of the modal height value. In such cases they were extrapolated to the modal height value. The mean basal area of the plots at the modal height was calculated simply as the average of the basal area evaluated from each plot regression for the modal height.

The slope of the combined regressions through the average basal area point was calculated over a 1·52 m (5 ft) height band (on which the modal height was central) by averaging the regression coefficients of the individual regressions occurring in that top height band. The slopes of successive 1·52 m bands were similarly calculated and a continuous line constructed from the modal height point.

The regression thus obtained was found to be satisfactory without further smoothing. The separation of the data into that of assessments carried out up to and including first thinning, and secondly, all assessments excluding the 'Q' series beyond the time in each series at which the 2·4 m spacing plot was thinned, yielded regressions which were found to be not significantly different. Figures 9–19 depict the latter regressions for the six species concerned for all trees and for trees of 7 cm dbh and above.

In broad terms closer spacing clearly produces greater basal area. As with height growth these differences are apparent at first assessments, reach a maximum at about 12–15 m top height and tend to remain constant in absolute terms thereafter.

It is noticeable that the exclusion of trees of less than 7 cm dbh has the effect of diminishing the basal area differences between spacings in the earlier phases of height covered by the analysis, but some recovery is observed with increased height. This is directly attributable to the fact that closer spacings have a high proportion of unmeasurable trees in these earlier periods, but recruitment to the 7 cm dbh class alters the position with time. Natural mortality of unmeasurable trees means that the basal area of trees of 7 cm and above can never attain the level of basal area of all trees, at least in the closer spacing.

Figures 9–19 show the levels of basal area production relative to the top height of each spacing. Since there are differences in top height between spacings, it follows that the *overall* effect of spacing on basal area production has to be considered. Figure 20 has been prepared to show the differences between spacings when top height differences have been incorporated. The values plotted are those occurring at a *common age* for each species. This is the age at which the widest spacing is first thinned in an average yield class for the species (Scots pine – yield class 8, Sitka spruce – yield class 12, Norway spruce – yield class 12, Japanese larch – yield class 8). In fact these differences remain approximately of the same order thereafter, irrespective of age or yield class.

5. Volume Production

The absence of reliable volume assessments from the northern series posed considerable problems in analysing the effects of spacing on volume production.

Although satisfactory volume assessments were available from the southern series, the numbers of these were considered inadequate to justify their exclusive use. The approach was therefore to assess the effects of spacing on form, effectively, from the southern series, and to reconstruct volume production data for the northern series on the basis of these results, together with the existing reliable data on height and basal area. The northern and southern series were then combined in the analysis of spacing effects on volume production.

In approaching the question of the effects of spacing on tree form, a number of alternative expressions were considered, e.g. tariff number, form factor, form height. It was found that *total crop form height* provided a convenient and most consistent parameter for the purpose required. Total crop form height is a wholly abstract term, quantified by dividing the total volume production by the total basal area production. Plotting total crop form height against top height from the southern series data produced regressions as illustrated in Figure 21 which shows the trends apparent in Japanese larch. These regressions were produced for each species, subsequently smoothed, and appropriate values of total crop form height obtained for individual assessments of the northern series data. Volume estimates were derived as the product of this value and the known total basal area production (of trees of 7 cm dbh and above) pertaining to each assessment.

Having established reasonable volume estimates for the northern series for each assessment, the volume data from all series was used to produce volume/top height regressions for each spacing of each species. The technique used was exactly that used for deriving basal area/top height regressions, that is, a linear regression was calculated for each plot and combined by the technique described previously.

Figures 22 to 27 show volume production trends derived from all assessment data, excluding data from 'Q' treatments beyond the time when the 2·4 m spacing plot, in each 'Q' series, was thinned.

The picture emerging is generally similar to that found with basal area, namely that closer spacings have higher volume production and that differences between spacings remain fairly constant in absolute terms *for a common top height*.

If the comparison between spacings is, however, made *at a common age* of a given yield class, the effect of height differences discussed previously has a significant impact on the overall volume production differences. A comparison made at the age of first thinning of the widest spacing for a typical yield class of each species is shown in Figure 28. A comparison made at the normal age of maximum mean annual increment of the same yield class for the species is shown in Figure 29. It can be seen here that the apparent differences are considerably greater than those occurring at the earlier age. This is simply a consequence of the fact that the normal top height/volume relationship is such that volume production per unit of height growth increases with increasing height. In general, therefore, the greater the *average* top height, the greater are the differences in volume production between spacings. Maximum mean annual increments occur at ages corresponding to lower top heights in lower yield classes. Thus the apparent 'loss' in production associated with wide spacings is marginally greater with higher yield classes, in the course of rotations defined by the age of maximum mean annual increment.

6. Diameter

Diameter at breast height has been measured in all series and the resultant data are largely adequate.

It was clearly important to distinguish between the effects of initial spacing and subsequent thinnings with diameter, more so than with any other parameter. Consequently the data were grouped into:

a. 'R' series plus all data up to and including 1st thinning

b. post-thinning 'P' series data

c. post-thinning 'Q' series data.

On account of the deficiencies of the 'Q' treatment series discussed previously, the post-thinning data have been discounted from total production considerations. The treatments nonetheless do provide a useful source of information on diameter growth in extremely low stand density conditions, and for that reason are considered here.

Figures 30–35 demonstrate the trends of mean dbh under the above categories, as far as data permit in each species. These regressions have been derived using the same technique of combining regressions as previously described. The mean diameters are those of *all* trees in the population.

The results show greater mean dbh with wider spacings at the time of first assessments. In absolute terms, these differences tend to increase with height in unthinned stands, do so more rapidly with the 'Q' series treatments, but tend to converge or remain constant in the 'P' series treatments.

Diameter Distribution

For a given *mean dbh* the range in dbh classes represented in the stand is greater with closer spacings. At a given *top height*, however, this situation is inverted as a consequence of the larger mean dbh associated with wider spacings.

The above statements are true of unthinned stands, and whilst this is also broadly true of stands subject to thinnings as depicted in the yield models (Appendix III) the type of thinning can clearly influence the nature of the subsequent dbh distribution. Using unthinned Sitka spruce as an example, the distributions of the 0·9 m and 2·4 m spacings have been compared in Figure 36 which shows the dbh distributions of each spacing at ten year intervals (Yield Class 16 assumed).

7. Form and Taper

Although some direct information on stem form is available from the southern series, it was considered better to derive values of this parameter in the process of constructing the yield models from the other essential parameters – volume, basal area, and height – rather than to attempt to analyse the limited and variable raw data on form.

Form factors for the main crop of each spacing at each specified age are shown in the yield models (Appendices II and III). (Crop form factor is the main crop volume divided by the product of mean height and basal area.) It is clear that lower form factors are associated with wider spacings, except in the earlier phases of height growth where the position tends to be inverted due to the frequency of small, low form factor trees and trees of less than 7 cm dbh in the closer spacings.

Taper, as distinct from form factor, is often more directly meaningful in practice. Studies of tree profiles of individuals taken from the more extreme treatments revealed no marked departures from those generally encountered in given height and dbh classes. In simple terms trees of the same height and dbh have the same general profile irrespective of spacing. Differences, however, occur between different dbh classes and of course the differences in both mean dbh, and in the dbh distributions of different spacings, affect the average tree profile. It is recognised also that species differences exist and this has governed the approach to deriving taper figures, described below.

Basic data were again only available from the southern series. Absolute form quotients were calculated for each of the ten maincrop volume sample trees which had been measured in sections at each assessment. The form quotient is defined as the ratio of the diameter measured midway between the breast height point and the top of the tree, to the diameter at breast height. The form quotients for each species, spacing, and subsequent thinning treatments have been plotted against top height (100) and a combined, smoothed regression derived. Thereafter, reference has been made to Behre's (1927) generalised taper curves from which taper at any point on the tree can be determined. These curves have been examined in British conditions by Macdonald (1932–34), and are considered adequate for this purpose. Essentially these are a series of stem profiles, the appropriate profile being dependent on form quotient.

From Behre's curves the taper between the top and mid-point of the first 6 m length (from the butt) has been calculated for the average tree in each spacing at top heights of 10, 15 and 20 m. (A standard 'low' thinning of marginal intensity is assumed.) These results, showing greatly increased taper with wider spacings are demonstrated in Figure 37.

8. Assortments

In order to establish the percentage of the total stand volume (to 7 cm top) to specified top diameters, a general stand volume assortment table may be used in conjunction with the mean diameter of the crop. Such a table is given in Forestry Commission Booklet 34 (Hamilton & Christie, 1971). Assortments derived in this way are generally applicable irrespective of spacing.

In the case of length assortments, a similar possibility is available with individual tree general length assortment tables. To use these, dbh and height are required. (A table of this kind will be included in "Forest Mensuration Handbook" to be published shortly by the Forestry Commission.)

In conjunction with tables of diameter distributions for each spacing, the individual tree assortment tables have been used to prepare Tables 6 and 7. Table 6 shows the average log length to a given top diameter, related to mean dbh for each of the four spacings of Sitka spruce subjected to the thinnings depicted in the yield models. Table 7 shows the average length to the same top diameter for the same species and thinning regime, but using top height rather than dbh as the basic parameter.

The effect of wider spacing is to increase the percentage volume and average length to a given top diameter for a given *age* or *top height*. For a *common dbh* however, the average length to a specified top diameter is greater with closer spacings.

TABLE 6
LENGTH ASSORTMENTS RELATIVE TO MEAN DBH (SITKA SPRUCE)

Spacing	Average length (m) to top diam. of 18 cm				Average length (m) to top diam. of 24 cm			
	0·9 m	1·4 m	1·8 m	2·4 m	0·9 m	1·4 m	1·8 m	2·4 m
Mean dbh (cm)								
15	0·7	0·4	0·4	0·4	—	—	—	—
20	3·7	3·4	3·1	2·9	0·7	0·5	0·5	0·4
25	8·2	7·7	7·0	6·6	3·0	2·6	2·4	2·3
30	12·7	11·7	10·7	10·1	6·3	5·9	5·4	5·2
35	16·0	15·3	14·2	13·4	10·0	9·5	8·9	8·4
40	18·7	18·0	16·9	16·1	13·2	12·7	11·9	11·4
45	21·0	20·1	18·9	18·1	16·1	15·5	14·5	13·8
50	23·4	22·1	20·6	19·8	19·1	18·0	16·9	16·0

TABLE 7
LENGTH ASSORTMENTS RELATIVE TO TOP HEIGHT (SITKA SPRUCE)

Spacing	Average length (m) to top diam. of 18 cm				Average length (m) to top diam. of 24 cm			
	0·9 m	1·4 m	1·8 m	2·4 m	0·9 m	1·4 m	1·8 m	2·4 m
Top height (m)								
10	—	—	—	—	—	—	—	—
12	—	0·2	0·2	0·9	—	—	—	—
14	—	0·8	1·3	2·4	—	—	—	0·2
16	1·0	2·0	3·1	4·6	—	—	0·5	1·2
18	2·4	4·0	5·5	7·2	0·2	0·8	1·6	2·7
20	5·0	6·9	8·3	10·1	1·3	2·4	3·6	5·2
22	8·2	10·0	11·3	12·8	3·0	4·6	6·1	7·8
24	11·7	13·1	14·2	15·6	5·4	7·2	8·9	10·7
26	15·1	16·0	16·9	18·1	8·8	10·1	11·9	13·8
28	18·2	18·8	19·3	20·3	12·5	13·5	15·2	16·7
30	21·0	21·5	21·8	22·5	16·1	17·2	18·2	19·4

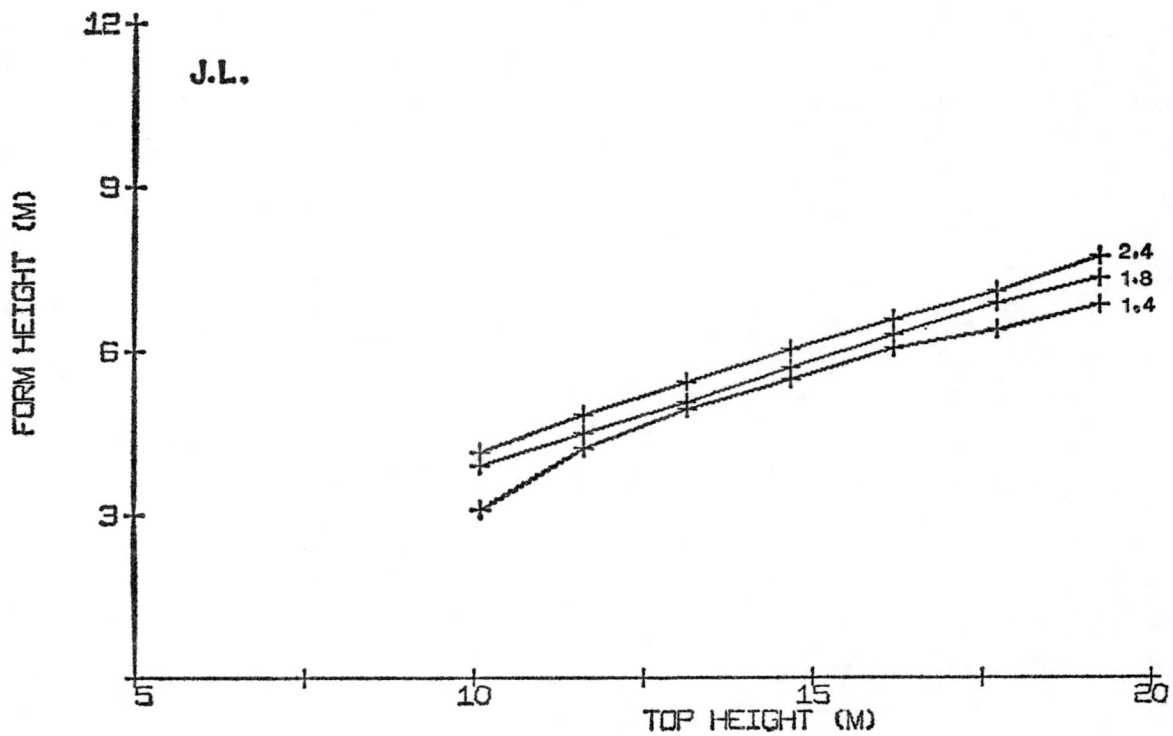

Figure 21. Total crop form heights of different spacings in Japanese larch, relative to top height.

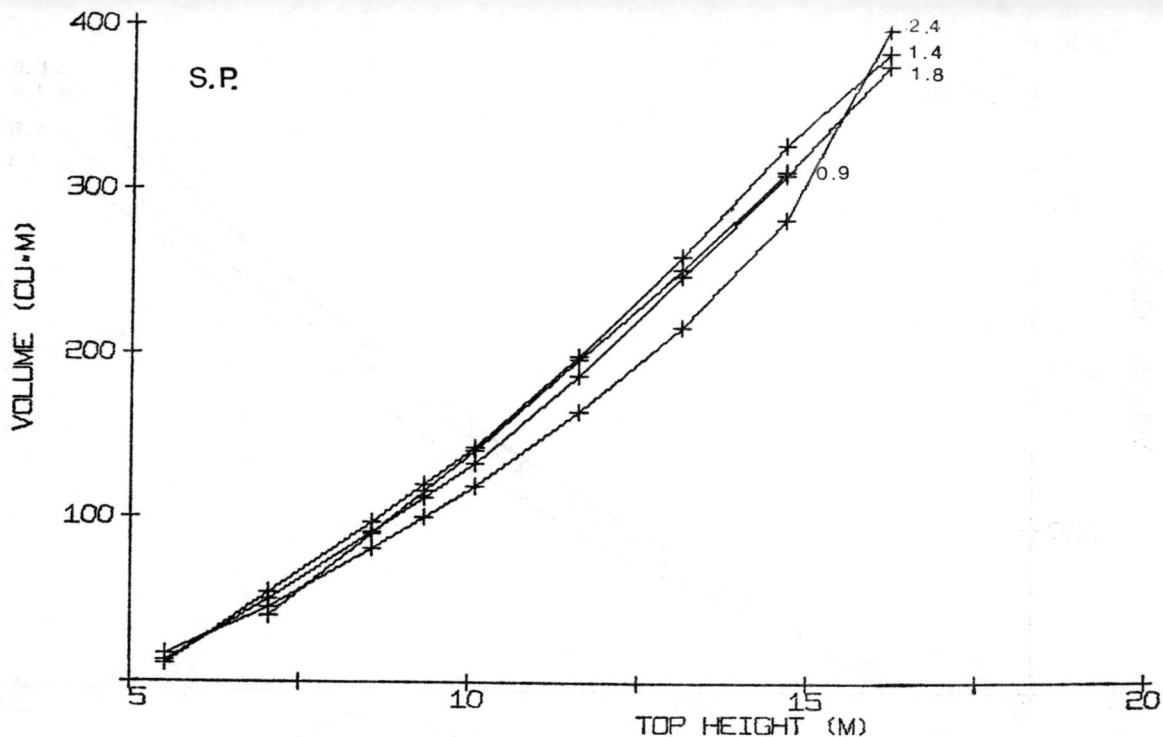

Figure 22. Relationship between total volume production and top height for different spacings in Scots pine.

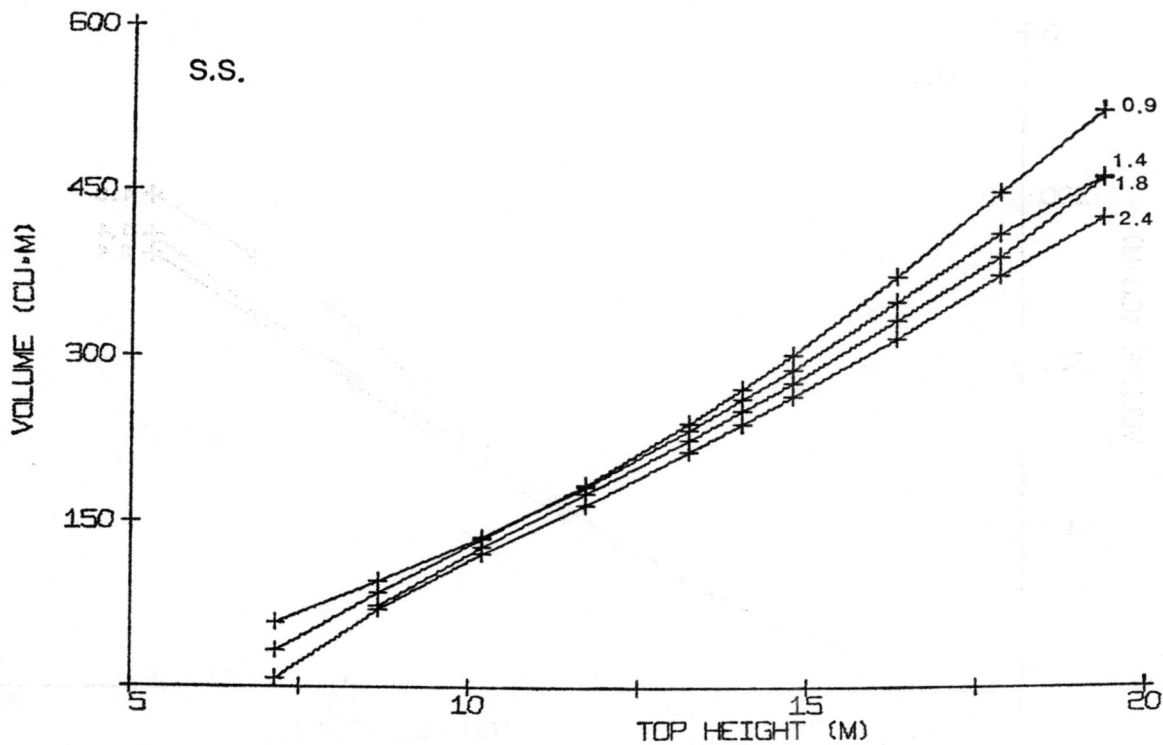

Figure 23. Relationship between total volume production and top height for different spacings in Sitka spruce.

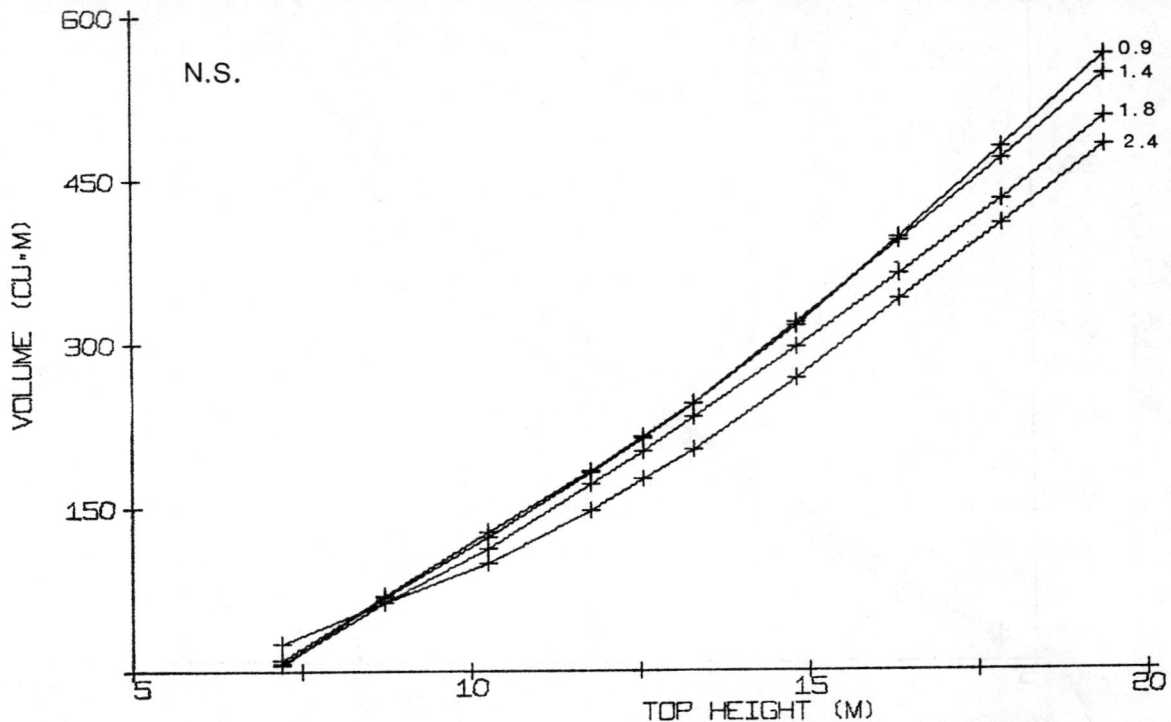

Figure 24.   Relationship between total volume production and top height for different spacings in Norway spruce.

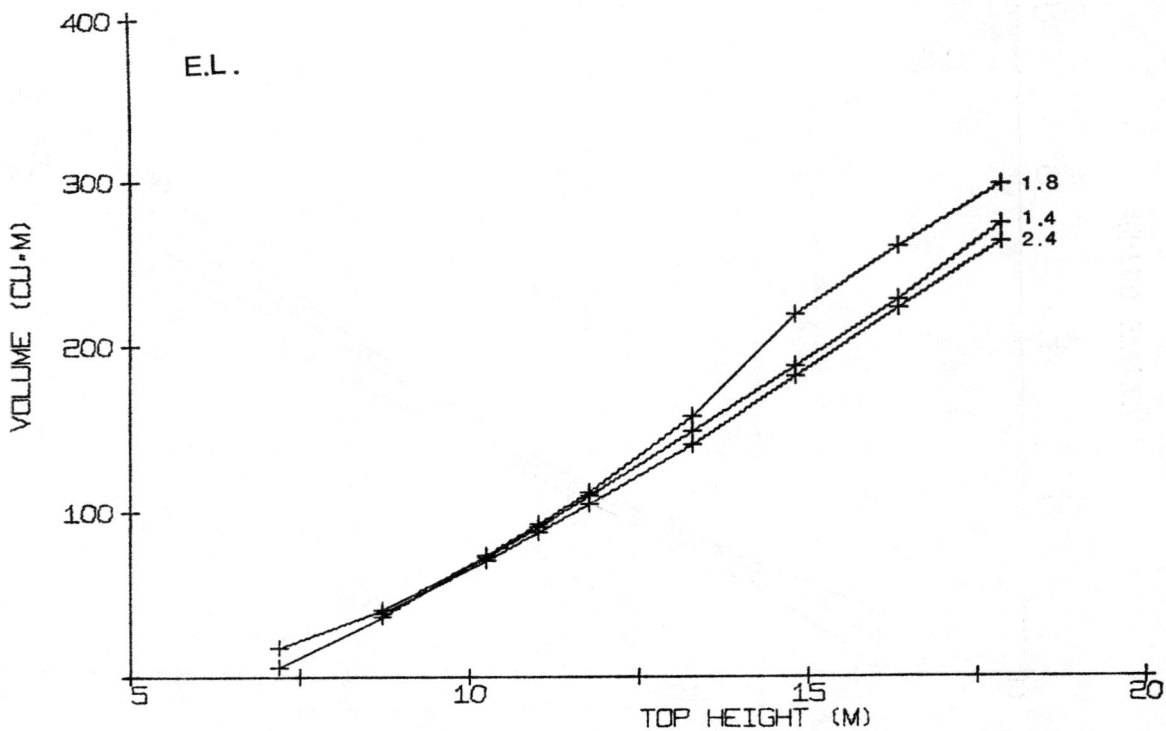

Figure 25.   Relationship between total volume production and top height for different spacings in European larch.

28

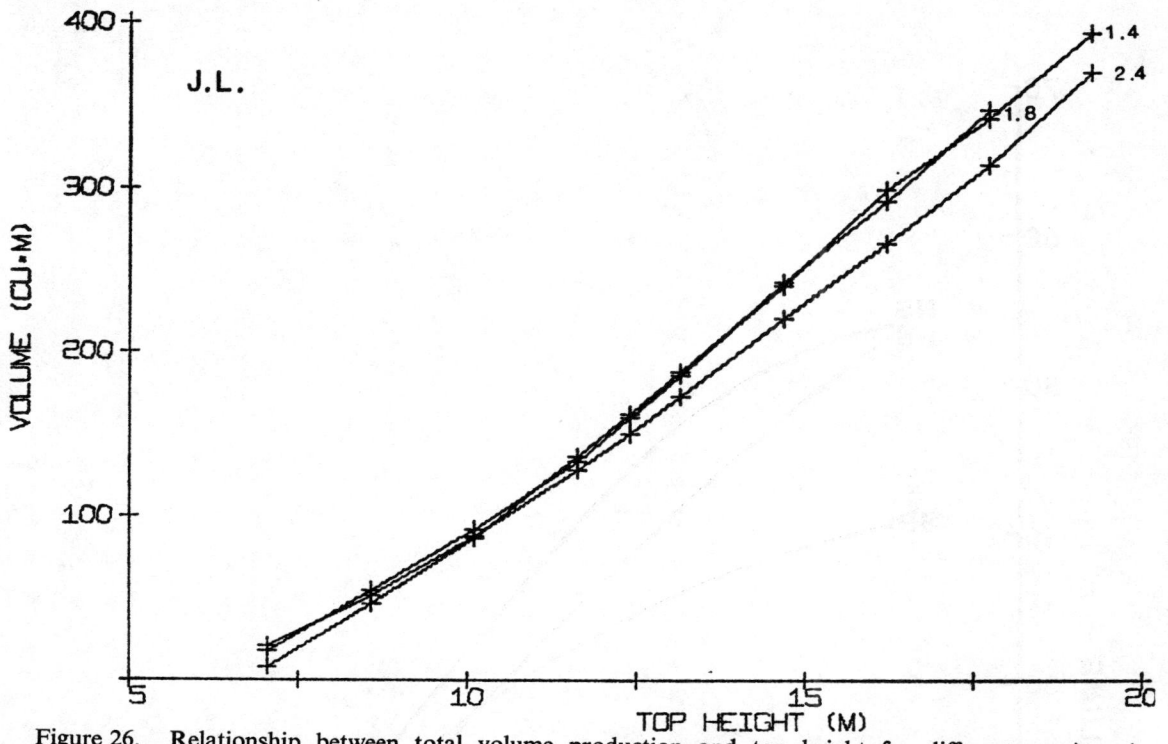

Figure 26. Relationship between total volume production and top height for different spacings in Japanese larch.

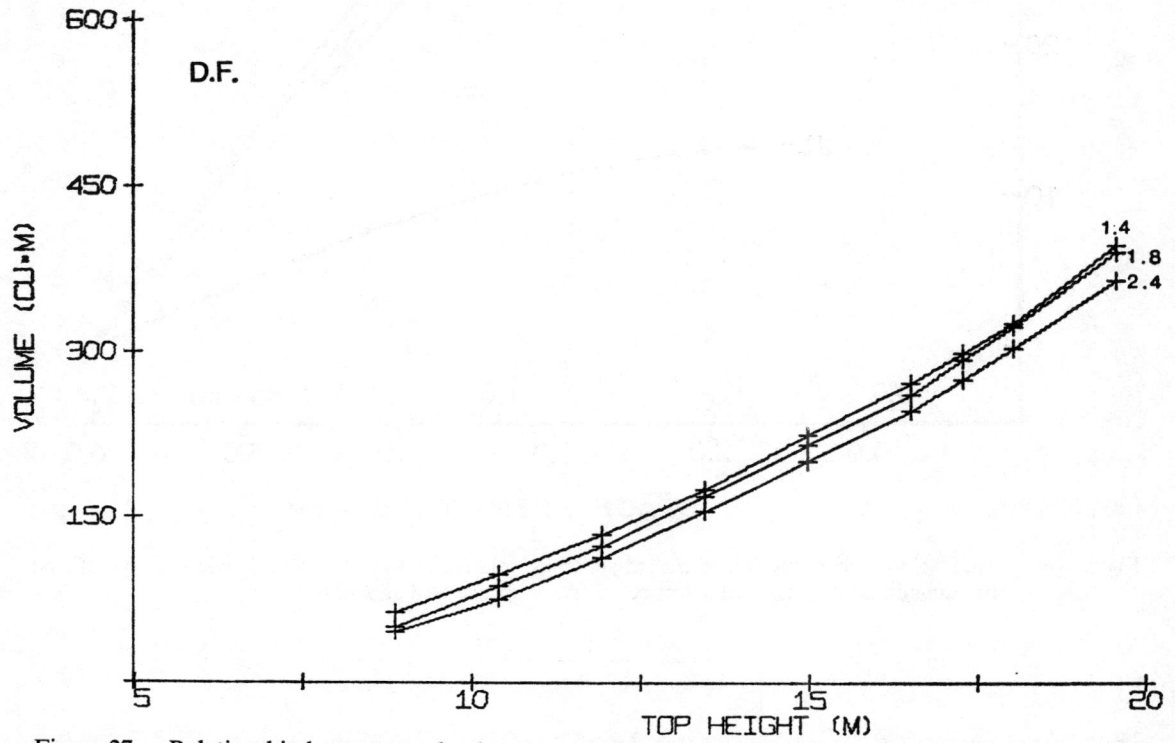

Figure 27. Relationship between total volume production and top height for different spacings in Douglas fir.

29

c

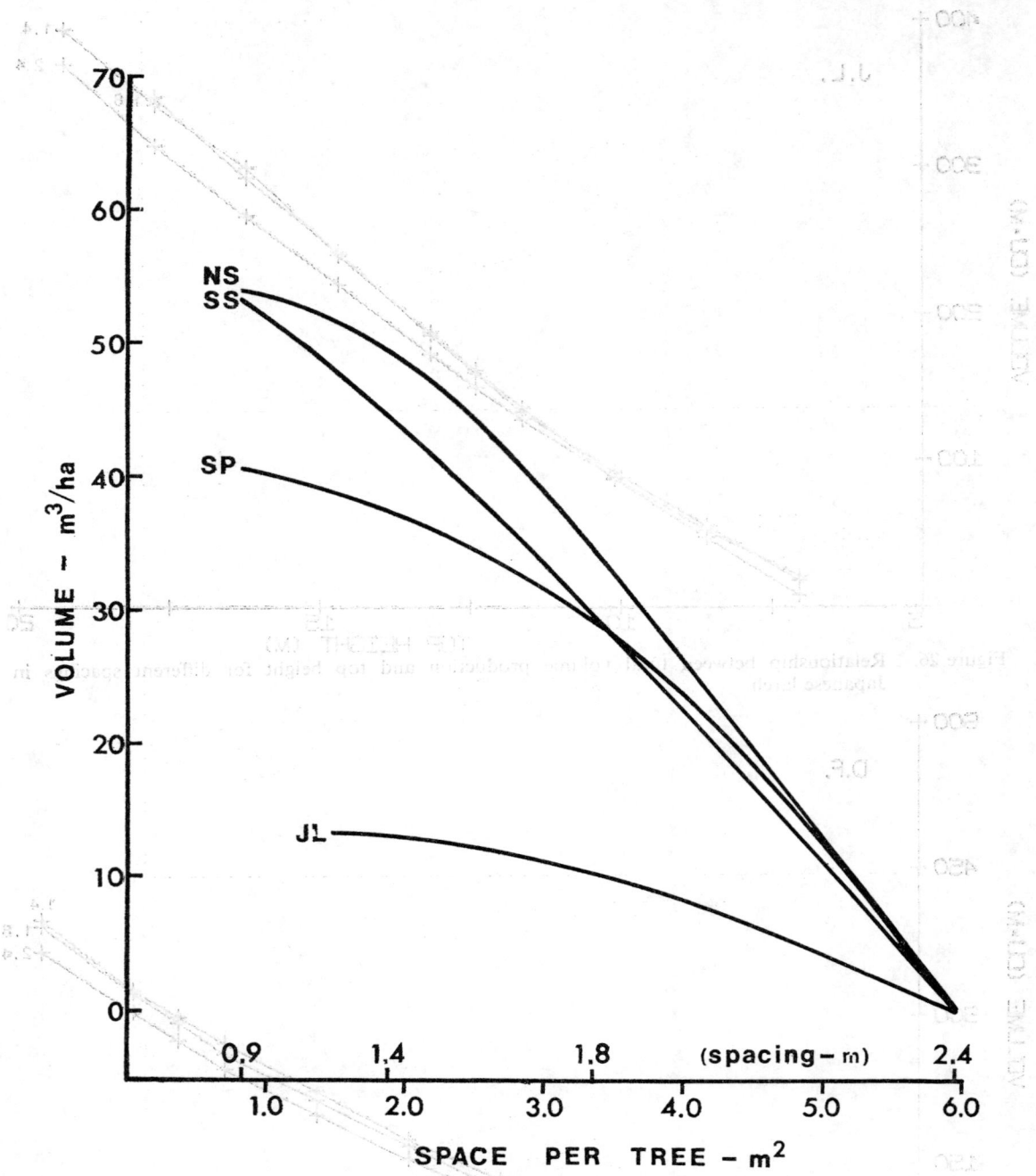

Figure 28. Total volume production of different spacings, relative to that of 2·4 m spacing, at age of first thinnings in Scots pine, Sitka spruce, Norway spruce and Japanese larch.

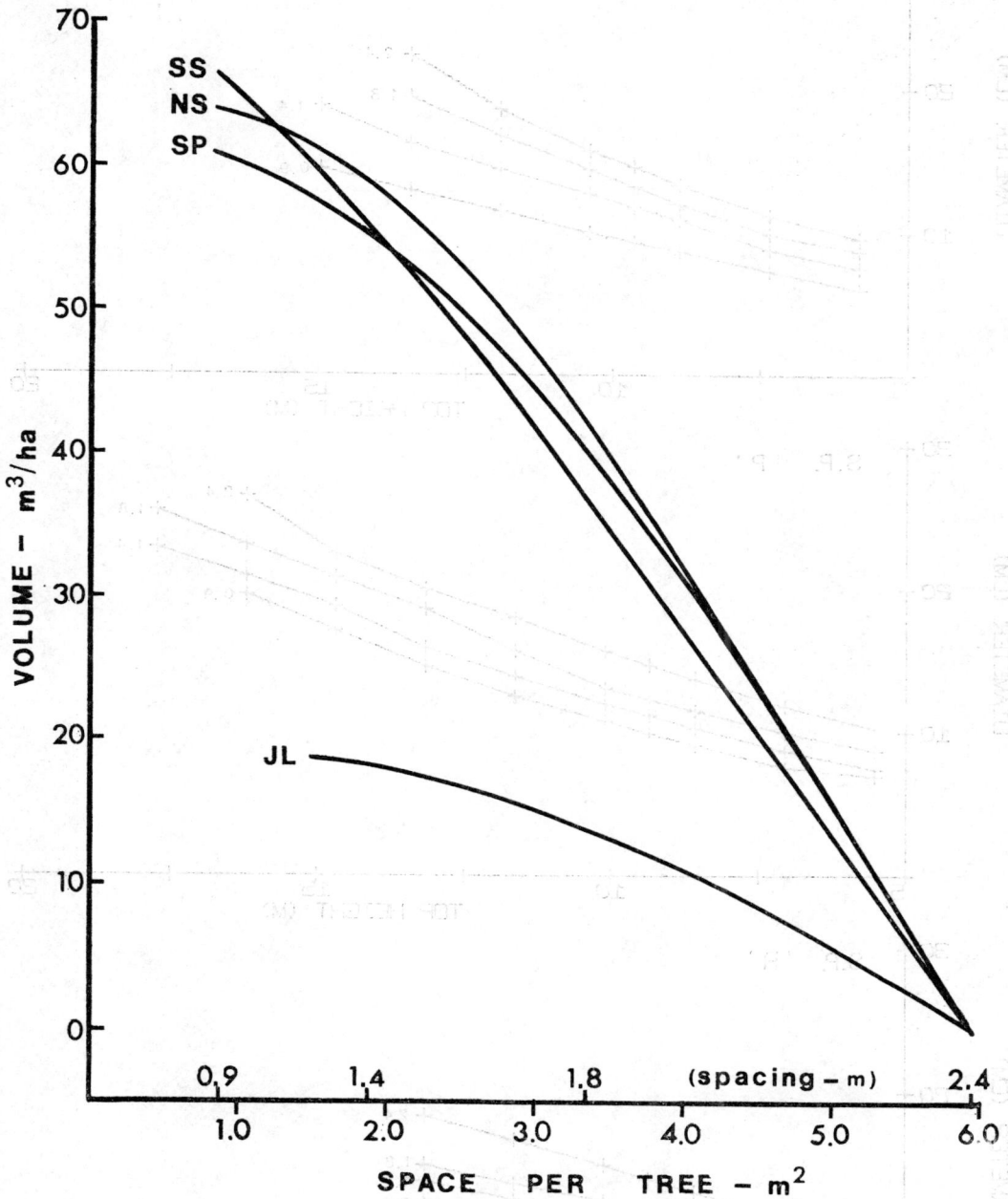

Figure 29. Total volume production of different spacings, relative to that of 2·4 m spacing, at age of maximum mean annual increment in Scots pine, Sitka spruce, Norway spruce and Japanese larch.

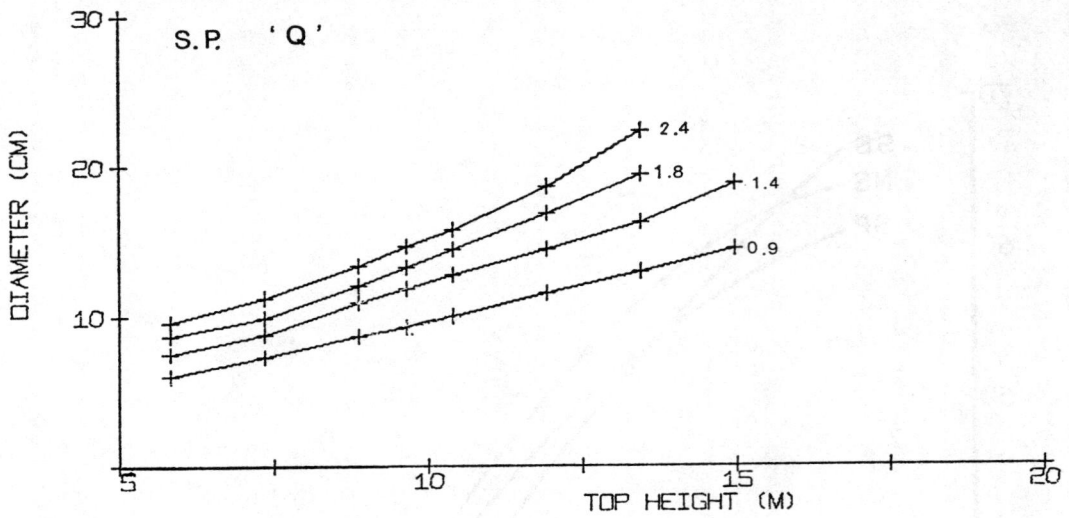

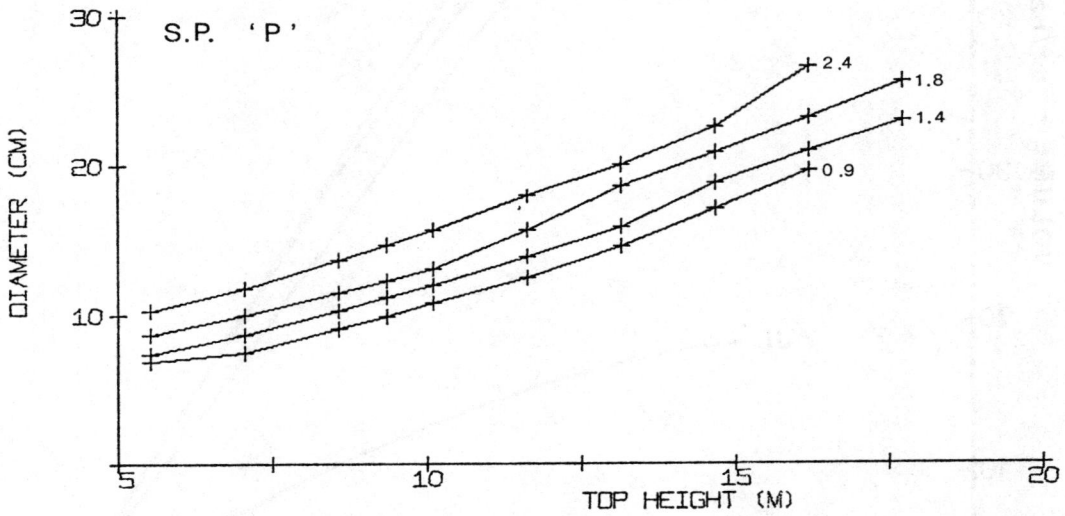

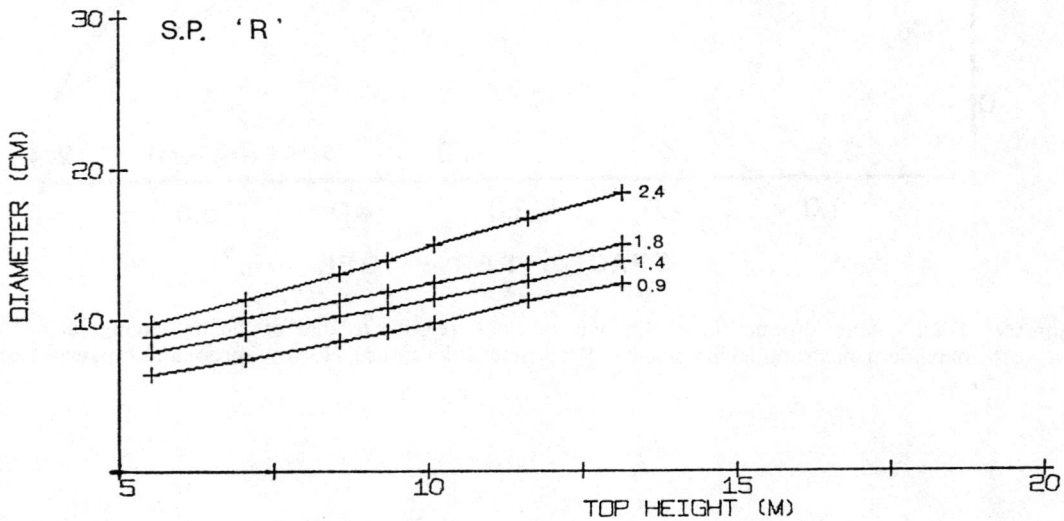

Figure 30.   Relationship between mean dbh and top height for 'Q', 'P' and 'R' thinning treatments in Scots pine.

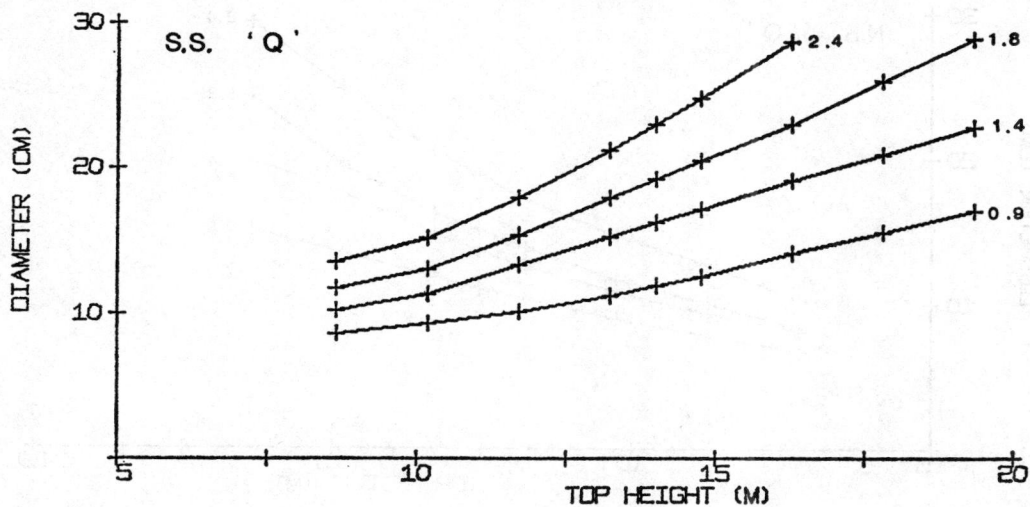

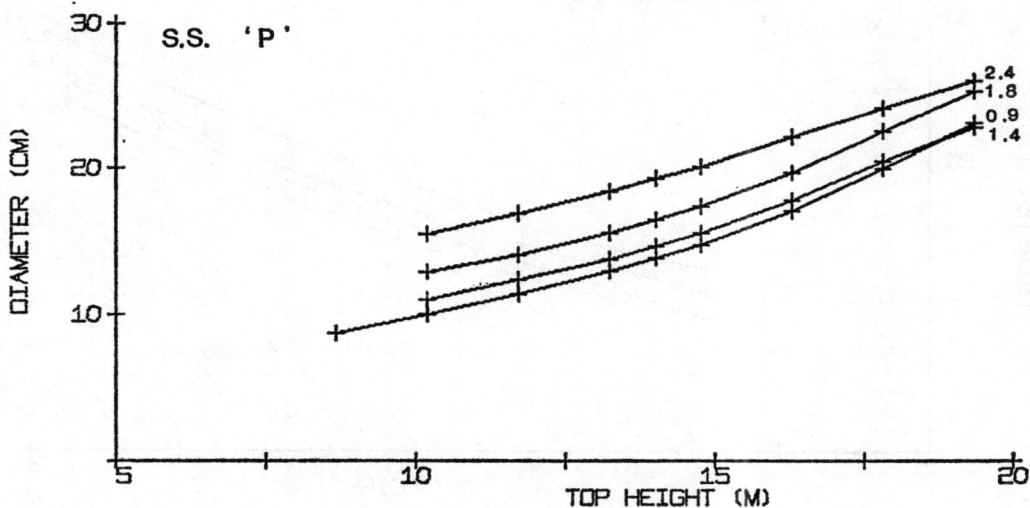

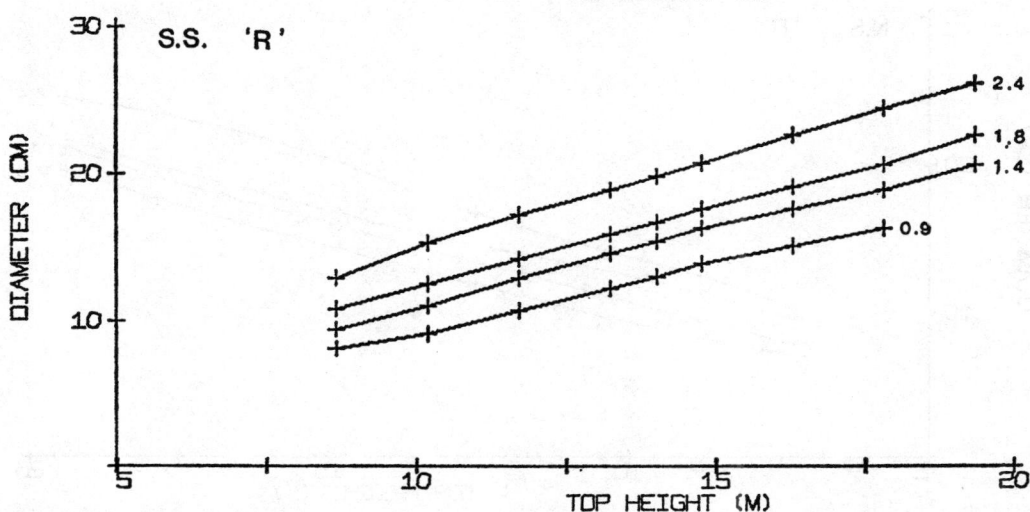

Figure 31.   Relationship between mean dbh and top height for 'Q', 'P' and 'R' thinning treatments in Sitka spruce.

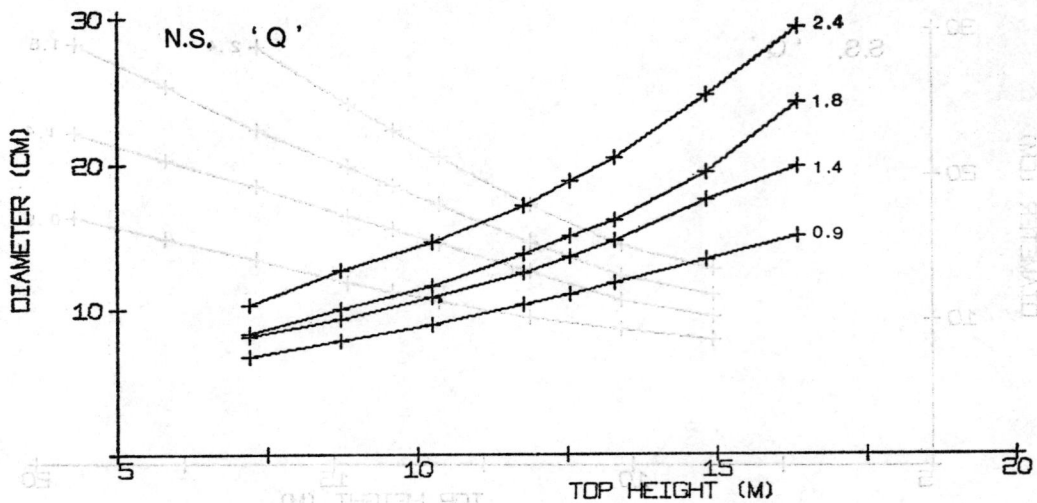

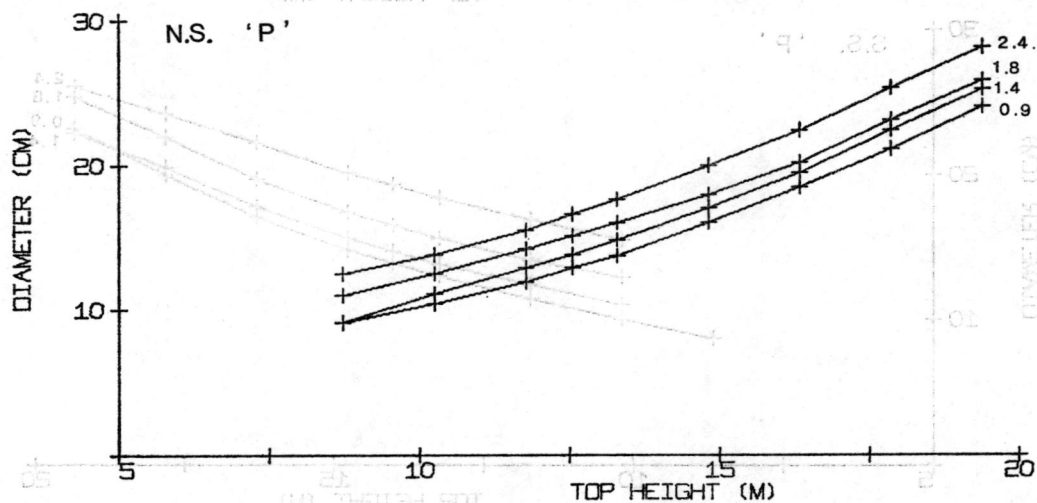

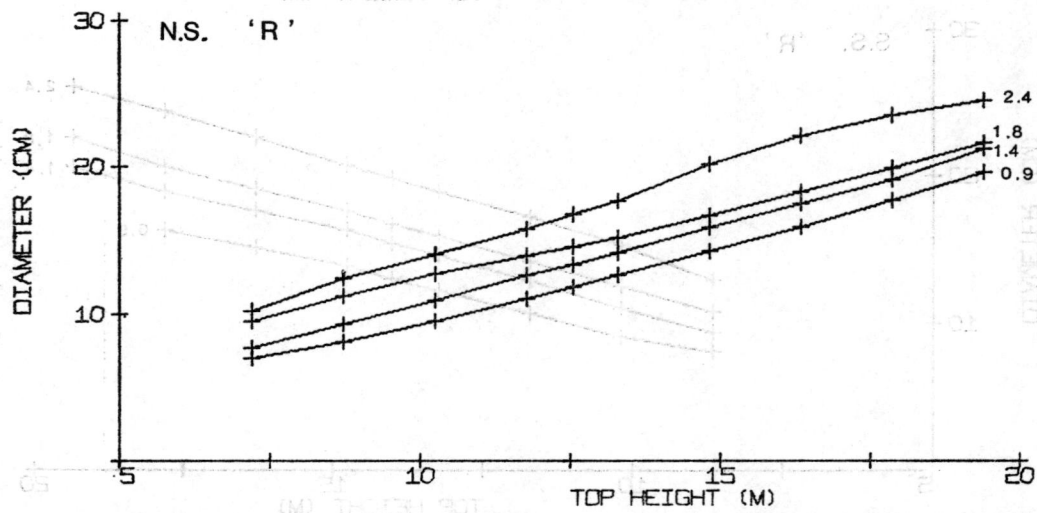

Figure 32. Relationship between mean dbh and top height for 'Q', 'P' and 'R' thinning treatments in Norway spruce.

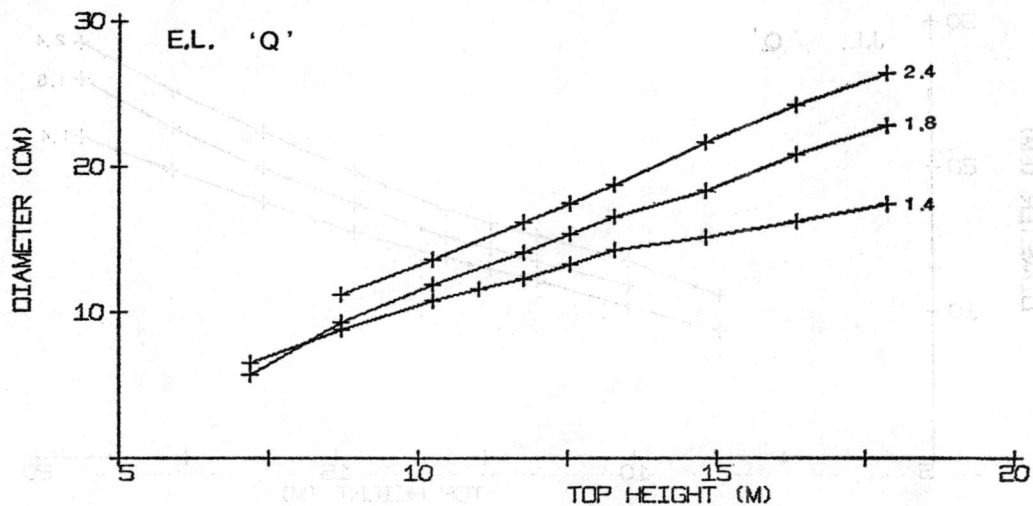

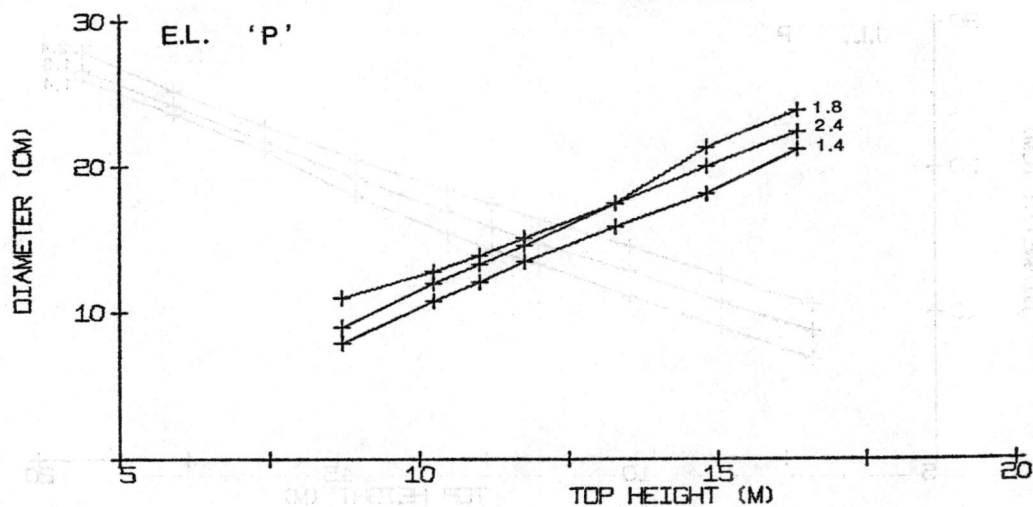

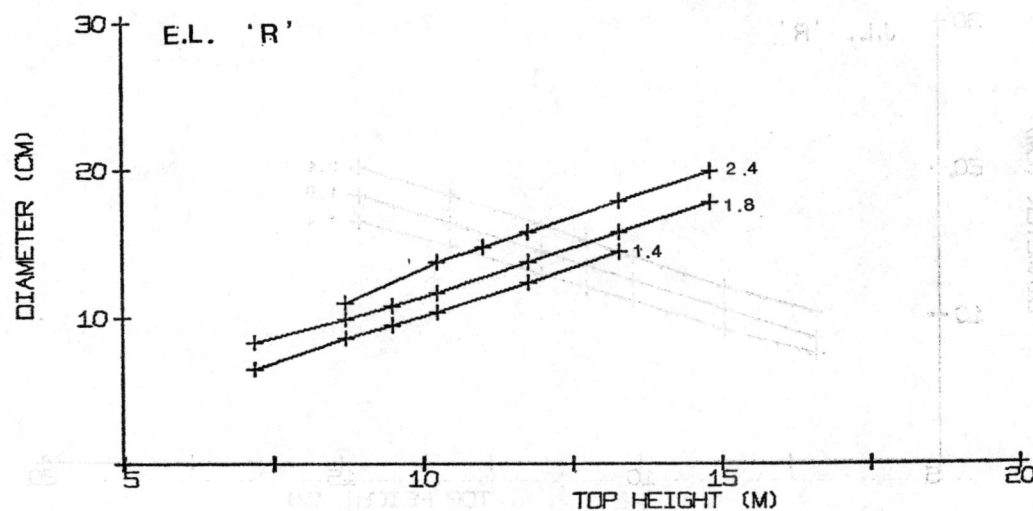

Figure 33. Relationship between mean dbh and top height for 'Q', 'P' and 'R' thinning treatments in European larch.

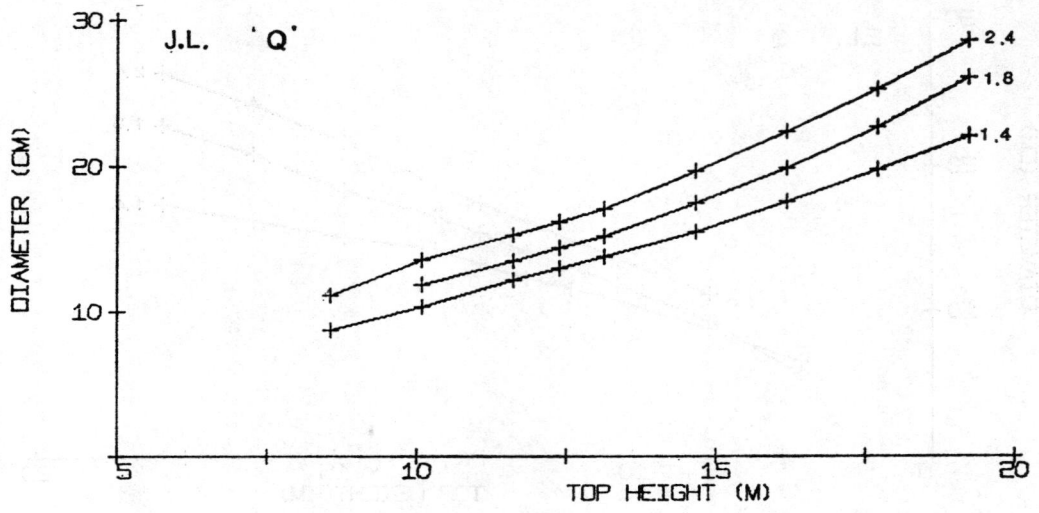

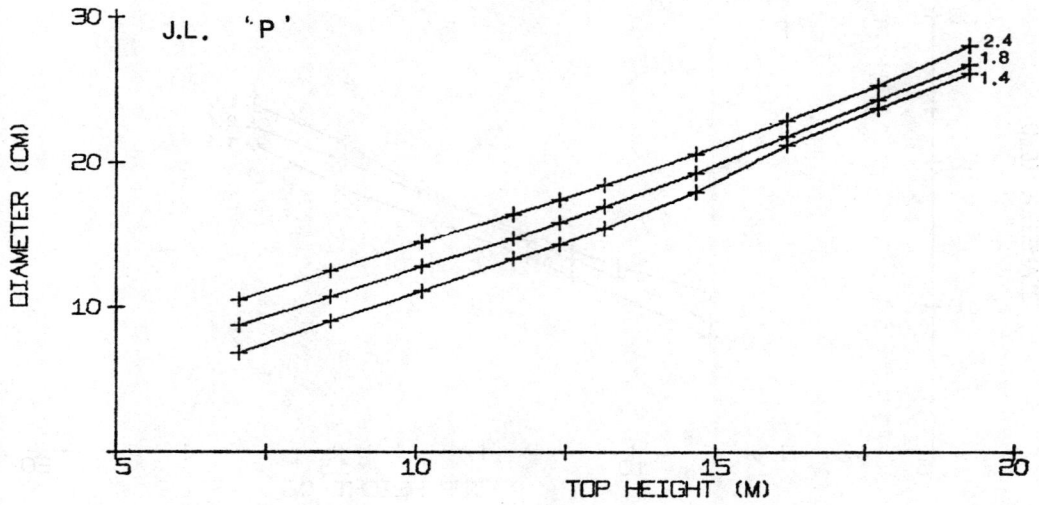

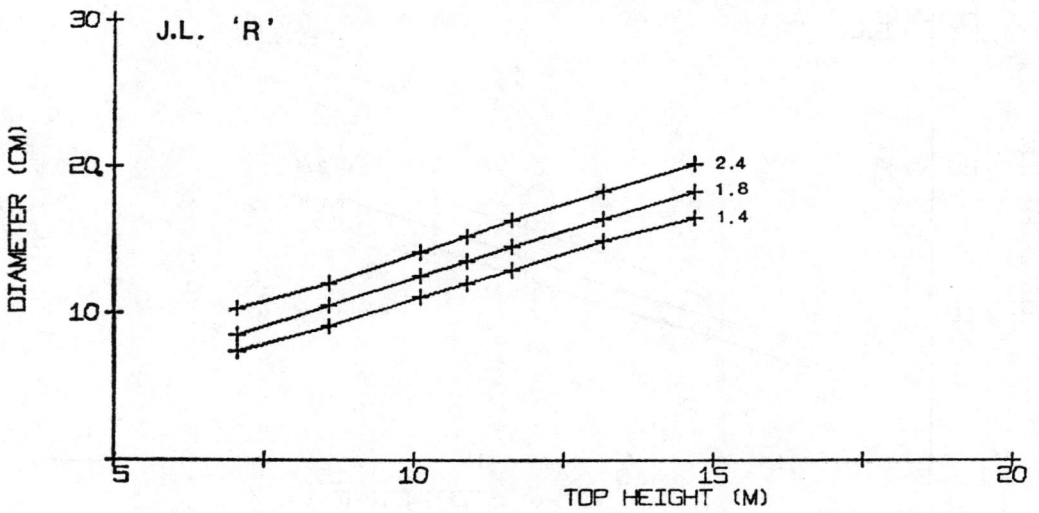

Figure 34.   Relationship between mean dbh and top height for 'Q', 'P' and 'R' thinning treatments in Japanese larch.

36

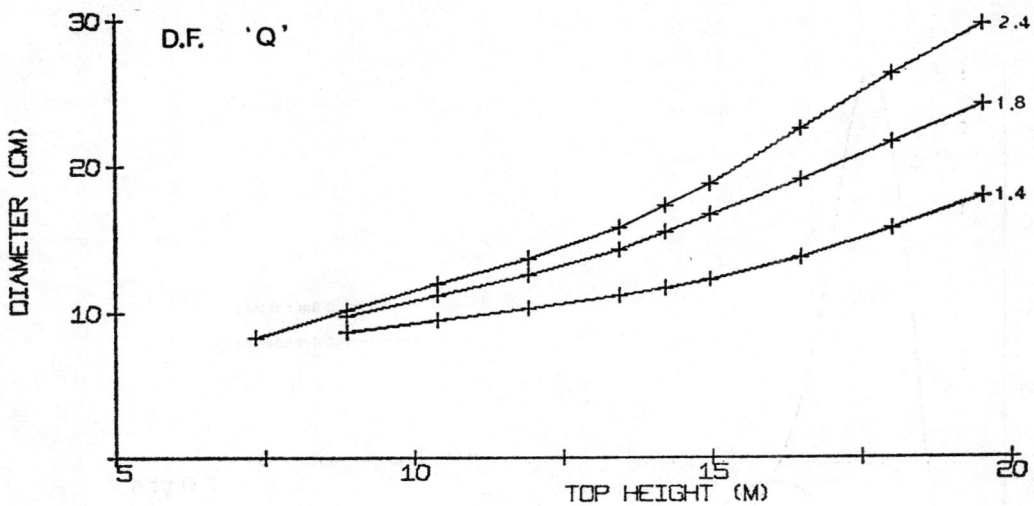

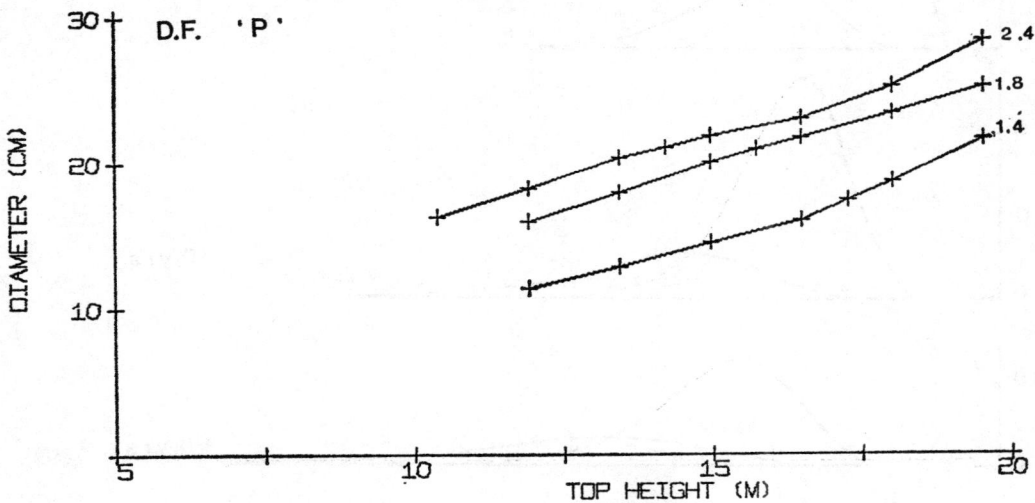

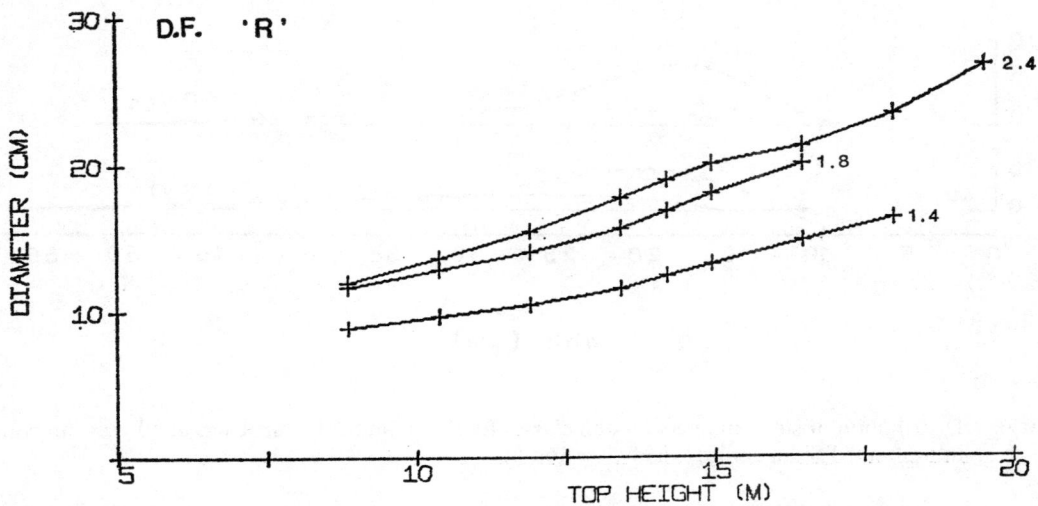

Figure 35. Relationship between mean dbh and top height for 'Q', 'P' and 'R' thinning treatments in Douglas fir.

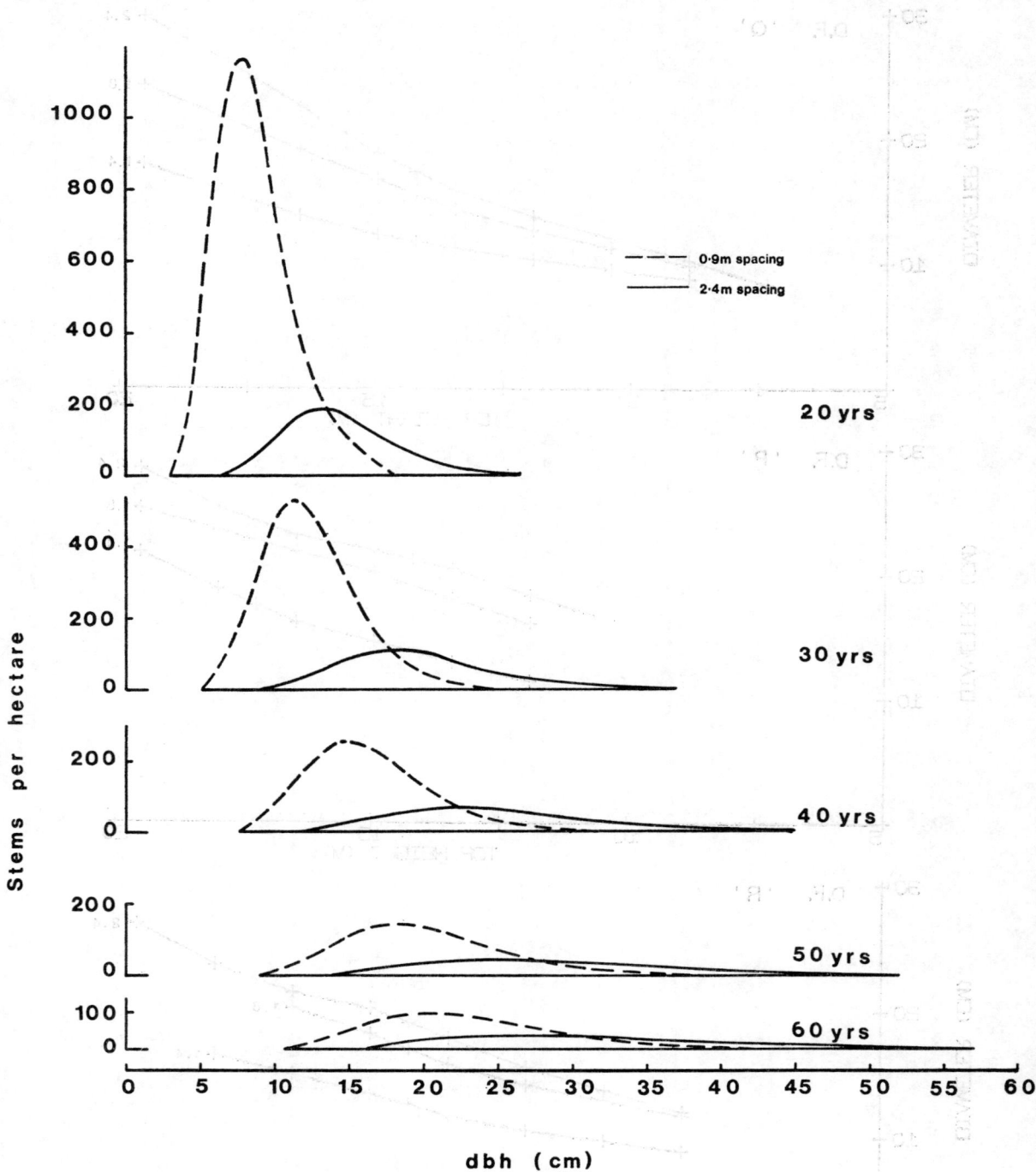

Figure 36. Distribution of stem numbers by dbh classes for 0·9 m and 2·4 m spacings at 10 year intervals, in unthinned Sitka spruce, yield class 16.

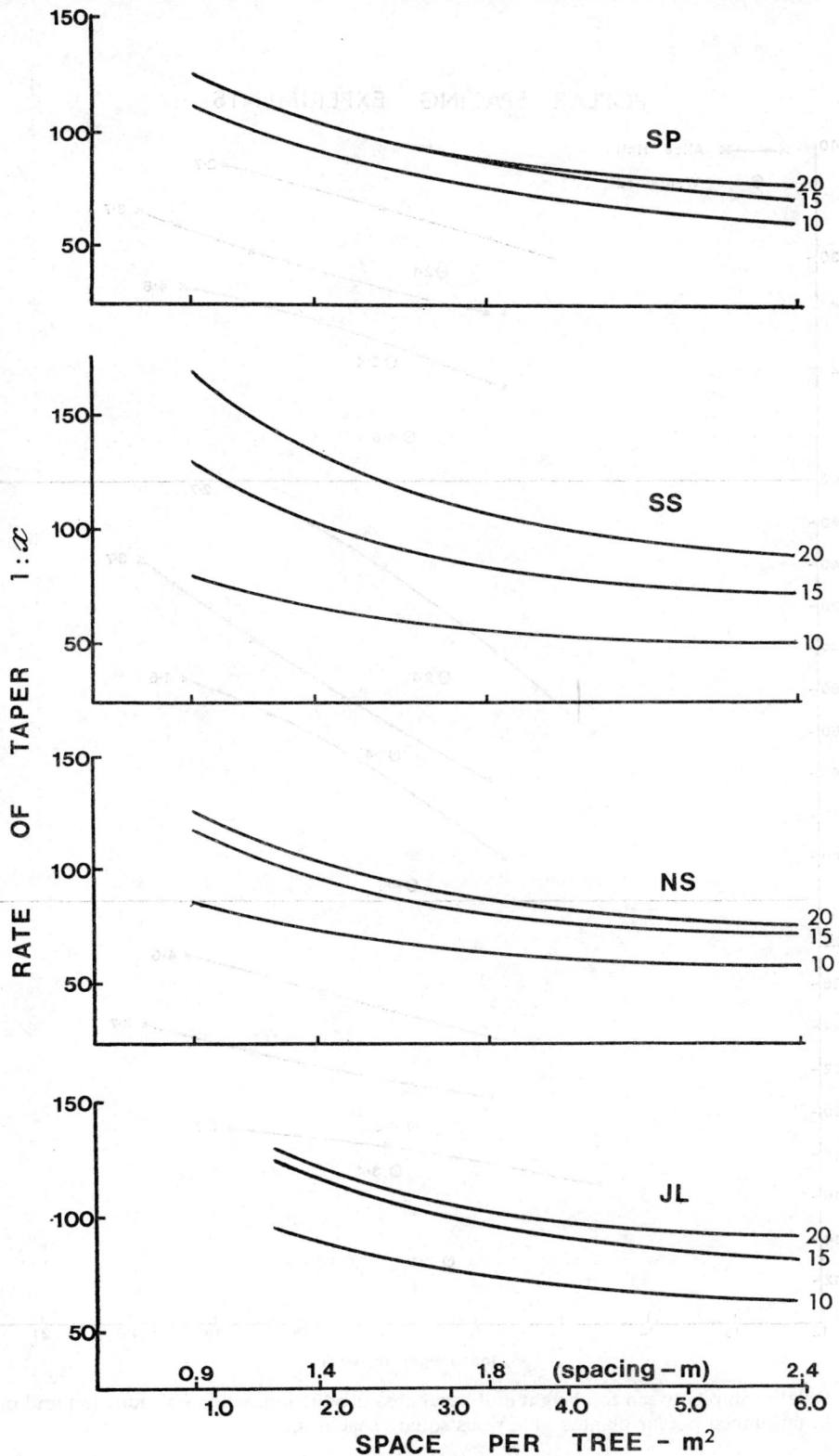

Figure 37. The influence of spacing on taper in the lower 6 m section of the average tree at top heights of 10, 15 and 20 metres in Scots pine, Sitka spruce, Norway spruce and Japanese larch. Normal intensity thinning is assumed.

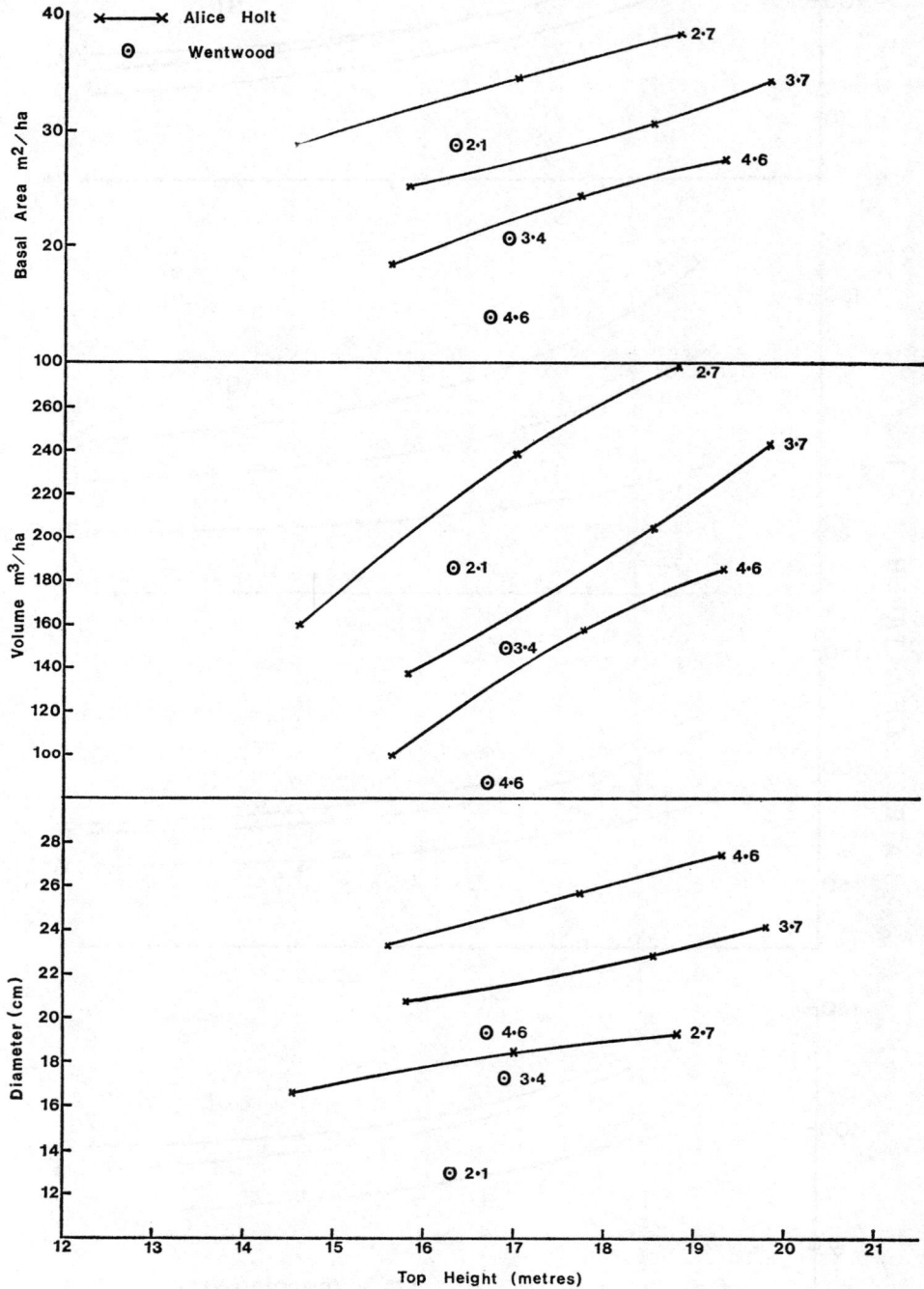

Figure 38. Relationship between top height and basal area production, volume production and mean dbh in unthinned poplar planted at various square spacings.

IV. YIELD MODELS

Presenting the effects of different spacings on crop characteristics in a familiar yield table format permits convenient comparison and evaluation of the different treatments.

In drawing together, in a yield model, the results of the analysis of individual components, there are three important features to be considered.

In the first place, most of the parameters analysed have been directly related to the top height of the individual plots. It was, however, recognised that top height differences existed between spacings. Consequently, to demonstrate the real differences in these parameters resulting from different spacings *on the same site* it was necessary to incorporate these differences in the models.

Secondly, question of the general growth *rate* or yield class has not figured prominently in the analysis to this point on account of the technique of relating parameters to top height irrespective of age. Consideration of yield class is essential however, and models for three alternative yield classes are presented in Appendices II and III for each species.

The third consideration concerns the subsequent thinning treatments. Current views on this subject differ from those evident at the time when the 'P', 'Q' and 'R' treatments were conceived. There are countless possible thinning treatments but only two basic treatments have been modelled here. These are first, no thinning at all (Appendix II), which is in effect the 'R' series treatment, and secondly, a standard 'low' thinning at an intensity currently adopted in field practice (Appendix III), usually termed normal Management Table intensity (Hamilton and Christie, 1971) which can be regarded as a more rational substitute for the 'P' treatments. Yield information is inadequate to model 'Q' treatments reliably.

No attempt has been made to construct models for European larch or Douglas fir due to the paucity of reliable data. Similarly, lack of 'R' treatments in Japanese larch made it difficult to produce adequate models of no-thinning treatment in that species.

A computer program designed to construct yield models of various treatments has for some time been in use and is being continually developed by the Mensuration Section. It was first used in con-structing the Commission's metric Normal Yield Tables. This program is described in detail in 'Construction and Application of Stand Yield Models' by Hamilton and Christie (1973), (Forestry Commission Research and Development Paper 96).

Its use was dependent on the mathematical characterisation of basic growth functions, e.g. top height/age, mean annual increment/age, etc. The characterisation of these basic functions is described by Christie (1972). For any given species, yield class, age of first thinning, thinning cycle, thinning type (crown or low), thinning intensity and initial plant stockings, the program will model the growth of a stand, tabulating the main crop and thinning parameters at specified ages.

In constructing the spacing models the standard top height/age, mean annual increment/age, form height/top height, and dbh/top height functions, were suitably modified according to the spacing and the results of the analyses. In all models the precise metric equivalents have been used, ie 2·44 m for 8 ft, etc.

Thereafter, by a process of trial and error the various parameters were harmonised to conform both to the accepted growth patterns for the species and yield class, and to the results of the analyses of the effects of spacing on these parameters. Certain experiments exhibited significant average deviations from the normal Production Class ('b') associated with the Normal Yield Tables (Hamilton & Christie, 1971). All yield models, however, have been constructed in terms of 'b' Production Class.

It is important to note that there can be no exact solution to the harmonising of different parameters, and this process inevitably involves an element of subjectivity. This follows from the main parameters being analysed independently, in turn a consequence of the nature of the basic data and the variation in treatments to which the experiments have been subject.

Parameters given most weight (in relation to height) were volume production and basal area. Depending on the particular model, mortality or thinning volumes were subsequently imposed, and the models derived from this information manipulated to accord with the evidence on the remaining parameters of dbh and form.

V. OTHER FORESTRY COMMISSION SPACING EXPERIMENTS

Two spacing series were established in Corsican pine in 1935/6. There are three series in Lodgepole pine. Site differences are particularly marked in the Corsican pine, and are present in the Lodgepole pine to such an extent that a formal analysis was considered to be unrewarding. The data does not indicate, however, any radical departure from the trends established with Scots pine, and it would seem not unreasonable to assume similar quantitative effects for these species.

Of two hardwood spacing experiments established at Fleet Forest in Kirkcudbrightshire, in 1935, one series in oak has survived. There were six spacings, ranging from 0·6 m x 0·9 m to 2·0 m x 2·0 m, but no replications. This experiment suffers both from site variation and inadequate assessments, such that no firm conclusions can be drawn from the data available.

Two more recently established hardwood spacing experiments, however, have provided useful and reliable data. Both are in poplar. One experiment at Alice Holt Forest, Hampshire, planted in 1957 at spacings of:

2·7 x 2·7 m (Actually 9 ft x 9 ft)
3·7 x 3·7 m   ,,   12 ft x 12 ft
4·6 x 4·6 m   ,,   15 ft x 15 ft

was replicated four times. The species is *Populus trichocarpa* 'CF'. Three assessments have been made in this experiment. The second experiment in poplar is in *Populus tacamahaca* x *trichocarpa* '32' at Wentwood, Monmouthshire, and has three spacings replicated three times. The spacings are:

2·1 x 2·1 m (Actually 7 ft x 7 ft)
3·3 x 3·3 m   ,,   11 ft x 11 ft
4·6 x 4·6 m   ,,   15 ft x 15 ft

Only one assessment has been made in this experiment. Neither of the above poplar spacing experiments have been thinned. Height differences are not significant. The relative basal area production, volume production and mean diameter are shown in Figure 38 in which these parameters are plotted against top height, separately for each experiment.

The differences in absolute terms are marked, and exceed those of the coniferous species, reflecting mainly the wider spacings employed.

VI. DISCUSSION

Perhaps the most useful reviews of the extensive literature on spacing are those of Sjolte-Jørgensen (1967), Bartoli and Decourt (1971) and Evert (1971). Whilst it is not intended to undertake a further comprehensive review of the subject here, it is of value to consider the results of the analysis described in this paper with some of the features emerging from these reviews and from other papers.

With regard to mortality, the experimental evidence reviewed by Bartoli and Decourt, and by Evert, displays marked variation in levels of survival at first assessments which could barely be accounted for solely by mutual competition. In common with Sjolte-Jørgensen's evidence, however, the theme of higher incidence of mortality with closer spacings is well established. Among the few papers reporting rates of mortality over an extended height range, two are of interest. Heding (1969) describing a spacing experiment in Norway spruce shows mortality, somewhat over-simplified, to be linearly related to top height. Heding's survival as a percentage of initial stocking is notably higher than the results obtained here at comparable top heights in Norway spruce. The same picture emerges in the

case of Stiell and Berry (1967), describing mortality in White spruce, *Picea alba*, in patterns more akin to those presented in Figure 1.

There is conflicting evidence on the effects of spacing on height growth, though the apparent contradictions are certainly due to some extent to the use of various expressions of stand height. The mean height of the total population tends to have attracted, perhaps unjustifiably, most attention. Although there are some reports of insignificant differences in mean height between varying spacings (Braathe (1952), Braastad (1970)), undoubtedly the bulk of experimental evidence indicates an increase in mean height with increased spacing (Eklund (1956), Bartoli (1971), Bartoli and Decourt (1971), Kjersgaard (1964), Cromer and Pawsey (1957)). It is, however, fairly clear that with the development of densely stocked stands, a higher proportion of trees occupy the lower canopy than in less dense stands. The consequent restriction of height growth of these individuals effectively depresses the mean height of the stand. The effect of spacing on dominant or top height is less clear from the literature. Cromer and Pawsey (1957) in their valuable studies in *Pinus radiata* show increases in dominant height with increased spacing, as does Reukema (1970). A notable source of support for the findings emerging from the analyses of Forestry Commission experiments is reported by Jack (1971). He describes a replicated re-spacing trial (spacing achieved by stem removal at 4 m mean height) in Sitka spruce in Northern Ireland in which top height clearly diminishes with increased spacing. It is not clear precisely why such conflicting evidence exists, though climatic variation is one explanation not easily discounted. The possibility that changes in relative heights may become apparent with age, discussed by Sjolte-Jørgensen (1967), is not consistently evident from the Forestry Commission experiments.

There is little doubt that basal area and volume production are diminished with increased spacing and the trends emerging from the analysis of Commission plots in this respect are heavily endorsed by the evidence presented by Bartoli and Decourt, Sjolte-Jørgensen and Evert. The main point of interest rests therefore, not so much with the indisputable trends but with the absolute differences in values of these parameters which are evident.

In drawing comparisons between the results of different experiments, it is important to consider the measurement limits applied in each case. The effect of imposing a dbh limit of 7 cm compared with no limit is well demonstrated in the basal area production figures. The smaller differences between the 0·9 m and 1·4 m spacings where a 7 cm dbh limit has been applied, stems from the fact that in the 0·9 m spacing a greater number of trees are suppressed and die before reaching this diameter. This situation is also apparent in the volume production figures where a top diameter limit of 7 cm is used. Without this limit applying, volume production would be relatively higher in the 0·9 m spacing plots. It is in fact possible to invert the volume production/spacing relationship by applying merchantable limits which are sufficiently high. The choice of merchantable limit can thus explain some apparently contradictory results evident in the literature.

Evert's summary of studies of basal area production relative to spacing, demonstrate differences on average very close to those presented here for Scots pine, Sitka spruce and Norway spruce over the same range of spacings. With volume production three studies are particularly noteworthy. The study of Cromer and Pawsey (1957) in *Pinus radiata* shows differences in total (to tip) volume over a comparative range of spacings at first thinnings to be rather less than experienced here with, for example, Scots pine considering the different measurement limits. A critical difference in the radiata study, however, is that height growth is shown to be greater in wider spacings, contrary to the findings here which of course have a notable effect on the relative levels of volume production. In a Norway spruce spacing study, Kjersgaard (1964) shows total volume (to tip) production differences which, again allowing for the difference accounted for by volume from 7 cm top diameter to the tip, are not dissimilar to those experienced with the same species here. Finally in Jack's (1972) study in Sitka spruce, volume production (to 8 cm top diameter) losses with wide spacings are again very similar to those found with Sitka spruce in this paper.

As with volume and basal area, a clear relationship between mean dbh and spacing is not in dispute. In this case, of course, the correlation is positive. Since mean dbh is a consequence not only of spacing but of mortality, subsequent thinning treatment and an inherent basal area/top height relationship, absolute comparisons between results presented here and those found in the literature is scarcely fruitful.

A reduction in crop form factor with increased spacing appears to be universally true. The more debatable aspect of this question is whether or not variation in form factor is wholly accounted for by variation in dbh. Cromer and Pawsey (1957) and Echeverria (1943) suggest this to be the case whilst Marsh (1957) has convincingly demonstrated that this is not his experience with *Pinus patula*. The evidence of the Forestry Commission spacing experiments could barely be described as conclusive, but it does tend to support the first mentioned viewpoint.

In general, many of the experiments described in the literature suffer from deficiencies not unlike those of the Forestry Commission experiments, i.e. inadequate replications in the face of site variation, incomplete assessments, limited range in spacings, etc. It is to be expected that more recently established experiments would eliminate these inadequacies and in due course improve on the knowledge of the effect of spacing outlined here.

VII. SUMMARY OF RESULTS

The results of analyses of Forestry Commission spacing experiments in Scots pine, Sitka spruce, Norway spruce, European larch, Japanese larch and Douglas fir demonstrate that:

a. closer spacings result in earlier competition with consequent higher rates of mortality prior to the thinning stage. At 10 m top height about 50% of the original stocking survives in 0·9 m spacing plots compared with about 90% in 2.4 m spacing plots.

b. marginally greater top heights are associated with closer spacings. Absolute differences between 0.9 m and 2.4 m spacings may be almost 1·0 m depending on the species.

c. greater total basal area production results from closer spacings. The absolute differences between 0·9 m and 2·4 m square spacings range from about 16–18 m^2/ha, in Scots pine, Sitka spruce and Norway spruce, but about 8 m^2/ha between the 1·2 and 2·4 m spacings in Japanese larch.

d. greater volume production results from closer spacings. The differences occurring at about the age of first thinning of the widest spacing (10–12 m top height) between the 0·9 and 2·4 m spacing are in the region of 40–55 m^3/ha for Scots pine, Sitka spruce and Norway spruce, rising to about 60–70 m^3/ha at the average age of maximum mean annual increment. In Japanese larch the corresponding differences between the 1·2 m and 2·4 m spacings are about 14 and 18 m^3/ha respectively.

e. greater diameter growth results from wider spacing.

f. crop form factors are lower in crops of wider spacing.

g. taper rate in the lower part of the stem increases with wider spacing.

VIII. REFERENCES

BARTOLI, M. (1971). Premiers resultats (á 11 et 15 ans) d'une experiénce de densité sur le Douglas. *Revue for. fr.* **XXII** (6), 605–608.

BARTOLI, M. and DECOURT, N. (1971). Densité de plantation. *Annls. Sci. for.*, **28**(1) 59–84.

BEHRE, C. E. (1927). Form class taper curves and volume tables and their application. *Jour. Agric. Res.* **35**(8) 673–744.

BRAASTAD, H. (1970). A spacing experiment with *Picea abies. Meddr. norske Skogsfors Ves.* Nr. 105. **XXVIII**(5) 298–329.

BRAATHE, P. (1952). The effect of different spacing upon stand development and yield in forests of Norway spruce. *Meddr. norske Skogsfor Ves.* No. 39, 213–301.

CHRISTIE, J. M. (1972). The characterisation of the relationships between basic crop parameters in yield table construction. Proc. 3rd *Conf. Adv. Gp. For. Stat. IUFRO.*

CROMER, D. A. N. and PAWSEY, C. K. (1957). *Initial spacing and growth of Pinus radiata* For. and Timber Bureau Bulletin 36, Canberra, Australia.

ECHEVERRIA, I. (1943). *Tratamiento del Pinus insignis* (*The management of Pinus insignis*). Inst. for. de Invest. y Exp., No. 26., Madrid.

EKLUND, B. (1956). An experiment in sowing and planting at different spacings. *Meddr. St. Skogsforsk. Inst.* **41**(1).

EVERT, F. (1971). *Spacing studies – a review.* Inform. Rep. FMR-X-37. Forest Management Inst. Can. For. Ser.

HAMILTON, G. J. (1964). *The thinning and espacement of spruce.* Hons. thesis, Edin. Univ.

HAMILTON, G. J. (1972). *Rep. Forest Res. Lond.* 1972 pages 122/3.

HAMILTON, G. J. and CHRISTIE, J. M. (1971). *Forest Management Tables* Bookl. 34 For. Commn, Lond. (HMSO.)

HAMILTON, G. J. and CHRISTIE, J. M. (1973). *Construction and application of stand yield models.* Res. Dev. Pap. 96, For. Commn, Lond.

HEDING, N. (1969). Stem number reduction and diameter development in non-thinned Norway spruce stands with various spacings. *Forst. Fors Vaes. Danm.* **XXXII** (2) 193–243.

HUMMEL, F. C. (1954). The definition of thinning treatments. *Proc. 11th Congr. IUFRO* Rome 1953.

JACK, W. H. (1971). The influence of tree spacing on Sitka spruce growth. *Irish Forestry* **28**(1) 13–33.

KJERSGAARD, O. (1964). An experiment in spacing of Norway spruce. *Forst. ForsVaes. Danm.* **XXIX** (1) 55–68.

MACDONALD, J. (1932). The form of the stem in coniferous trees *Forestry* **VI**(1)

(1932)	,,	,,	,,	**VI**(2)
(1933)	,,	,,	,,	**VII**(1)
(1933)	,,	,,	,,	**VII**(2)
(1934)	,,	,,	,,	**VIII**(1)

MARSH, E. K. (1957). *Some preliminary results from O'Connor's CCT experiments on thinnings and espacements and their practical significance.* Cmmn. Forest Conf. 1957.

REUKEMA, D. L. (1970). Forty-year development of Douglas fir stands planted at various spacings, U.S.D.A. Forest Service Research Paper PNW 100.

ROWAN, A. A. and SKINNER, J. R. (1949) *Report on spacing experiments.* Internal Forestry Commission report.

SJOLTE-JØRGENSEN, J. (1967). Influence of spacing on coniferous plantations. *Int. Rev. For. Res.* **2**, 43–94.

STIELL, W. M. and BERRY, A. B. (1967). *White spruce growth and yield at the Petawawa Forest Experiment Station.* Can. Dept. For. Bch Dept Publication No. 1200.

D

APPENDIX I

LIST OF EXPERIMENTS

Species	Expt Nos.	Forest	Treatment	P Year	Average General Yield Class
Scots pine	2086–2089	Tintern	P	1935	14
	2093–2096	Llanover, Ebbw	P	1935	10
	3344–3347	Roseisle, Laigh of Moray	P	1935	12
	Expt 6 Block III	Roseisle, Laigh of Moray	P	1936	10
	Expt 7 Block I & II	Findon, Black Isle	P	1935	8 & 10
	Expt 1	Slaley	P	1936	9
	1374–1377	Thetford	Q	1935	10
	Expt 6 Block I & II	Roseisle, Laigh of Moray	Q	1936	9
	Expt 3	Glengarry	Q	1935	9
	Expt 7	Findon, Black Isle	Q	1935	9
	Expt 1	Slaley	Q	1936	9
	3410–3413	Findon, Black Isle	R	1936	9
	3422–3425	Roseisle, Laigh of Moray	R	1935	9
	Expt 1	Slaley	R	1936	9
Sitka spruce	Expt 14	Ae	P	1935	17
	Expt 70	Kielder North	P	1936	14
	Expt 2	Barcaldine	P	1935	20
	Expt 5	Knapdale	P	1936	18
	Expt 5	Glen Garry	P	1935	19
	2121–2124	Brecon, Brycheiniog	Q	1935	17
	2125–2128	Radnor	Q	1935	16
	2174–2177	Rheola	Q	1935	12
	Expt 14	Ae	Q	1936	17
	Expt 3	Durris, Banchory	Q	1935	17
	2180–2183	Gwydyr	R	1935	8
	2184–2187	Clocaenog	R	1935	13
	3351–3353	Inverinan, Inverliever	R	1935	22
	Expt 6	Loch Ard	R	1936	17
Norway spruce	2108–2111	Ceri	P	1935	13
	Expt 2	Kershope	P	1936	16
	Expt 69	Kielder North	P	1936	13
	Expt 15	Ae	P	1935	14
	Expt 1	Loch Ard	P	1936	19
	Expt 3	Inverinan, Inverliever	P	1936	14
	Expt 1	Fiunary, Sunart	P	1935	14
	Expt 2	Barcaldine	P	1936	20

Species	Expt Nos.	Forest	Treatment	P Year	Average General Yield Class
Norway spruce	2098–2101	Clocaenog	Q	1935	12
—*continued*	2158–2161	Rheola	Q	1935	13
	Expt 69	Kielder North	Q	1936	13
	Expt 16	Ae	Q	1936	15
	Expt 3	Inverinan, Inverliever	Q	1936	15
	Expt 4	Glen Livet	Q	1935	11
	Expt 4	Glen Garry	Q	1935	14
	Expt 2	Durris, Banchory	Q	1935	12
	3417–3420	Glen Livet	R	1935	12
	3426–3429	Clunes, Leanachan	R	1935	19
	Expt 4	Glen Garry	R	1935	16
Japanese larch	1357–1359	Bodmin, Kernow	P	1935	10
	2065–2067	Crychan	P	1935	12
	2069–2071	Rheola	P	1935	12
	2090–2092	Llanover, Ebbw	P	1935	7
	2105–2107	Gwydyr	P	1935	7
	3280–3283	Drumtochty, Mearns	P	1935	6
	3295–3298	Dalbeattie, Solway	P	1936	12
	Expt 1	Barcaldine	P	1935	13
	Expt 2	Fiunary, Sunart	P	1942	7
	1393–1395	Brendon	Q	1935	10
	2118–2120	Caeo	Q	1935	12
	2135–2137	Brechfa	Q	1935	12
	Expt 1	Barcaldine	Q	1935	13
European larch	1400–1402	Mortimer	P	1935	6
	2102–2104	Clocaenog	P	1935	7
	3261–3264	Fleet	P	1936	9
	Expt 26	Clashindarroch, Huntly	P	1937	5
	1414–1416	Dean	Q	1935	9
	2129–2131	Radnor	Q	1935	5
	Expt 45	Clashindarroch, Huntly	Q	1935	4
Douglas fir	Expt 2	Iverinan, Inverliever	P	1936	16
	1382–1385	Eggesford	Q	1935	18
	2115–2117	Ystwyth	Q	1935	16
	2132–2134	Brechfa	Q	1935	15

SCOTS PINE   YIELD CLASS 10   UNTHINNED

0.9 x 0.9 m spacing

Age	MAIN CROP After Thinning									Yield from THINNINGS						TOTAL YIELD		INCREMENT			Age
	No. of Trees	Top Ht. m	Mean Diam cm	Basal Area m²	Form Factor	Mean Vol. per Tree m³	Volume in cubic metres to top diameters of– 7 cm	18 cm	24 cm	No. of Trees	Mean Diam cm	Mean Vol. per Tree m³	7 cm	18 cm	24 cm	Basal Area m²	Vol. to 7 cm m³	CAI Basal Area m²	CAI Vol. to 7 cm m³	MAI Vol. to 7 cm m³	
20	7205	8.2	7.4	31.1	0.30	0.01	66	0	0	0	0.0	0.00	0	0	0	31.1	66	1.21	8.2	3.3	20
25	5828	10.3	8.9	35.9	0.36	0.02	115	0	0	0	0.0	0.00	0	0	0	35.9	115	0.86	10.7	4.6	25
30	4473	12.2	10.6	39.7	0.42	0.04	173	0	0	0	0.0	0.00	0	0	0	39.7	173	0.71	11.9	5.8	30
35	3695	14.0	12.2	43.1	0.46	0.06	234	1	0	0	0.0	0.00	0	0	0	43.1	234	0.68	12.1	6.7	35
40	3078	15.7	13.9	46.5	0.48	0.10	294	9	0	0	0.0	0.00	0	0	0	46.5	294	0.67	11.8	7.4	40
45	2598	17.2	15.6	49.7	0.49	0.14	352	32	0	0	0.0	0.00	0	0	0	49.7	352	0.62	11.2	7.8	45
50	2223	18.6	17.4	52.7	0.49	0.18	407	76	1	0	0.0	0.00	0	0	0	52.7	407	0.59	10.5	8.1	50
55	1932	19.9	19.1	55.6	0.49	0.24	457	152	16	0	0.0	0.00	0	0	0	55.6	457	0.54	9.6	8.3	55
60	1707	21.0	20.8	58.2	0.49	0.29	503	207	31	0	0.0	0.00	0	0	0	58.2	503	0.47	8.6	8.4	60
65	1518	22.1	22.5	60.2	0.49	0.36	543	298	70	0	0.0	0.00	0	0	0	60.2	543	0.41	7.6	8.4	65
70	1379	23.0	24.0	62.3	0.48	0.42	579	350	98	0	0.0	0.00	0	0	0	62.3	579	0.37	6.6	8.3	70
75	1267	23.8	25.4	64.0	0.48	0.48	609	427	165	0	0.0	0.00	0	0	0	64.0	609	0.31	5.6	8.1	75
80	1174	24.6	26.6	65.3	0.48	0.54	635	469	208	0	0.0	0.00	0	0	0	65.3	635	0.25	4.7	7.9	80

1.4 x 1.4 m spacing

Age	MAIN CROP After Thinning									Yield from THINNINGS						TOTAL YIELD		INCREMENT			Age
	No. of Trees	Top Ht. m	Mean Diam cm	Basal Area m²	Form Factor	Mean Vol. per Tree m³	Volume in cubic metres to top diameters of– 7 cm	18 cm	24 cm	No. of Trees	Mean Diam cm	Mean Vol. per Tree m³	7 cm	18 cm	24 cm	Basal Area m²	Vol. to 7 cm m³	CAI Basal Area m²	CAI Vol. to 7 cm m³	MAI Vol. to 7 cm m³	
20	4186	8.1	8.8	25.3	0.36	0.02	64	0	0	0	0.0	0.00	0	0	0	25.3	64	1.35	8.1	3.2	20
25	3667	10.2	10.6	32.1	0.39	0.03	112	0	0	0	0.0	0.00	0	0	0	32.1	112	1.20	10.5	4.5	25
30	3125	12.1	12.3	37.3	0.43	0.05	170	1	0	0	0.0	0.00	0	0	0	37.3	170	0.99	11.9	5.7	30
35	2713	13.9	14.0	42.0	0.45	0.09	231	13	0	0	0.0	0.00	0	0	0	42.0	231	0.91	12.3	6.6	35
40	2345	15.6	15.9	46.3	0.47	0.12	293	26	0	0	0.0	0.00	0	0	0	46.3	293	0.81	12.0	7.3	40
45	2030	17.1	17.7	50.1	0.48	0.17	352	65	1	0	0.0	0.00	0	0	0	50.1	352	0.71	11.5	7.8	45
50	1771	18.5	19.6	53.4	0.48	0.23	408	136	15	0	0.0	0.00	0	0	0	53.4	408	0.64	10.7	8.2	50
55	1560	19.8	21.5	56.4	0.48	0.29	459	222	42	0	0.0	0.00	0	0	0	56.4	459	0.57	9.7	8.3	55
60	1392	20.9	23.3	59.1	0.47	0.36	505	305	85	0	0.0	0.00	0	0	0	59.1	505	0.51	8.7	8.4	60
65	1259	22.0	25.0	61.6	0.47	0.43	546	359	119	0	0.0	0.00	0	0	0	61.6	546	0.43	7.7	8.4	65
70	1143	22.9	26.6	63.4	0.47	0.51	582	429	191	0	0.0	0.00	0	0	0	63.4	582	0.36	6.7	8.3	70
75	1056	23.7	28.0	65.1	0.46	0.58	613	490	269	0	0.0	0.00	0	0	0	65.1	613	0.32	5.8	8.2	75
80	985	24.5	29.3	66.6	0.46	0.65	640	527	315	0	0.0	0.00	0	0	0	66.6	640	0.27	5.0	8.0	80

1.8 x 1.8 m spacing

	MAIN CROP — After Thinning									Yield from THINNINGS						TOTAL YIELD		INCREMENT CAI MAI			
Age	No. of Trees	Top Ht. m	Mean Diam cm	Basal Area m²	Form Factor	Mean Vol. per Tree m³	Vol 7 cm	Vol 18 cm	Vol 24 cm	No. of Trees	Mean Diam cm	Mean Vol. per Tree m³	Vol 7 cm	Vol 18 cm	Vol 24 cm	Basal Area m²	Vol to 7 cm m³	Basal Area m²	Vol to 7 cm m³	Vol to 7 cm m³	Age
21	2580	8.3	10.3	21.7	0.40	0.03	65	0	0	0	0.0	0.00	0	0	0	21.7	65	1.41	8.2	3.1	21
26	2408	10.4	12.2	28.3	0.45	0.05	113	0	0	0	0.0	0.00	0	0	0	28.3	113	1.26	10.6	4.3	26
31	2154	12.3	14.2	34.3	0.45	0.08	171	9	0	0	0.0	0.00	0	0	0	34.3	171	1.13	12.2	5.5	31
36	1930	14.0	16.2	39.7	0.46	0.12	235	31	0	0	0.0	0.00	0	0	0	39.7	235	1.06	12.8	6.5	36
41	1745	15.7	18.1	44.9	0.47	0.17	299	76	5	0	0.0	0.00	0	0	0	44.9	299	0.97	12.7	7.3	41
46	1571	17.2	20.0	49.4	0.47	0.23	362	149	22	0	0.0	0.00	0	0	0	49.4	362	0.83	12.1	7.9	46
51	1413	18.6	21.9	53.2	0.46	0.30	421	203	39	0	0.0	0.00	0	0	0	53.2	421	0.71	11.2	8.2	51
56	1276	19.8	23.7	56.5	0.46	0.37	474	286	80	0	0.0	0.00	0	0	0	56.5	474	0.62	10.2	8.5	56
61	1165	21.0	25.5	59.5	0.46	0.45	523	367	142	0	0.0	0.00	0	0	0	59.5	523	0.57	9.4	8.6	61
66	1078	22.0	27.1	62.1	0.45	0.53	568	438	219	0	0.0	0.00	0	0	0	62.1	568	0.48	8.6	8.6	66
71	1001	22.9	28.6	64.3	0.45	0.61	609	487	267	0	0.0	0.00	0	0	0	64.3	609	0.41	7.7	8.6	71
76	944	23.7	29.9	66.3	0.45	0.68	645	532	317	0	0.0	0.00	0	0	0	66.3	645	0.37	6.9	8.5	76
81	897	24.4	31.1	68.0	0.44	0.76	677	585	398	0	0.0	0.00	0	0	0	68.0	677	0.32	6.1	8.4	81

2.4 x 2.4 m spacing

	MAIN CROP — After Thinning									Yield from THINNINGS						TOTAL YIELD		INCREMENT CAI MAI			
Age	No. of Trees	Top Ht. m	Mean Diam cm	Basal Area m²	Form Factor	Mean Vol. per Tree m³	Vol 7 cm	Vol 18 cm	Vol 24 cm	No. of Trees	Mean Diam cm	Mean Vol. per Tree m³	Vol 7 cm	Vol 18 cm	Vol 24 cm	Basal Area m²	Vol to 7 cm m³	Basal Area m²	Vol to 7 cm m³	Vol to 7 cm m³	Age
24	1485	9.1	13.3	20.5	0.41	0.05	70	2	0	0	0.0	0.00	0	0	0	20.5	70	1.60	9.0	2.9	24
29	1441	11.1	15.9	28.1	0.42	0.09	121	10	0	0	0.0	0.00	0	0	0	28.1	121	1.50	11.0	4.2	29
34	1349	12.9	18.3	35.4	0.42	0.13	180	45	3	0	0.0	0.00	0	0	0	35.4	180	1.42	12.4	5.3	34
39	1285	14.6	20.5	42.2	0.43	0.19	244	100	15	0	0.0	0.00	0	0	0	42.2	244	1.27	13.0	6.3	39
44	1211	16.1	22.5	48.2	0.43	0.26	310	170	39	0	0.0	0.00	0	0	0	48.2	310	1.09	12.9	7.0	44
49	1132	17.5	24.5	53.2	0.43	0.33	374	245	81	0	0.0	0.00	0	0	0	53.2	374	0.93	12.3	7.6	49
54	1053	18.9	26.4	57.4	0.43	0.41	433	320	142	0	0.0	0.00	0	0	0	57.4	433	0.78	11.3	8.0	54
59	978	20.0	28.2	61.0	0.42	0.50	487	390	214	0	0.0	0.00	0	0	0	61.0	487	0.66	10.2	8.3	59
64	914	21.1	29.9	64.0	0.42	0.59	536	442	264	0	0.0	0.00	0	0	0	64.0	536	0.57	9.4	8.4	64
69	858	22.1	31.5	66.7	0.42	0.68	581	501	342	0	0.0	0.00	0	0	0	66.7	581	0.51	8.7	8.4	69
74	818	22.9	32.8	69.2	0.42	0.76	623	547	393	0	0.0	0.00	0	0	0	69.2	623	0.46	7.9	8.4	74
79	784	23.6	34.0	71.2	0.41	0.84	660	597	462	0	0.0	0.00	0	0	0	71.2	660	0.39	7.0	8.4	79

0.9 x 0.9m spacing

	MAIN CROP						After Thinning			Yield from THINNINGS						TOTAL YIELD		INCREMENT			
Age	No. of Trees	Top Ht. (m)	Mean Diam (cm)	Basal Area (m²)	Form Factor	Mean Vol. per Tree (m³)	7 cm	18 cm	24 cm	No. of Trees	Mean Diam (cm)	Mean Vol. per Tree (m³)	7 cm	18 cm	24 cm	Basal Area (m²)	Vol. to 7 cm (m³)	CAI Basal Area (m²)	CAI Vol. to 7 cm (m³)	MAI Vol. to 7 cm (m³)	Age
19	8440	6.3	6.3	26.3	0.25	0.00	35	0	0	0	0.0	0.00	0	0	0	26.3	35	0.53	4.9	1.8	19
24	7186	8.2	7.4	30.7	0.30	0.01	66	0	0	0	0.0	0.00	0	0	0	30.7	66	0.90	7.3	2.8	24
29	5995	10.1	8.7	35.3	0.35	0.02	108	0	0	0	0.0	0.00	0	0	0	35.3	108	0.81	9.2	3.7	29
34	4856	11.7	10.1	38.8	0.40	0.03	158	0	0	0	0.0	0.00	0	0	0	38.8	158	0.64	10.3	4.6	34
39	4095	13.3	11.4	41.7	0.44	0.05	211	0	0	0	0.0	0.00	0	0	0	41.7	211	0.59	10.5	5.4	39
44	3496	14.8	12.8	44.7	0.47	0.08	263	2	0	0	0.0	0.00	0	0	0	44.7	263	0.58	10.2	6.0	44
49	3011	16.1	14.2	47.5	0.48	0.10	313	18	0	0	0.0	0.00	0	0	0	47.5	313	0.54	9.7	6.4	49
54	2623	17.3	15.6	50.1	0.49	0.14	360	32	0	0	0.0	0.00	0	0	0	50.1	360	0.50	9.0	6.7	54
59	2314	18.4	17.0	52.5	0.50	0.17	403	75	1	0	0.0	0.00	0	0	0	52.5	403	0.47	8.3	6.8	59
64	2068	19.5	18.4	54.8	0.50	0.21	443	112	7	0	0.0	0.00	0	0	0	54.8	443	0.44	7.5	6.9	64
69	1870	20.4	19.7	56.9	0.49	0.26	478	159	17	0	0.0	0.00	0	0	0	56.9	478	0.38	6.5	6.9	69
74	1709	21.2	20.9	58.6	0.49	0.30	508	209	31	0	0.0	0.00	0	0	0	58.6	508	0.30	5.4	6.9	74
79	1576	21.9	22.0	59.9	0.49	0.34	532	292	68	0	0.0	0.00	0	0	0	59.9	532	0.20	4.2	6.7	79
84	1451	22.5	23.1	60.6	0.48	0.38	550	332	93	0	0.0	0.00	0	0	0	60.6	550	0.13	3.2	6.6	84

1.4 x 1.4m spacing

	MAIN CROP						After Thinning			Yield from THINNINGS						TOTAL YIELD		INCREMENT			
Age	No. of Trees	Top Ht. (m)	Mean Diam (cm)	Basal Area (m²)	Form Factor	Mean Vol. per Tree (m³)	7 cm	18 cm	24 cm	No. of Trees	Mean Diam (cm)	Mean Vol. per Tree (m³)	7 cm	18 cm	24 cm	Basal Area (m²)	Vol. to 7 cm (m³)	CAI Basal Area (m²)	CAI Vol. to 7 cm (m³)	MAI Vol. to 7 cm (m³)	Age
19	4652	6.2	7.3	19.3	0.33	0.01	34	0	0	0	0.0	0.00	0	0	0	19.3	34	0.80	4.8	1.8	19
24	4179	8.1	8.7	25.0	0.36	0.02	64	0	0	0	0.0	0.00	0	0	0	25.0	64	1.19	7.2	2.7	24
29	3710	10.0	10.3	31.2	0.38	0.03	105	0	0	0	0.0	0.00	0	0	0	31.2	105	1.06	8.9	3.6	29
34	3244	11.6	11.8	35.7	0.42	0.05	153	0	0	0	0.0	0.00	0	0	0	35.7	153	0.88	10.1	4.5	34
39	2882	13.2	13.3	40.0	0.45	0.07	206	6	0	0	0.0	0.00	0	0	0	40.0	206	0.81	10.6	5.3	39
44	2553	14.7	14.8	43.8	0.46	0.10	259	15	0	0	0.0	0.00	0	0	0	43.8	259	0.72	10.4	5.9	44
49	2262	16.0	16.3	47.2	0.47	0.14	310	41	0	0	0.0	0.00	0	0	0	47.2	310	0.64	9.8	6.3	49
54	2014	17.2	17.8	50.2	0.48	0.18	357	66	1	0	0.0	0.00	0	0	0	50.2	357	0.57	9.2	6.6	54
59	1806	18.3	19.3	52.9	0.48	0.22	402	134	14	0	0.0	0.00	0	0	0	52.9	402	0.52	8.5	6.8	59
64	1634	19.4	20.8	55.4	0.48	0.27	442	182	27	0	0.0	0.00	0	0	0	55.4	442	0.47	7.6	6.9	64
69	1492	20.3	22.2	57.6	0.48	0.32	478	262	61	0	0.0	0.00	0	0	0	57.6	478	0.40	6.6	6.9	69
74	1373	21.1	23.5	59.5	0.47	0.37	508	307	86	0	0.0	0.00	0	0	0	59.5	508	0.33	5.5	6.9	74
79	1274	21.8	24.7	60.8	0.47	0.42	533	350	116	0	0.0	0.00	0	0	0	60.8	533	0.22	4.4	6.7	79
84	1180	22.4	25.8	61.6	0.47	0.47	552	387	150	0	0.0	0.00	0	0	0	61.6	552	0.15	3.3	6.6	84

1.8 x 1.8 m spacing

	MAIN CROP					After Thinning				Yield from THINNINGS						TOTAL YIELD		INCREMENT			
							Volume in cubic metres to top of diameters of-						Volume in cubic metres to top of diameters of-					CAI	CAI	MAI	
Age	No. of Trees	Top Ht. (m)	Mean Diam (cm)	Basal Area (m²)	Form Factor	Mean Vol. per Tree (m³)	7 cm	18 cm	24 cm	No. of Trees	Mean Diam (cm)	Mean Vol. per Tree (m³)	7 cm	18 cm	24 cm	Basal Area (m²)	Vol. to 7 cm (m³)	Basal Area (m²)	Vol. to 7 cm (m³)	Vol. to 7 cm (m³)	Age
20	2710	6.4	8.5	15.3	0.39	0.01	33	0	0	0	0.0	0.00	0	0	0	15.3	33	0.91	4.7	1.7	20
25	2582	8.3	10.3	21.3	0.40	0.02	64	0	0	0	0.0	0.00	0	0	0	21.3	64	1.14	7.1	2.5	25
30	2389	10.1	11.9	26.7	0.43	0.04	105	0	0	0	0.0	0.00	0	0	0	26.7	105	1.09	9.0	3.5	30
35	2192	11.8	13.7	32.2	0.45	0.07	154	4	0	0	0.0	0.00	0	0	0	32.2	154	1.06	10.3	4.4	35
40	2019	13.3	15.3	37.4	0.46	0.10	208	18	0	0	0.0	0.00	0	0	0	37.4	208	0.99	10.8	5.2	40
45	1857	14.7	17.0	42.1	0.46	0.14	262	35	0	0	0.0	0.00	0	0	0	42.1	262	0.87	10.8	5.8	45
50	1706	16.1	18.6	46.1	0.47	0.19	316	80	5	0	0.0	0.00	0	0	0	46.1	316	0.76	10.4	6.3	50
55	1566	17.3	20.1	49.6	0.47	0.23	366	150	22	0	0.0	0.00	0	0	0	49.6	366	0.66	9.7	6.7	55
60	1439	18.4	21.6	52.7	0.47	0.29	413	200	38	0	0.0	0.00	0	0	0	52.7	413	0.58	8.8	6.9	60
65	1329	19.3	23.0	55.4	0.46	0.34	455	275	77	0	0.0	0.00	0	0	0	55.4	455	0.51	7.9	7.0	65
70	1234	20.2	24.4	57.7	0.46	0.40	492	323	107	0	0.0	0.00	0	0	0	57.7	492	0.44	7.0	7.0	70
75	1156	21.0	25.7	59.8	0.45	0.45	524	367	142	0	0.0	0.00	0	0	0	59.8	524	0.36	6.0	7.0	75
80	1090	21.7	26.8	61.3	0.45	0.51	552	407	181	0	0.0	0.00	0	0	0	61.3	552	0.26	5.0	6.9	80
85	1027	22.3	27.8	62.4	0.45	0.56	574	443	221	0	0.0	0.00	0	0	0	62.4	574	0.19	4.0	6.8	85

2.4 x 2.4 m spacing

	MAIN CROP					After Thinning				Yield from THINNINGS						TOTAL YIELD		INCREMENT			
							Volume in cubic metres to top of diameters of-						Volume in cubic metres to top of diameters of-					CAI	CAI	MAI	
Age	No. of Trees	Top Ht. (m)	Mean Diam (cm)	Basal Area (m²)	Form Factor	Mean Vol. per Tree (m³)	7 cm	18 cm	24 cm	No. of Trees	Mean Diam (cm)	Mean Vol. per Tree (m³)	7 cm	18 cm	24 cm	Basal Area (m²)	Vol. to 7 cm (m³)	Basal Area (m²)	Vol. to 7 cm (m³)	Vol. to 7 cm (m³)	Age
24	1522	7.5	11.1	14.6	0.41	0.03	40	0	0	0	0.0	0.00	0	0	0	14.6	40	1.14	5.4	1.6	24
29	1482	9.3	13.4	21.0	0.42	0.05	73	2	0	0	0.0	0.00	0	0	0	21.0	73	1.27	7.8	2.5	29
34	1398	11.0	15.8	27.3	0.42	0.08	117	10	0	0	0.0	0.00	0	0	0	27.3	117	1.31	9.5	3.4	34
39	1360	12.5	17.9	34.1	0.42	0.12	168	31	0	0	0.0	0.00	0	0	0	34.1	168	1.27	10.5	4.3	39
44	1309	14.0	19.7	40.1	0.42	0.17	222	74	8	0	0.0	0.00	0	0	0	40.1	222	1.12	10.8	5.0	44
49	1250	15.3	21.5	45.3	0.43	0.22	276	133	25	0	0.0	0.00	0	0	0	45.3	276	0.97	10.7	5.6	49
54	1187	16.6	23.1	49.7	0.43	0.28	329	199	55	0	0.0	0.00	0	0	0	49.7	329	0.83	10.3	6.1	54
59	1123	17.7	24.6	53.5	0.43	0.34	379	249	83	0	0.0	0.00	0	0	0	53.5	379	0.71	9.6	6.4	59
64	1062	18.7	26.1	56.9	0.42	0.40	425	314	139	0	0.0	0.00	0	0	0	56.9	425	0.61	8.7	6.6	64
69	1005	19.6	27.5	59.6	0.42	0.46	466	360	179	0	0.0	0.00	0	0	0	59.6	466	0.52	7.7	6.8	69
74	953	20.4	28.8	62.1	0.42	0.53	502	401	220	0	0.0	0.00	0	0	0	62.1	502	0.45	6.7	6.8	74
79	909	21.1	30.0	64.1	0.42	0.59	533	439	262	0	0.0	0.00	0	0	0	64.1	533	0.36	5.7	6.7	79
84	871	21.7	31.0	65.7	0.42	0.64	559	472	303	0	0.0	0.00	0	0	0	65.7	559	0.26	4.8	6.7	84

51

SCOTS PINE   YIELD CLASS 6   UNTHINNED

0.9 x 0.9 m spacing

	MAIN CROP — After Thinning									Yield from THINNINGS						TOTAL YIELD		INCREMENT C.A.I.		M.A.I.	
Age	No. of Trees	Top Ht. (m)	Mean Diam (cm)	Basal Area (m²)	Form Factor	Mean Vol. per Tree (m³)	Vol. to 7 cm (m³)	Vol. to 18 cm (m³)	Vol. to 24 cm (m³)	No. of Trees	Mean Diam (cm)	Mean Vol. per Tree (m³)	Vol. to 7 cm (m³)	Vol. to 18 cm (m³)	Vol. to 24 cm (m³)	Basal Area (m²)	Vol. to 7 cm (m³)	Basal Area (m²)	Vol. to 7 cm (m³)	Vol. to 7 cm (m³)	Age
23	8572	6.1	6.3	26.6	0.25	0.00	33	0	0	0	0.0	0.00	0	0	0	26.6	33	0.36	4.0	1.4	23
28	7477	7.8	7.1	29.5	0.29	0.01	58	0	0	0	0.0	0.00	0	0	0	29.5	58	0.69	5.7	2.1	28
33	6436	9.4	8.1	33.5	0.33	0.01	90	0	0	0	0.0	0.00	0	0	0	33.5	90	0.77	7.1	2.7	33
38	5473	10.8	9.3	37.2	0.37	0.02	129	0	0	0	0.0	0.00	0	0	0	37.2	129	0.68	8.1	3.4	38
43	4396	12.2	10.8	40.3	0.41	0.04	172	0	0	0	0.0	0.00	0	0	0	40.3	172	0.59	8.6	4.0	43
48	3876	13.4	11.9	43.0	0.44	0.06	215	0	0	0	0.0	0.00	0	0	0	43.0	215	0.54	8.5	4.4	48
53	3443	14.6	13.0	45.6	0.45	0.07	257	2	0	0	0.0	0.00	0	0	0	45.6	257	0.49	8.2	4.8	53
58	3074	15.6	14.1	47.9	0.47	0.10	297	17	0	0	0.0	0.00	0	0	0	47.9	297	0.43	7.7	5.1	58
63	2764	16.6	15.2	50.0	0.48	0.12	334	30	0	0	0.0	0.00	0	0	0	50.0	334	0.39	7.1	5.3	63
68	2506	17.5	16.2	51.8	0.48	0.15	367	49	1	0	0.0	0.00	0	0	0	51.8	367	0.35	6.3	5.4	68
73	2296	18.2	17.2	53.5	0.48	0.17	397	74	1	0	0.0	0.00	0	0	0	53.5	397	0.32	5.5	5.4	73
78	2123	18.9	18.2	55.0	0.48	0.20	423	107	7	0	0.0	0.00	0	0	0	55.0	423	0.27	4.6	5.4	78
83	1979	19.5	19.0	56.2	0.48	0.22	443	147	16	0	0.0	0.00	0	0	0	56.2	443	0.19	3.6	5.3	83
88	1854	20.0	19.8	56.9	0.48	0.25	458	153	16	0	0.0	0.00	0	0	0	56.9	458	0.12	2.7	5.2	88

1.4 x 1.4 m spacing

	MAIN CROP — After Thinning									Yield from THINNINGS						TOTAL YIELD		INCREMENT C.A.I.		M.A.I.	
Age	No. of Trees	Top Ht. (m)	Mean Diam (cm)	Basal Area (m²)	Form Factor	Mean Vol. per Tree (m³)	Vol. to 7 cm (m³)	Vol. to 18 cm (m³)	Vol. to 24 cm (m³)	No. of Trees	Mean Diam (cm)	Mean Vol. per Tree (m³)	Vol. to 7 cm (m³)	Vol. to 18 cm (m³)	Vol. to 24 cm (m³)	Basal Area (m²)	Vol. to 7 cm (m³)	Basal Area (m²)	Vol. to 7 cm (m³)	Vol. to 7 cm (m³)	Age
23	4702	6.0	7.2	19.3	0.33	0.01	32	0	0	0	0.0	0.00	0	0	0	19.3	32	0.75	3.9	1.4	23
28	4289	7.7	8.4	23.7	0.35	0.01	56	0	0	0	0.0	0.00	0	0	0	23.7	56	0.91	5.6	2.0	28
33	3896	9.3	9.6	28.4	0.38	0.02	88	0	0	0	0.0	0.00	0	0	0	28.4	88	0.89	7.0	2.7	33
38	3578	10.8	10.8	32.5	0.41	0.04	126	0	0	0	0.0	0.00	0	0	0	32.5	126	0.80	8.0	3.3	38
43	3237	12.1	12.0	36.4	0.44	0.05	168	0	0	0	0.0	0.00	0	0	0	36.4	168	0.74	8.5	3.9	43
48	2943	13.3	13.2	40.0	0.45	0.07	211	6	0	0	0.0	0.00	0	0	0	40.0	211	0.68	8.6	4.4	48
53	2678	14.5	14.3	43.2	0.47	0.09	254	14	0	0	0.0	0.00	0	0	0	43.2	254	0.60	8.3	4.8	53
58	2437	15.5	15.5	46.0	0.47	0.12	294	26	0	0	0.0	0.00	0	0	0	46.0	294	0.52	7.8	5.1	58
63	2223	16.5	16.6	48.3	0.48	0.15	332	44	0	0	0.0	0.00	0	0	0	48.3	332	0.45	7.2	5.3	63
68	2039	17.4	17.8	50.5	0.48	0.18	366	68	1	0	0.0	0.00	0	0	0	50.5	366	0.40	6.5	5.4	68
73	1886	18.1	18.8	52.4	0.48	0.21	397	101	7	0	0.0	0.00	0	0	0	52.4	397	0.36	5.6	5.4	73
78	1758	18.8	19.8	54.0	0.48	0.24	422	141	15	0	0.0	0.00	0	0	0	54.0	422	0.29	4.7	5.4	78
83	1649	19.4	20.7	55.3	0.48	0.27	444	182	27	0	0.0	0.00	0	0	0	55.3	444	0.22	3.7	5.3	83
88	1549	19.9	21.5	56.2	0.48	0.30	459	222	42	0	0.0	0.00	0	0	0	56.2	459	0.15	2.8	5.2	88

1.8 x 1.8 m spacing

	MAIN CROP After Thinning									Yield from THINNINGS						TOTAL YIELD		INCREMENT			
							Volume in cubic metres to top diameters of-						Volume in cubic metres to top diameters of-					C A I		M A I	
Age	No. of Trees	Top Ht. (m)	Mean Diam (cm)	Basal Area (m²)	Form Factor	Mean Vol. per Tree (m³)	7 cm	18 cm	24 cm	No. of Trees	Mean Diam (cm)	Mean Vol. per Tree (m³)	7 cm	18 cm	24 cm	Basal Area (m²)	Vol. to 7 cm (m³)	Basal Area (m²)	Vol. to 7 cm (m³)	Vol. to 7 cm (m³)	Age
24	2727	6.2	8.4	15.0	0.39	0.01	31	0	0	0	0.0	0.00	0	0	0	15.0	31	0.81	3.7	1.3	24
29	2615	7.8	9.8	19.7	0.40	0.02	55	0	0	0	0.0	0.00	0	0	0	19.7	55	0.96	5.5	1.9	29
34	2470	9.4	11.3	24.6	0.41	0.03	86	0	0	0	0.0	0.00	0	0	0	24.6	86	0.94	6.9	2.5	34
39	2278	10.8	12.8	29.1	0.43	0.05	124	0	0	0	0.0	0.00	0	0	0	29.1	124	0.90	7.9	3.2	39
44	2128	12.1	14.2	33.6	0.45	0.08	166	9	0	0	0.0	0.00	0	0	0	33.6	166	0.85	8.5	3.8	44
49	1996	13.3	15.5	37.7	0.46	0.10	209	19	0	0	0.0	0.00	0	0	0	37.7	209	0.82	8.7	4.3	49
54	1875	14.5	16.8	41.7	0.46	0.13	253	33	0	0	0.0	0.00	0	0	0	41.7	253	0.74	8.6	4.7	54
59	1759	15.5	18.1	45.1	0.46	0.17	295	75	5	0	0.0	0.00	0	0	0	45.1	295	0.62	8.2	5.0	59
64	1650	16.5	19.2	47.9	0.46	0.20	335	111	12	0	0.0	0.00	0	0	0	47.9	335	0.54	7.6	5.2	64
69	1552	17.3	20.3	50.4	0.46	0.24	371	152	22	0	0.0	0.00	0	0	0	50.4	371	0.46	6.8	5.4	69
74	1464	18.1	21.4	52.6	0.46	0.28	403	195	37	0	0.0	0.00	0	0	0	52.6	403	0.39	5.9	5.4	74
79	1388	18.7	22.3	54.4	0.46	0.31	430	235	55	0	0.0	0.00	0	0	0	54.4	430	0.33	4.9	5.4	79
84	1321	19.3	23.2	55.8	0.46	0.34	452	273	76	0	0.0	0.00	0	0	0	55.8	452	0.25	4.0	5.4	84
89	1260	19.8	24.0	56.9	0.45	0.37	470	284	79	0	0.0	0.00	0	0	0	56.9	470	0.18	3.2	5.3	89

2.4 x 2.4 m spacing

	MAIN CROP After Thinning									Yield from THINNINGS						TOTAL YIELD		INCREMENT			
							Volume in cubic metres to top diameters of-						Volume in cubic metres to top diameters of-					C A I		M A I	
Age	No. of Trees	Top Ht. (m)	Mean Diam (cm)	Basal Area (m²)	Form Factor	Mean Vol. per Tree (m³)	7 cm	18 cm	24 cm	No. of Trees	Mean Diam (cm)	Mean Vol. per Tree (m³)	7 cm	18 cm	24 cm	Basal Area (m²)	Vol. to 7 cm (m³)	Basal Area (m²)	Vol. to 7 cm (m³)	Vol. to 7 cm (m³)	Age
29	1524	7.3	11.0	14.4	0.41	0.03	38	0	0	0	0.0	0.00	0	0	0	14.4	38	0.84	4.1	1.3	29
34	1490	8.9	12.9	19.5	0.41	0.04	65	0	0	0	0.0	0.00	0	0	0	19.5	65	0.97	6.0	1.9	34
39	1389	10.3	14.9	24.1	0.43	0.07	98	5	0	0	0.0	0.00	0	0	0	24.1	98	1.04	7.3	2.5	39
44	1366	11.7	16.7	29.8	0.43	0.10	138	18	0	0	0.0	0.00	0	0	0	29.8	138	1.11	8.1	3.1	44
49	1337	12.9	18.3	35.2	0.43	0.13	180	45	3	0	0.0	0.00	0	0	0	35.2	180	1.01	8.5	3.7	49
54	1300	14.0	19.8	40.0	0.43	0.17	223	74	8	0	0.0	0.00	0	0	0	40.0	223	0.90	8.3	4.1	54
59	1257	15.0	21.2	44.2	0.43	0.21	265	128	24	0	0.0	0.00	0	0	0	44.2	265	0.78	8.3	4.5	59
64	1211	16.0	22.4	47.8	0.43	0.25	306	167	39	0	0.0	0.00	0	0	0	47.8	306	0.66	7.8	4.8	64
69	1164	16.9	23.6	50.8	0.43	0.29	343	207	58	0	0.0	0.00	0	0	0	50.8	343	0.56	7.1	5.0	69
74	1121	17.6	24.6	53.4	0.43	0.34	377	248	82	0	0.0	0.00	0	0	0	53.4	377	0.47	6.3	5.1	74
79	1081	18.3	25.6	55.5	0.43	0.38	406	285	110	0	0.0	0.00	0	0	0	55.5	406	0.40	5.4	5.1	79
84	1045	18.8	26.4	57.3	0.42	0.41	431	318	141	0	0.0	0.00	0	0	0	57.3	431	0.34	4.6	5.1	84
89	1012	19.3	27.2	58.9	0.42	0.45	452	349	174	0	0.0	0.00	0	0	0	58.9	452	0.27	3.9	5.1	89

SITKA SPRUCE YIELD CLASS 16 UNTHINNED

0.9 x 0.9 m spacing

| | MAIN CROP | | | | | After Thinning | | | | Yield from THINNINGS | | | | | | TOTAL YIELD | | INCREMENT CAI MAI | | | |
	No. of Trees	Top Ht. m	Mean Diam cm	Basal Area m²	Form Factor	Mean Vol per Tree m³	Volume in cubic metres to top diameters of– 7 cm	18 cm	24 cm	No. of Trees	Mean Diam cm	Mean Vol per Tree m³	Volume in cubic metres to top diameters of– 7 cm	18 cm	24 cm	Basal Area m²	Vol to 7 cm m³	Basal Area m²	Vol to 7 cm m³	Vol to 7 cm m³	Age
15	8777	6.8	7.1	34.8	0.39	0.01	67	0	0	0	0.0	0.00	0	0	0	34.8	67	2.30	14.4	4.5	15
20	6840	10.0	9.3	46.2	0.40	0.02	147	0	0	0	0.0	0.00	0	0	0	46.2	147	1.53	17.8	7.4	20
25	5314	13.1	11.0	50.1	0.46	0.05	245	10	0	0	0.0	0.00	0	0	0	50.1	245	0.69	20.3	9.8	25
30	3971	16.1	13.0	53.0	0.50	0.09	350	41	0	0	0.0	0.00	0	0	0	53.0	350	0.55	20.7	11.7	30
35	3074	18.9	15.2	55.6	0.52	0.15	452	102	0	0	0.0	0.00	0	0	0	55.6	452	0.50	19.6	12.9	35
40	2467	21.5	17.3	58.0	0.53	0.22	546	210	1	0	0.0	0.00	0	0	0	58.0	546	0.44	17.7	13.7	40
45	2060	23.7	19.3	60.1	0.53	0.31	629	340	23	0	0.0	0.00	0	0	0	60.1	629	0.41	15.6	14.0	45
50	1787	25.7	21.0	62.1	0.53	0.39	702	420	65	0	0.0	0.00	0	0	0	62.1	702	0.42	13.7	14.0	50
55	1602	27.3	22.6	64.3	0.52	0.48	767	498	98	0	0.0	0.00	0	0	0	64.3	767	0.43	12.2	13.9	55
60	1472	28.6	24.0	66.4	0.52	0.56	824		140	0	0.0	0.00	0	0	0	66.4	824	0.43	13.6	13.7	60

1.4 x 1.4 m spacing

| | MAIN CROP | | | | | After Thinning | | | | Yield from THINNINGS | | | | | | TOTAL YIELD | | INCREMENT CAI MAI | | | |
	No. of Trees	Top Ht. m	Mean Diam cm	Basal Area m²	Form Factor	Mean Vol per Tree m³	Volume in cubic metres to top diameters of– 7 cm	18 cm	24 cm	No. of Trees	Mean Diam cm	Mean Vol per Tree m³	Volume in cubic metres to top diameters of– 7 cm	18 cm	24 cm	Basal Area m²	Vol to 7 cm m³	Basal Area m²	Vol to 7 cm m³	Vol to 7 cm m³	Age
15	4641	6.7	8.8	28.0	0.45	0.01	63	0	0	0	0.0	0.00	0	0	0	28.0	63	2.36	13.2	4.2	15
20	4000	9.8	11.2	39.1	0.44	0.04	140	0	0	0	0.0	0.00	0	0	0	39.1	140	1.96	17.1	7.0	20
25	3426	13.0	13.3	47.7	0.47	0.07	234	7	0	0	0.0	0.00	0	0	0	47.7	234	1.52	19.9	9.4	25
30	2823	16.0	15.7	54.4	0.49	0.12	339	30	0	0	0.0	0.00	0	0	0	54.4	339	1.27	20.9	11.3	30
35	2360	18.8	18.0	60.3	0.50	0.19	443	113	7	0	0.0	0.00	0	0	0	60.3	443	1.09	20.0	12.7	35
40	2007	21.4	20.4	65.3	0.50	0.27	539	222	33	0	0.0	0.00	0	0	0	65.3	539	0.90	18.1	13.5	40
45	1755	23.6	22.4	69.3	0.50	0.36	625	342	80	0	0.0	0.00	0	0	0	69.3	625	0.78	16.0	13.9	45
50	1579	25.5	24.3	73.0	0.49	0.44	699	460	153	0	0.0	0.00	0	0	0	73.0	699	0.71	14.1	14.0	50
55	1457	27.1	25.8	76.4	0.49	0.53	765	537	208	0	0.0	0.00	0	0	0	76.4	765	0.66	12.4	13.9	55
60	1374	28.5	27.2	79.6	0.48	0.60	824	636	317	0	0.0	0.00	0	0	0	79.6	824	0.64	10.6	13.7	60

1.8 x 1.8m spacing

	MAIN CROP After Thinning						Volume in cubic metres to top diameters of-			Yield from THINNINGS			Volume in cubic metres to top diameters of-			TOTAL YIELD		INCREMENT CAI		MAI	
Age	No. of Trees	Top Ht. m	Mean Diam cm	Basal Area m²	Form Factor	Mean Vol. per Tree m³	7 cm	18 cm	24 cm	No. of Trees	Mean Diam cm	Mean Vol. per Tree m³	7 cm	18 cm	24 cm	Basal Area m²	Vol. to 7 cm m³	Basal Area m²	Vol. 7 cm to 7 cm m³	Vol. to 7 cm m³	Age
16	2797	7.1	10.7	25.3	0.46	0.02	66	0	0	0	0.0	0.00	0	0	0	25.3	66	2.35	13.3	4.1	16
21	2616	10.3	13.4	37.0	0.44	0.06	144	4	0	0	0.0	0.00	0	0	0	37.0	144	1.99	17.7	6.9	21
26	2328	13.4	15.7	45.2	0.46	0.10	244	22	0	0	0.0	0.00	0	0	0	45.2	244	1.44	21.0	9.4	26
31	1967	16.4	18.2	51.4	0.47	0.18	354	90	6	0	0.0	0.00	0	0	0	51.4	354	1.06	21.9	11.4	31
36	1683	19.1	20.6	55.9	0.48	0.27	462	190	28	0	0.0	0.00	0	0	0	55.9	462	0.81	20.6	12.8	36
41	1460	21.6	22.8	59.5	0.48	0.38	561	307	72	0	0.0	0.00	0	0	0	59.5	561	0.66	18.5	13.7	41
46	1297	23.8	24.8	62.4	0.48	0.50	647	425	141	0	0.0	0.00	0	0	0	62.4	647	0.56	16.3	14.1	46
51	1182	25.7	26.5	65.1	0.47	0.61	724	535	238	0	0.0	0.00	0	0	0	65.1	724	0.52	14.5	14.2	51
56	1102	27.2	28.0	67.7	0.47	0.72	793	612	305	0	0.0	0.00	0	0	0	67.7	793	0.51	13.0	14.2	56
61	1046	28.5	29.2	70.2	0.46	0.82	854	704	420	0	0.0	0.00	0	0	0	70.2	854	0.50	11.5	14.0	61

2.4 x 2.4m spacing

	MAIN CROP After Thinning						Volume in cubic metres to top diameters of-			Yield from THINNINGS			Volume in cubic metres to top diameters of-			TOTAL YIELD		INCREMENT CAI		MAI	
Age	No. of Trees	Top Ht. m	Mean Diam cm	Basal Area m²	Form Factor	Mean Vol. per Tree m³	7 cm	18 cm	24 cm	No. of Trees	Mean Diam cm	Mean Vol. per Tree m³	7 cm	18 cm	24 cm	Basal Area m²	Vol. to 7 cm m³	Basal Area m²	Vol. 7 cm to 7 cm m³	Vol. to 7 cm m³	Age
19	1597	8.6	14.1	24.9	0.47	0.05	86	4	0	0	0.0	0.00	0	0	0	24.9	86	2.42	15.0	4.5	19
24	1562	11.7	17.3	36.8	0.45	0.11	174	32	0	0	0.0	0.00	0	0	0	36.8	174	2.05	19.2	7.2	24
29	1395	14.8	20.4	45.4	0.45	0.20	278	114	17	0	0.0	0.00	0	0	0	45.4	278	1.50	21.5	9.6	29
34	1224	17.6	23.2	51.9	0.46	0.32	389	235	66	0	0.0	0.00	0	0	0	51.9	389	1.16	21.8	11.4	34
39	1088	20.3	25.8	57.0	0.46	0.46	496	348	134	0	0.0	0.00	0	0	0	57.0	496	0.89	20.3	12.7	39
44	980	22.6	28.1	60.7	0.46	0.60	593	474	260	0	0.0	0.00	0	0	0	60.7	593	0.67	18.1	13.5	44
49	898	24.5	30.1	63.7	0.46	0.75	677	572	367	0	0.0	0.00	0	0	0	63.7	677	0.56	15.9	13.8	49
54	840	26.2	31.7	66.4	0.46	0.89	752	649	442	0	0.0	0.00	0	0	0	66.4	752	0.51	14.0	13.9	54
59	797	27.6	33.1	68.8	0.45	1.03	818	730	546	0	0.0	0.00	0	0	0	68.8	818	0.47	12.4	13.9	59
64	766	28.8	34.4	71.1	0.45	1.14	876	793	614	0	0.0	0.00	0	0	0	71.1	876	0.43	11.0	13.7	64

SITKA SPRUCE YIELD CLASS 12 UNTHINNED

0.9 x 0.9 m spacing

Age	MAIN CROP No. of Trees	Top Ht. (m)	Mean Diam (cm)	Basal Area (m²)	Form Factor	Mean Vol. per Tree (m³)	After Thinning Vol. to 7 cm (m³)	18 cm	24 cm	Yield from THINNINGS No. of Trees	Mean Diam (cm)	Mean Vol. per Tree (m³)	Vol. 7 cm	18 cm	24 cm	TOTAL YIELD Basal Area (m²)	Vol. to 7 cm (m³)	INCREMENT CAI Basal Area (m²)	CAI Vol. to 7 cm (m³)	MAI Vol. to 7 cm (m³)	Age
22	7562	8.8	8.4	41.9	0.40	0.02	115	0	0	0	0.0	0.00	0	0	0	41.9	115	1.91	14.5	5.2	22
27	5922	11.4	10.5	50.9	0.41	0.03	194	0	0	0	0.0	0.00	0	0	0	50.9	194	1.26	15.4	7.2	27
32	4736	14.0	12.1	54.5	0.45	0.06	279	2	0	0	0.0	0.00	0	0	0	54.5	279	0.58	16.8	8.7	32
37	3820	16.3	13.7	56.6	0.48	0.09	363	11	0	0	0.0	0.00	0	0	0	56.6	363	0.36	16.1	9.8	37
42	3133	18.4	15.4	58.1	0.50	0.14	440	40	0	0	0.0	0.00	0	0	0	58.1	440	0.29	14.7	10.5	42
47	2637	20.4	17.0	59.5	0.51	0.19	509	68	0	0	0.0	0.00	0	0	0	59.5	509	0.26	12.8	10.8	47
52	2278	22.0	18.4	60.7	0.52	0.25	568	144	10	0	0.0	0.00	0	0	0	60.7	568	0.24	10.8	10.9	52
57	2022	23.5	19.7	61.9	0.52	0.31	618	206	22	0	0.0	0.00	0	0	0	61.9	618	0.24	9.0	10.8	57
62	1838	24.6	20.9	63.1	0.52	0.36	658	271	40	0	0.0	0.00	0	0	0	63.1	658	0.24	7.2	10.6	62

1.4 x 1.4 m spacing

Age	MAIN CROP No. of Trees	Top Ht. (m)	Mean Diam (cm)	Basal Area (m²)	Form Factor	Mean Vol. per Tree (m³)	After Thinning Vol. to 7 cm (m³)	18 cm	24 cm	Yield from THINNINGS No. of Trees	Mean Diam (cm)	Mean Vol. per Tree (m³)	Vol. 7 cm	18 cm	24 cm	TOTAL YIELD Basal Area (m²)	Vol. to 7 cm (m³)	INCREMENT CAI Basal Area (m²)	CAI Vol. to 7 cm (m³)	MAI Vol. to 7 cm (m³)	Age
18	4675	6.5	8.6	26.9	0.44	0.01	57	0	0	0	0.0	0.00	0	0	0	26.9	57	2.18	11.7	3.2	18
23	4144	9.2	10.8	37.7	0.43	0.03	123	0	0	0	0.0	0.00	0	0	0	37.7	123	1.83	14.5	5.3	23
28	3717	11.8	12.5	45.3	0.46	0.05	202	1	0	0	0.0	0.00	0	0	0	45.3	202	1.35	16.4	7.2	28
33	3224	14.3	14.2	51.2	0.49	0.09	287	16	0	0	0.0	0.00	0	0	0	51.2	287	1.09	16.8	8.7	33
38	2772	16.6	16.1	56.2	0.50	0.13	370	49	0	0	0.0	0.00	0	0	0	56.2	370	0.91	16.1	9.7	38
43	2419	18.7	17.8	60.3	0.51	0.18	448	83	1	0	0.0	0.00	0	0	0	60.3	448	0.74	14.6	10.4	43
48	2131	20.6	19.5	63.6	0.51	0.24	516	172	19	0	0.0	0.00	0	0	0	63.6	516	0.61	12.7	10.7	48
53	1913	22.2	21.0	66.4	0.51	0.30	575	278	53	0	0.0	0.00	0	0	0	66.4	575	0.53	10.8	10.8	53
58	1752	23.6	22.4	68.9	0.50	0.36	624	342	80	0	0.0	0.00	0	0	0	68.9	624	0.47	9.0	10.8	58
63	1632	24.7	23.6	71.1	0.50	0.41	664	401	112	0	0.0	0.00	0	0	0	71.1	664	0.41	7.4	10.5	63

1.8 x 1.8 m spacing

	MAIN CROP After Thinning									Yield from THINNINGS						TOTAL YIELD		INCREMENT			
							Volume in cubic metres to top diameters of–						Volume in cubic metres to top diameters of–						CAI		MAI
Age	No. of Trees	Top Ht. (m)	Mean Diam (cm)	Basal Area (m²)	Form Factor	Mean Vol. per Tree (m³)	7 cm (m³)	18 cm (m³)	24 cm (m³)	No. of Trees	Mean Diam (cm)	Mean Vol. per Tree (m³)	7 cm (m³)	18 cm (m³)	24 cm (m³)	Basal Area (m²)	Vol. to 7 cm (m³)	Basal Area (m²)	Vol. to 7 cm (m³)	Vol. to 7 cm (m³)	Age
20	2781	7.4	10.9	25.9	0.46	0.03	71	0	0	0	0.0	0.00	0	0	0	25.9	71	2.16	12.0	3.5	20
25	2627	10.1	13.3	36.4	0.44	0.05	139	4	0	0	0.0	0.00	0	0	0	36.4	139	1.85	15.0	5.5	25
30	2452	12.7	15.2	44.3	0.45	0.09	220	20	0	0	0.0	0.00	0	0	0	44.3	220	1.30	17.0	7.3	30
35	2152	15.1	17.1	49.4	0.47	0.14	308	57	0	0	0.0	0.00	0	0	0	49.4	308	0.91	17.3	8.8	35
40	1895	17.3	19.0	53.4	0.48	0.21	394	100	7	0	0.0	0.00	0	0	0	53.4	394	0.69	16.4	9.8	40
45	1687	19.3	20.6	56.3	0.48	0.28	472	194	29	0	0.0	0.00	0	0	0	56.3	472	0.54	14.6	10.5	45
50	1516	21.1	22.2	58.8	0.48	0.36	540	296	69	0	0.0	0.00	0	0	0	58.8	540	0.45	12.5	10.8	50
55	1385	22.6	23.6	60.7	0.48	0.43	597	361	101	0	0.0	0.00	0	0	0	60.7	597	0.36	10.5	10.9	55
60	1287	23.9	24.9	62.4	0.48	0.50	645	424	141	0	0.0	0.00	0	0	0	62.4	645	0.32	8.8	10.8	60
65	1213	24.9	25.9	63.9	0.47	0.56	685	481	186	0	0.0	0.00	0	0	0	63.9	685	0.30	7.2	10.5	65

2.4 x 2.4 m spacing

	MAIN CROP After Thinning									Yield from THINNINGS						TOTAL YIELD		INCREMENT			
							Volume in cubic metres to top diameters of–						Volume in cubic metres to top diameters of–						CAI		MAI
Age	No. of Trees	Top Ht. (m)	Mean Diam (cm)	Basal Area (m²)	Form Factor	Mean Vol. per Tree (m³)	7 cm (m³)	18 cm (m³)	24 cm (m³)	No. of Trees	Mean Diam (cm)	Mean Vol. per Tree (m³)	7 cm (m³)	18 cm (m³)	24 cm (m³)	Basal Area (m²)	Vol. to 7 cm (m³)	Basal Area (m²)	Vol. to 7 cm (m³)	Vol. to 7 cm (m³)	Age
23	1597	8.6	14.1	24.8	0.47	0.05	85	4	0	0	0.0	0.00	0	0	0	24.8	85	2.11	12.6	3.7	23
28	1568	11.2	16.9	35.0	0.45	0.10	158	21	0	0	0.0	0.00	0	0	0	35.0	158	1.84	15.6	5.6	28
33	1473	13.7	19.3	43.2	0.45	0.16	241	80	8	0	0.0	0.00	0	0	0	43.2	241	1.37	16.9	7.3	33
38	1325	16.0	21.6	48.7	0.46	0.25	327	158	30	0	0.0	0.00	0	0	0	48.7	327	1.00	16.9	8.6	38
43	1205	18.1	23.7	53.2	0.46	0.34	410	247	69	0	0.0	0.00	0	0	0	53.2	410	0.78	15.8	9.5	43
48	1101	20.0	25.6	56.5	0.46	0.44	485	340	131	0	0.0	0.00	0	0	0	56.5	485	0.58	14.1	10.1	48
53	1018	21.6	27.2	59.0	0.46	0.54	551	425	212	0	0.0	0.00	0	0	0	59.0	551	0.45	12.0	10.4	53
59	953	23.0	28.5	61.0	0.46	0.64	606	485	266	0	0.0	0.00	0	0	0	61.0	606	0.37	10.1	10.4	58
63	904	24.1	29.7	62.7	0.46	0.72	651	537	321	0	0.0	0.00	0	0	0	62.7	651	0.33	8.6	10.3	63
68	866	25.0	30.8	64.3	0.45	0.80	691	583	375	0	0.0	0.00	0	0	0	64.3	691	0.30	7.3	10.2	68

SITKA SPRUCE YIELD CLASS 8 UNTHINNED

0.9 x 0.9 m spacing

Age	MAIN CROP No. of Trees	Top Ht. m	Mean Diam cm	Basal Area m²	Form Factor	After Thinning Mean Vol. per Tree m³	Vol. 7 cm	Vol. 18 cm	Vol. 24 cm	Yield from THINNINGS No. of Trees	Mean Diam cm	Mean Vol. per Tree m³	Vol. 7 cm	Vol. 18 cm	Vol. 24 cm	TOTAL YIELD Basal Area m²	Vol. to 7 cm m³	INCREMENT CAI Basal Area m²	CAI Vol. to 7 cm m³	MAI Vol. to 7 cm m³	Age
26	8092	8.0	7.8	39.0	0.40	0.01	93	0	0	0	0.0	0.00	0	0	0	39.0	93	1.48	10.2	3.6	26
31	6791	10.0	9.3	45.7	0.40	0.02	149	0	0	0	0.0	0.00	0	0	0	45.7	149	1.08	11.8	4.8	31
36	5907	12.0	10.4	49.8	0.43	0.04	211	0	0	0	0.0	0.00	0	0	0	49.8	211	0.66	12.5	5.9	36
41	5058	13.8	11.5	52.4	0.46	0.05	274	0	0	0	0.0	0.00	0	0	0	52.4	274	0.43	12.3	6.7	41
46	4330	15.4	12.6	54.1	0.49	0.08	334	2	0	0	0.0	0.00	0	0	0	54.1	334	0.28	11.2	7.3	46
51	3750	16.9	13.7	55.1	0.50	0.10	386	11	0	0	0.0	0.00	0	0	0	55.1	386	0.19	9.8	7.6	51
56	3319	18.2	14.7	56.0	0.51	0.13	431	25	0	0	0.0	0.00	0	0	0	56.0	431	0.17	8.3	7.7	56
61	2982	19.3	15.6	56.9	0.51	0.16	469	42	0	0	0.0	0.00	0	0	0	56.9	469	0.15	6.8	7.7	61
66	2726	20.2	16.4	57.5	0.52	0.18	499	66	0	0	0.0	0.00	0	0	0	57.5	499	0.10	5.3	7.6	66
71	2517	20.9	17.1	57.9	0.52	0.21	522	97	1	0	0.0	0.00	0	0	0	57.9	522	0.05	3.9	7.3	71

1.4 x 1.4 m spacing

Age	MAIN CROP No. of Trees	Top Ht. m	Mean Diam cm	Basal Area m²	Form Factor	After Thinning Mean Vol. per Tree m³	Vol. 7 cm	Vol. 18 cm	Vol. 24 cm	Yield from THINNINGS No. of Trees	Mean Diam cm	Mean Vol. per Tree m³	Vol. 7 cm	Vol. 18 cm	Vol. 24 cm	TOTAL YIELD Basal Area m²	Vol. to 7 cm m³	INCREMENT CAI Basal Area m²	CAI Vol. to 7 cm m³	MAI Vol. to 7 cm m³	Age
23	4681	6.5	8.7	27.8	0.45	0.01	60	0	0	0	0.0	0.00	0	0	0	27.8	60	1.56	8.5	2.6	23
28	4250	8.7	10.3	35.6	0.44	0.03	108	0	0	0	0.0	0.00	0	0	0	35.6	108	1.54	10.6	3.9	28
33	3844	10.7	12.0	43.2	0.44	0.04	166	0	0	0	0.0	0.00	0	0	0	43.2	166	1.32	12.0	5.0	33
38	3557	12.6	13.2	48.8	0.46	0.06	229	7	0	0	0.0	0.00	0	0	0	48.8	229	1.01	12.5	6.0	38
43	3229	14.3	14.5	53.2	0.48	0.09	291	16	0	0	0.0	0.00	0	0	0	53.2	291	0.77	11.9	6.8	43
48	2913	15.9	15.7	56.5	0.49	0.12	348	31	0	0	0.0	0.00	0	0	0	56.5	348	0.58	10.8	7.2	48
53	2646	17.3	16.9	59.1	0.50	0.15	398	53	0	0	0.0	0.00	0	0	0	59.1	398	0.46	9.3	7.5	53
58	2432	18.5	17.9	61.1	0.50	0.18	441	82	1	0	0.0	0.00	0	0	0	61.1	441	0.38	7.8	7.6	58
63	2257	19.5	18.8	62.9	0.50	0.21	477	121	8	0	0.0	0.00	0	0	0	62.9	477	0.31	6.3	7.6	63
68	2115	20.4	19.7	64.3	0.50	0.24	504	168	18	0	0.0	0.00	0	0	0	64.3	504	0.24	5.0	7.4	68
73	1990	21.1	20.4	65.3	0.49	0.26	527	216	32	0	0.0	0.00	0	0	0	65.3	527	0.18	4.0	7.2	73

1.8 x 1.8m spacing

Age	MAIN CROP — After Thinning									Yield from THINNINGS						TOTAL YIELD		INCREMENT			Age
	No. of Trees	Top Ht. (m)	Mean Diam (cm)	Basal Area (m²)	Form Factor	Mean Vol. per Tree (m³)	Vol. to 7 cm (m³)	18 cm	24 cm	No. of Trees	Mean Diam (cm)	Mean Vol. per Tree (m³)	7 cm	18 cm	24 cm	Basal Area (m²)	Vol. to 7 cm (m³)	CAI Basal Area (m²)	CAI Vol. to 7 cm (m³)	MAI Vol. to 7 cm (m³)	
25	2794	7.2	10.8	25.4	0.47	0.02	68	0	0	0	0.0	0.00	0	0	0	25.4	68	1.60	8.6	2.7	25
30	2671	9.3	12.6	33.4	0.45	0.04	117	0	0	0	0.0	0.00	0	0	0	33.4	117	1.54	10.7	3.9	30
35	2649	11.3	14.0	40.8	0.44	0.07	175	10	0	0	0.0	0.00	0	0	0	40.8	175	1.25	12.1	5.0	35
40	2447	13.1	15.4	45.8	0.45	0.10	238	21	0	0	0.0	0.00	0	0	0	45.8	238	0.88	12.6	6.0	40
45	2237	14.8	16.8	49.6	0.46	0.13	301	40	0	0	0.0	0.00	0	0	0	49.6	301	0.63	12.0	6.7	45
50	2045	16.3	18.0	52.2	0.47	0.18	358	91	6	0	0.0	0.00	0	0	0	52.2	358	0.46	10.7	7.2	50
55	1888	17.6	19.1	54.2	0.48	0.22	408	136	15	0	0.0	0.00	0	0	0	54.2	408	0.35	9.2	7.4	55
60	1760	18.8	20.1	55.7	0.48	0.26	450	185	27	0	0.0	0.00	0	0	0	55.7	450	0.28	7.7	7.5	60
65	1655	19.7	20.9	56.9	0.48	0.29	485	199	30	0	0.0	0.00	0	0	0	56.9	485	0.22	6.3	7.5	65
70	1568	20.5	21.7	57.9	0.48	0.33	513	248	47	0	0.0	0.00	0	0	0	57.9	513	0.15	5.1	7.3	70
75	1489	21.2	22.4	58.5	0.48	0.36	536	294	69	0	0.0	0.00	0	0	0	58.5	536	0.11	3.8	7.2	75

2.4 x 2.4m spacing

Age	MAIN CROP — After Thinning									Yield from THINNINGS						TOTAL YIELD		INCREMENT			Age
	No. of Trees	Top Ht. (m)	Mean Diam (cm)	Basal Area (m²)	Form Factor	Mean Vol. per Tree (m³)	Vol. to 7 cm (m³)	18 cm	24 cm	No. of Trees	Mean Diam (cm)	Mean Vol. per Tree (m³)	7 cm	18 cm	24 cm	Basal Area (m²)	Vol. to 7 cm (m³)	CAI Basal Area (m²)	CAI Vol. to 7 cm (m³)	MAI Vol. to 7 cm (m³)	
29	1598	8.5	13.9	24.1	0.47	0.05	83	2	0	0	0.0	0.00	0	0	0	24.1	83	1.64	9.0	2.9	29
34	1576	10.5	16.1	32.0	0.45	0.09	135	18	0	0	0.0	0.00	0	0	0	32.0	135	1.52	11.2	4.0	34
39	1555	12.3	18.0	39.4	0.45	0.13	195	36	0	0	0.0	0.00	0	0	0	39.4	195	1.26	12.1	5.0	39
44	1460	14.0	19.7	44.5	0.45	0.18	256	85	9	0	0.0	0.00	0	0	0	44.5	256	0.89	11.9	5.8	44
49	1359	15.6	21.3	48.3	0.45	0.23	314	152	29	0	0.0	0.00	0	0	0	48.3	314	0.64	11.0	6.4	49
54	1270	16.9	22.6	51.0	0.46	0.29	366	200	47	0	0.0	0.00	0	0	0	51.0	366	0.48	9.7	6.8	54
59	1200	18.1	23.7	53.1	0.46	0.34	411	248	69	0	0.0	0.00	0	0	0	53.1	411	0.38	8.2	7.0	59
64	1140	19.1	24.7	54.8	0.46	0.39	448	294	98	0	0.0	0.00	0	0	0	54.8	448	0.30	6.9	7.0	64
69	1092	19.9	25.6	56.1	0.46	0.44	479	336	130	0	0.0	0.00	0	0	0	56.1	479	0.24	5.8	6.9	69
74	1049	20.6	26.4	57.2	0.46	0.48	507	374	166	0	0.0	0.00	0	0	0	57.2	507	0.18	4.8	6.8	74

NORWAY SPRUCE　　YIELD CLASS 16　　UNTHINNED

0.9 x 0.9 m spacing

| | MAIN CROP | | | | | | After Thinning | | | Yield from THINNINGS | | | | | | TOTAL YIELD | | INCREMENT | | | |
							Volume in cubic metres to top diameters of-						Volume in cubic metres to top diameters of-					CAI		MAI	
Age	No. of Trees	Top Ht. (m)	Mean Diam (cm)	Basal Area (m²)	Form Factor	Mean Vol. per Tree (m³)	7 cm	18 cm	24 cm	No. of Trees	Mean Diam (cm)	Mean Vol. per Tree (m³)	7 cm	18 cm	24 cm	Basal Area (m²)	Vol. to 7 cm (m³)	Basal Area (m²)	Vol. to 7 cm (m³)	Vol. to 7 cm (m³)	Age
17	7982	7.8	6.6	27.6	0.35	0.01	55	0	0	0	0.0	0.00	0	0	0	27.6	55	2.89	12.8	3.2	17
22	6256	10.6	9.2	41.5	0.39	0.02	136	0	0	0	0.0	0.00	0	0	0	41.5	136	2.08	18.3	6.2	22
27	4941	13.4	11.2	48.3	0.46	0.05	237	0	0	0	0.0	0.00	0	0	0	48.3	237	1.23	20.7	8.8	27
32	3928	16.0	13.2	53.8	0.50	0.09	343	10	0	0	0.0	0.00	0	0	0	53.8	343	0.98	21.0	10.7	32
37	3153	18.3	15.3	58.1	0.52	0.14	447	40	0	0	0.0	0.00	0	0	0	58.1	447	0.84	20.0	12.1	37
42	2630	20.4	17.4	62.3	0.53	0.21	543	101	1	0	0.0	0.00	0	0	0	62.3	543	0.75	18.5	12.9	42
47	2208	22.3	19.5	65.6	0.53	0.29	632	210	23	0	0.0	0.00	0	0	0	65.6	632	0.67	16.8	13.4	47
52	1911	24.0	21.4	68.9	0.53	0.37	711	344	66	0	0.0	0.00	0	0	0	68.9	711	0.65	15.1	13.7	52
57	1685	25.5	23.3	72.1	0.52	0.46	782	473	132	0	0.0	0.00	0	0	0	72.1	782	0.62	13.4	13.7	57
62	1511	26.9	25.2	75.1	0.51	0.56	845	593	229	0	0.0	0.00	0	0	0	75.1	845	0.58	11.8	13.6	62
67	1373	28.1	26.9	77.9	0.51	0.66	900	665	296	0	0.0	0.00	0	0	0	77.9	900	0.53	10.5	13.4	67
72	1262	29.2	28.5	80.4	0.50	0.75	950	760	417	0	0.0	0.00	0	0	0	80.4	950	0.50	9.5	13.2	72

1.4 x 1.4 m spacing

| | MAIN CROP | | | | | | After Thinning | | | Yield from THINNINGS | | | | | | TOTAL YIELD | | INCREMENT | | | |
							Volume in cubic metres to top diameters of-						Volume in cubic metres to top diameters of-					CAI		MAI	
Age	No. of Trees	Top Ht. (m)	Mean Diam (cm)	Basal Area (m²)	Form Factor	Mean Vol. per Tree (m³)	7 cm	18 cm	24 cm	No. of Trees	Mean Diam (cm)	Mean Vol. per Tree (m³)	7 cm	18 cm	24 cm	Basal Area (m²)	Vol. to 7 cm (m³)	Basal Area (m²)	Vol. to 7 cm (m³)	Vol. to 7 cm (m³)	Age
18	4321	8.3	8.7	25.4	0.39	0.02	65	0	0	0	0.0	0.00	0	0	0	25.4	65	2.90	14.5	3.6	18
23	3666	11.2	11.7	39.4	0.42	0.05	152	0	0	0	0.0	0.00	0	0	0	39.4	152	2.41	19.0	6.6	23
28	3209	13.9	14.0	49.5	0.45	0.08	256	14	0	0	0.0	0.00	0	0	0	49.5	256	1.73	21.2	9.1	28
33	2695	16.4	16.4	56.7	0.47	0.13	364	48	0	0	0.0	0.00	0	0	0	56.7	364	1.30	21.3	11.0	33
38	2269	18.7	18.7	62.5	0.49	0.21	468	119	8	0	0.0	0.00	0	0	0	62.5	468	1.10	20.2	12.3	38
43	1967	20.7	20.9	67.7	0.49	0.29	565	232	35	0	0.0	0.00	0	0	0	67.7	565	0.93	18.6	13.1	43
48	1697	22.6	23.2	71.7	0.49	0.39	654	395	111	0	0.0	0.00	0	0	0	71.7	654	0.80	17.0	13.6	48
53	1505	24.3	25.3	75.7	0.48	0.49	735	515	199	0	0.0	0.00	0	0	0	75.7	735	0.77	15.3	13.9	53
58	1356	25.8	27.3	79.4	0.48	0.60	807	624	311	0	0.0	0.00	0	0	0	79.4	807	0.71	13.7	13.9	58
63	1238	27.1	29.2	82.8	0.47	0.70	872	719	429	0	0.0	0.00	0	0	0	82.8	872	0.65	12.2	13.8	63
68	1144	28.3	30.9	86.0	0.46	0.81	930	785	504	0	0.0	0.00	0	0	0	86.0	930	0.60	11.0	13.7	68
73	1066	29.4	32.6	88.8	0.46	0.92	982	863	620	0	0.0	0.00	0	0	0	88.8	982	0.56	10.0	13.4	73

1.8 x 1.8m spacing

	MAIN CROP					After Thinning				Yield from THINNINGS						TOTAL YIELD		INCREMENT CAI / MAI			
Age	No. of Trees	Top Ht. m	Mean Diam cm	Basal Area m²	Form Factor	Mean Vol. per Tree m³	Vol. to 7 cm	to 18 cm	to 24 cm	No. of Trees	Mean Diam cm	Mean Vol. per Tree m³	7 cm	18 cm	24 cm	Basal Area m²	Vol. to 7 cm m³	Basal Area m² (CAI)	Vol. 7 cm to m³ (CAI)	Vol. 7 cm to m³ (MAI)	Age
19	2700	8.8	10.5	23.5	0.42	0.03	72	0	0	0	0.0	0.00	0	0	0	23.5	72	2.72	14.8	3.8	19
24	2573	11.6	13.4	36.1	0.44	0.06	159	4	0	0	0.0	0.00	0	0	0	36.1	159	2.30	19.3	6.6	24
29	2319	14.3	16.0	46.5	0.46	0.11	265	24	0	0	0.0	0.00	0	0	0	46.5	265	1.78	21.5	9.1	29
34	1992	16.8	18.6	53.9	0.48	0.19	374	95	6	0	0.0	0.00	0	0	0	53.9	374	1.34	21.6	11.0	34
39	1727	19.0	21.0	59.9	0.48	0.28	481	233	44	0	0.0	0.00	0	0	0	59.9	481	1.12	20.7	12.3	39
44	1518	21.0	23.4	65.1	0.49	0.38	581	351	98	0	0.0	0.00	0	0	0	65.1	581	0.98	19.4	13.2	44
49	1359	22.8	25.6	69.7	0.48	0.50	674	473	183	0	0.0	0.00	0	0	0	69.7	674	0.89	17.9	13.8	49
54	1232	24.5	27.6	73.9	0.48	0.62	759	587	293	0	0.0	0.00	0	0	0	73.9	759	0.79	16.2	14.1	54
59	1129	25.9	29.6	77.6	0.47	0.74	836	690	412	0	0.0	0.00	0	0	0	77.6	836	0.73	14.7	14.2	59
64	1047	27.2	31.4	81.2	0.47	0.87	906	782	533	0	0.0	0.00	0	0	0	81.2	906	0.67	13.3	14.2	64
69	980	28.4	33.1	84.4	0.46	0.99	969	866	648	0	0.0	0.00	0	0	0	84.4	969	0.62	12.1	14.0	69
74	924	29.5	34.7	87.3	0.45	1.11	1027	930	719	0	0.0	0.00	0	0	0	87.3	1027	0.57	11.1	13.9	74

2.4 x 2.4 m spacing

	MAIN CROP					After Thinning				Yield from THINNINGS						TOTAL YIELD		INCREMENT CAI / MAI			
Age	No. of Trees	Top Ht. m	Mean Diam cm	Basal Area m²	Form Factor	Mean Vol. per Tree m³	Vol. to 7 cm	to 18 cm	to 24 cm	No. of Trees	Mean Diam cm	Mean Vol. per Tree m³	7 cm	18 cm	24 cm	Basal Area m²	Vol. to 7 cm m³	Basal Area m² (CAI)	Vol. 7 cm to m³ (CAI)	Vol. 7 cm to m³ (MAI)	Age
22	1571	10.3	13.7	23.3	0.43	0.06	89	2	0	0	0.0	0.00	0	0	0	23.3	89	2.82	17.0	4.1	22
27	1563	13.0	17.3	36.7	0.43	0.12	185	34	0	0	0.0	0.00	0	0	0	36.7	185	2.37	20.5	6.9	27
32	1448	15.6	20.3	46.9	0.45	0.20	294	121	18	0	0.0	0.00	0	0	0	46.9	294	1.73	21.9	9.2	32
37	1301	17.9	23.0	54.1	0.46	0.31	404	244	68	0	0.0	0.00	0	0	0	54.1	404	1.30	21.5	10.9	37
42	1184	20.0	25.4	59.9	0.46	0.43	509	357	138	0	0.0	0.00	0	0	0	59.9	509	1.06	20.5	12.1	42
47	1077	21.6	27.6	64.6	0.47	0.57	609	470	234	0	0.0	0.00	0	0	0	64.6	609	0.89	19.2	12.9	47
52	995	23.6	29.7	68.8	0.47	0.70	701	578	345	0	0.0	0.00	0	0	0	68.8	701	0.78	17.7	13.5	52
57	926	25.1	31.6	72.4	0.47	0.85	786	678	462	0	0.0	0.00	0	0	0	72.4	786	0.69	16.1	13.8	57
62	870	26.5	33.3	75.7	0.47	0.99	862	770	576	0	0.0	0.00	0	0	0	75.7	862	0.62	14.6	13.9	62
67	823	27.7	34.9	78.7	0.46	1.13	932	844	653	0	0.0	0.00	0	0	0	78.7	932	0.56	13.3	13.9	67
72	783	28.9	36.4	81.3	0.46	1.27	995	920	753	0	0.0	0.00	0	0	0	81.3	995	0.51	12.2	13.8	72
77	749	29.9	37.7	83.8	0.45	1.41	1053	981	821	0	0.0	0.00	0	0	0	83.8	1053	0.47	10.8	13.7	77

E

NORWAY SPRUCE   YIELD CLASS 12   UNTHINNED

0.9 x 0.9 m spacing

Age	MAIN CROP After Thinning No. of Trees	Top Ht. m	Mean Diam cm	Basal Area m²	Form Factor	Mean Vol. per Tree m³	Vol. 7 cm	Vol. 18 cm	Vol. 24 cm	Yield from Thinnings No. of Trees	Mean Diam cm	Mean Vol. per Tree m³	Vol. 7 cm	Vol. 18 cm	Vol. 24 cm	TOTAL YIELD Basal Area m²	Vol. to 7 cm m³	INCREMENT CAI Basal Area m²	CAI Vol. to 7 cm m³	MAI Vol. to 7 cm m³	Age
20	8033	7.7	6.6	27.2	0.34	0.01	53	0	0	0	0.0	0.00	0	0	0	27.2	53	2.53	11.2	2.6	20
25	6554	10.2	8.7	39.2	0.38	0.02	120	0	0	0	0.0	0.00	0	0	0	39.2	120	1.81	14.8	4.8	25
30	5393	12.5	10.3	45.3	0.44	0.04	201	0	0	0	0.0	0.00	0	0	0	45.3	201	1.13	16.4	6.7	30
35	4549	14.6	11.9	50.5	0.48	0.06	284	0	0	0	0.0	0.00	0	0	0	50.5	284	0.90	16.4	8.1	35
40	3806	16.4	13.5	54.3	0.51	0.10	365	11	0	0	0.0	0.00	0	0	0	54.3	365	0.71	15.8	9.1	40
45	3232	18.2	15.1	57.6	0.52	0.14	442	40	0	0	0.0	0.00	0	0	0	57.6	442	0.64	14.9	9.8	45
50	2807	19.7	16.6	60.8	0.53	0.18	514	68	0	0	0.0	0.00	0	0	0	60.8	514	0.56	13.8	10.3	50
55	2453	21.2	18.1	63.3	0.53	0.24	580	147	10	0	0.0	0.00	0	0	0	63.3	580	0.50	12.5	10.5	55
60	2187	22.4	19.6	65.7	0.53	0.29	639	213	23	0	0.0	0.00	0	0	0	65.7	639	0.48	11.1	10.6	60
65	1975	23.6	20.9	68.0	0.53	0.35	691	284	42	0	0.0	0.00	0	0	0	68.0	691	0.45	9.9	10.6	65
70	1803	24.6	22.3	70.2	0.53	0.41	738	404	95	0	0.0	0.00	0	0	0	70.2	738	0.42	9.0	10.5	70
75	1660	25.6	23.5	72.2	0.52	0.47	780	472	132	0	0.0	0.00	0	0	0	72.2	780	0.38	8.1	10.4	75

1.4 x 1.4 m spacing

Age	MAIN CROP After Thinning No. of Trees	Top Ht. m	Mean Diam cm	Basal Area m²	Form Factor	Mean Vol. per Tree m³	Vol. 7 cm	Vol. 18 cm	Vol. 24 cm	Yield from Thinnings No. of Trees	Mean Diam cm	Mean Vol. per Tree m³	Vol. 7 cm	Vol. 18 cm	Vol. 24 cm	TOTAL YIELD Basal Area m²	Vol. to 7 cm m³	INCREMENT CAI Basal Area m²	CAI Vol. to 7 cm m³	MAI Vol. to 7 cm m³	Age
21	4358	8.1	8.5	24.7	0.39	0.01	61	0	0	0	0.0	0.00	0	0	0	24.7	61	2.52	12.1	2.9	21
26	3800	10.6	11.1	36.6	0.41	0.03	132	0	0	0	0.0	0.00	0	0	0	36.6	132	2.04	15.2	5.1	26
31	3364	12.8	13.1	45.1	0.45	0.06	213	6	0	0	0.0	0.00	0	0	0	45.1	213	1.52	16.5	6.9	31
36	2983	14.9	14.9	51.8	0.47	0.10	297	17	0	0	0.0	0.00	0	0	0	51.8	297	1.19	16.5	8.2	36
41	2609	16.7	16.7	57.0	0.48	0.15	379	50	0	0	0.0	0.00	0	0	0	57.0	379	0.96	16.0	9.2	41
46	2298	18.4	18.4	61.4	0.49	0.20	456	116	8	0	0.0	0.00	0	0	0	61.4	456	0.84	15.1	9.9	46
51	2058	20.0	20.1	65.4	0.49	0.26	529	217	32	0	0.0	0.00	0	0	0	65.4	529	0.71	13.9	10.4	51
56	1839	21.4	21.8	68.5	0.49	0.32	595	288	55	0	0.0	0.00	0	0	0	68.5	595	0.61	12.6	10.6	56
61	1673	22.6	23.3	71.5	0.49	0.39	655	396	111	0	0.0	0.00	0	0	0	71.5	655	0.57	11.2	10.7	61
66	1538	23.8	24.8	74.2	0.49	0.46	708	465	155	0	0.0	0.00	0	0	0	74.2	708	0.53	10.1	10.7	66
71	1426	24.8	26.2	76.8	0.48	0.53	756	558	248	0	0.0	0.00	0	0	0	76.8	756	0.50	9.2	10.6	71
76	1331	25.7	27.5	79.2	0.48	0.60	800	618	308	0	0.0	0.00	0	0	0	79.2	800	0.46	8.3	10.5	76

1.8 x 1.8 m spacing

	MAIN CROP After Thinning									Yield from THINNINGS						TOTAL YIELD		INCREMENT CAI MAI			
	No. of Trees	Top Ht. (m)	Mean Diam (cm)	Basal Area (m²)	Form Factor	Mean Vol. per Tree (m³)	Volume in cubic metres to top diameters of—			No. of Trees	Mean Diam (cm)	Mean Vol. per Tree (m³)	Volume in cubic metres to top diameters of—			Basal Area (m²)	Vol. to 7 cm (m³)	Basal Area (m²)	Vol. to 7 cm (m³)	Vol. to 7 cm (m³)	
Age							7 cm	18 cm	24 cm				7 cm	18 cm	24 cm						Age
22	2718	8.5	10.3	22.4	0.42	0.02	66	0	0	0	0.0	0.00	0	0	0	22.4	66	2.35	12.0	3.0	22
27	2578	11.0	12.8	32.9	0.44	0.05	136	1	0	0	0.0	0.00	0	0	0	32.9	136	1.97	15.0	5.0	27
32	2437	13.2	14.8	42.1	0.46	0.09	217	12	0	0	0.0	0.00	0	0	0	42.1	217	1.60	16.5	6.8	32
37	2192	15.2	16.9	48.9	0.47	0.14	301	40	0	0	0.0	0.00	0	0	0	48.9	301	1.21	16.7	8.1	37
42	1954	17.0	18.8	54.2	0.48	0.20	383	97	6	0	0.0	0.00	0	0	0	54.2	383	0.99	16.2	9.1	42
47	1758	18.6	20.7	58.9	0.48	0.26	462	190	28	0	0.0	0.00	0	0	0	58.9	462	0.88	15.4	9.8	47
52	1607	20.2	22.4	63.0	0.48	0.33	537	294	69	0	0.0	0.00	0	0	0	63.0	537	0.75	14.3	10.3	52
57	1462	21.5	24.0	66.4	0.48	0.41	606	398	132	0	0.0	0.00	0	0	0	66.4	606	0.64	13.1	10.6	57
62	1354	22.8	25.6	69.5	0.48	0.49	668	469	181	0	0.0	0.00	0	0	0	69.5	668	0.60	11.9	10.8	62
67	1264	23.9	27.0	72.4	0.48	0.57	725	560	279	0	0.0	0.00	0	0	0	72.4	725	0.56	10.9	10.8	67
72	1188	24.9	28.4	75.0	0.47	0.65	777	622	341	0	0.0	0.00	0	0	0	75.0	777	0.51	10.0	10.8	72
77	1121	25.8	29.7	77.5	0.47	0.74	825	680	406	0	0.0	0.00	0	0	0	77.5	825	0.47	9.2	10.7	77

2.4 x 2.4 m spacing

	MAIN CROP After Thinning									Yield from THINNINGS						TOTAL YIELD		INCREMENT CAI MAI			
	No. of Trees	Top Ht. (m)	Mean Diam (cm)	Basal Area (m²)	Form Factor	Mean Vol. per Tree (m³)	Volume in cubic metres to top diameters of—			No. of Trees	Mean Diam (cm)	Mean Vol. per Tree (m³)	Volume in cubic metres to top diameters of—			Basal Area (m²)	Vol. to 7 cm (m³)	Basal Area (m²)	Vol. to 7 cm (m³)	Vol. to 7 cm (m³)	
Age							7 cm	18 cm	24 cm				7 cm	18 cm	24 cm						Age
26	1572	10.3	13.7	23.2	0.43	0.06	89	2	0	0	0.0	0.00	0	0	0	23.2	89	2.27	13.6	3.4	26
31	1559	12.5	16.7	34.0	0.43	0.11	164	22	0	0	0.0	0.00	0	0	0	34.0	164	1.97	15.9	5.3	31
36	1498	14.6	19.1	43.0	0.44	0.17	248	82	9	0	0.0	0.00	0	0	0	43.0	248	1.54	16.7	6.9	36
41	1389	16.4	21.3	49.4	0.45	0.24	331	160	30	0	0.0	0.00	0	0	0	49.4	331	1.15	16.4	8.1	41
46	1283	18.1	23.3	54.5	0.46	0.32	412	249	70	0	0.0	0.00	0	0	0	54.5	412	0.95	15.8	9.0	46
51	1197	19.6	25.0	58.9	0.46	0.41	489	343	133	0	0.0	0.00	0	0	0	58.9	489	0.78	15.0	9.6	51
56	1113	21.0	26.7	62.3	0.47	0.50	562	414	184	0	0.0	0.00	0	0	0	62.3	562	0.66	13.9	10.0	56
61	1049	22.3	28.2	65.5	0.47	0.60	628	502	276	0	0.0	0.00	0	0	0	65.5	628	0.60	12.7	10.3	61
66	994	23.4	29.6	68.3	0.47	0.69	688	567	339	0	0.0	0.00	0	0	0	68.3	688	0.54	11.6	10.4	66
71	947	24.4	30.9	70.9	0.47	0.79	744	628	403	0	0.0	0.00	0	0	0	70.9	744	0.49	10.8	10.5	71
76	905	25.4	32.1	73.2	0.47	0.88	797	700	503	0	0.0	0.00	0	0	0	73.2	797	0.43	9.9	10.5	76
81	867	26.3	33.2	75.1	0.46	0.97	843	753	563	0	0.0	0.00	0	0	0	75.1	843	0.38	9.0	10.4	81

NORWAY SPRUCE YIELD CLASS 8 UNTHINNED

0.9 x 0.9m spacing

Age	MAIN CROP After Thinning									Yield from THINNINGS						TOTAL YIELD		INCREMENT CAI		MAI	Age
	No. of Trees	Top Ht. (m)	Mean Diam (cm)	Basal Area (m²)	Form Factor	Mean Vol. per Tree (m³)	Vol. 7 cm	Vol. 18 cm	Vol. 24 cm	No. of Trees	Mean Diam (cm)	Mean Vol. per Tree (m³)	Vol. 7 cm	Vol. 18 cm	Vol. 24 cm	Basal Area (m²)	Vol. to 7 cm (m³)	Basal Area (m²)	Vol. to 7 cm (m³)	Vol. to 7 cm (m³)	
30	6912	9.6	8.2	36.5	0.37	0.01	102	0	0	0	0.0	0.00	0	0	0	36.5	102	1.75	10.7	3.4	30
35	5893	11.3	9.8	44.6	0.39	0.03	158	0	0	0	0.0	0.00	0	0	0	44.6	158	1.19	11.5	4.5	35
40	5114	12.8	11.0	48.4	0.44	0.04	217	0	0	0	0.0	0.00	0	0	0	48.4	217	0.73	11.7	5.4	40
45	4543	14.3	12.1	51.9	0.46	0.06	275	2	0	0	0.0	0.00	0	0	0	51.9	275	0.62	11.4	6.1	45
50	4020	15.6	13.2	54.6	0.48	0.08	331	10	0	0	0.0	0.00	0	0	0	54.6	331	0.50	10.9	6.6	50
55	3585	16.8	14.2	56.9	0.50	0.11	384	22	0	0	0.0	0.00	0	0	0	56.9	384	0.45	10.2	7.0	55
60	3231	17.9	15.3	59.1	0.51	0.13	433	39	0	0	0.0	0.00	0	0	0	59.1	433	0.39	9.5	7.2	60
65	2938	18.9	16.2	60.9	0.51	0.16	479	64	0	0	0.0	0.00	0	0	0	60.9	479	0.35	8.7	7.4	65
70	2702	19.9	17.2	62.6	0.52	0.19	520	97	1	0	0.0	0.00	0	0	0	62.6	520	0.33	7.9	7.4	70
75	2518	20.7	18.0	64.1	0.52	0.22	558	142	10	0	0.0	0.00	0	0	0	64.1	558	0.29	7.2	7.4	75
80	2317	21.5	19.0	65.5	0.52	0.26	592	150	10	0	0.0	0.00	0	0	0	65.5	592	0.27	6.5	7.4	80

1.4 x 1.4 m spacing

Age	MAIN CROP After Thinning									Yield from THINNINGS						TOTAL YIELD		INCREMENT CAI		MAI	Age
	No. of Trees	Top Ht. (m)	Mean Diam (cm)	Basal Area (m²)	Form Factor	Mean Vol. per Tree (m³)	Vol. 7 cm	Vol. 18 cm	Vol. 24 cm	No. of Trees	Mean Diam (cm)	Mean Vol. per Tree (m³)	Vol. 7 cm	Vol. 18 cm	Vol. 24 cm	Basal Area (m²)	Vol. to 7 cm (m³)	Basal Area (m²)	Vol. to 7 cm (m³)	Vol. to 7 cm (m³)	
26	4382	8.0	8.4	24.2	0.39	0.01	59	0	0	0	0.0	0.00	0	0	0	24.2	59	1.87	9.0	2.3	26
31	3965	9.9	10.3	33.3	0.40	0.03	109	0	0	0	0.0	0.00	0	0	0	33.3	109	1.72	10.6	3.5	31
36	3583	11.5	12.1	41.4	0.42	0.05	166	1	0	0	0.0	0.00	0	0	0	41.4	166	1.38	11.6	4.6	36
41	3315	13.1	13.5	47.1	0.44	0.07	224	6	0	0	0.0	0.00	0	0	0	47.1	224	1.03	11.7	5.5	41
46	3047	14.5	14.7	51.7	0.46	0.09	283	16	0	0	0.0	0.00	0	0	0	51.7	283	0.84	11.4	6.1	46
51	2781	15.8	15.9	55.5	0.47	0.12	339	30	0	0	0.0	0.00	0	0	0	55.5	339	0.70	10.9	6.6	51
56	2548	17.0	17.1	58.7	0.48	0.15	392	73	1	0	0.0	0.00	0	0	0	58.7	392	0.61	10.3	7.0	56
61	2348	18.1	18.3	61.6	0.48	0.19	442	112	7	0	0.0	0.00	0	0	0	61.6	442	0.52	9.6	7.2	61
66	2175	19.1	19.3	63.9	0.49	0.22	488	162	18	0	0.0	0.00	0	0	0	63.9	488	0.46	8.8	7.4	66
71	2035	20.0	20.3	66.1	0.49	0.26	530	210	32	0	0.0	0.00	0	0	0	66.1	530	0.42	7.9	7.5	71
76	1925	20.8	21.2	68.1	0.49	0.29	567	275	52	0	0.0	0.00	0	0	0	68.1	567	0.38	7.3	7.5	76
81	1793	21.5	22.3	70.0	0.48	0.34	603	330	77	0	0.0	0.00	0	0	0	70.0	603	0.35	6.7	7.4	81

1.8 x 1.8 m spacing

	MAIN CROP After Thinning						Volume in cubic metres to top diameters of-			Yield from THINNINGS			Volume in cubic metres to top diameters of-			TOTAL YIELD		INCREMENT CAI		MAI	
Age	No. of Trees	Top Ht. m	Mean Diam cm	Basal Area m²	Form Factor	Mean Vol. per Tree m³	7 cm	18 cm	24 cm	No. of Trees	Mean Diam cm	Mean Vol. per Tree m³	7 cm	18 cm	24 cm	Basal Area m²	Vol. to 7 cm m³	Basal Area m²	Vol. to 7 cm m³	Vol. to 7 cm m³	Age
27	2735	8.3	10.0	21.5	0.42	0.02	61	0	0	0	0.0	0.00	0	0	0	21.5	61	1.73	8.6	2.3	27
32	2602	10.1	12.1	29.9	0.43	0.04	109	0	0	0	0.0	0.00	0	0	0	29.9	109	1.59	10.3	3.4	32
37	2558	11.7	13.6	37.4	0.44	0.06	164	5	0	0	0.0	0.00	0	0	0	37.4	164	1.37	11.4	4.4	37
42	2438	13.3	15.1	43.6	0.45	0.09	223	20	0	0	0.0	0.00	0	0	0	43.6	223	1.10	11.7	5.3	42
47	2264	14.7	16.5	48.4	0.46	0.12	282	37	0	0	0.0	0.00	0	0	0	48.4	282	0.87	11.5	6.0	47
52	2093	16.0	17.8	52.3	0.47	0.16	338	63	1	0	0.0	0.00	0	0	0	52.3	338	0.72	11.0	6.5	52
57	1942	17.1	19.1	55.6	0.47	0.20	392	130	14	0	0.0	0.00	0	0	0	55.6	392	0.62	10.4	6.9	57
62	1813	18.2	20.3	58.5	0.48	0.24	442	181	27	0	0.0	0.00	0	0	0	58.5	442	0.54	9.7	7.1	62
67	1701	19.2	21.4	61.0	0.48	0.29	489	237	45	0	0.0	0.00	0	0	0	61.0	489	0.48	9.0	7.3	67
72	1611	20.1	22.4	63.3	0.48	0.33	532	291	68	0	0.0	0.00	0	0	0	63.3	532	0.46	8.2	7.4	72
77	1541	20.8	23.3	65.6	0.48	0.37	571	345	97	0	0.0	0.00	0	0	0	65.6	571	0.43	7.5	7.4	77
82	1449	21.6	24.4	67.6	0.48	0.42	607	399	132	0	0.0	0.00	0	0	0	67.6	607	0.40	6.8	7.4	82

2.4 x 2.4 m spacing

	MAIN CROP After Thinning						Volume in cubic metres to top diameters of-			Yield from THINNINGS			Volume in cubic metres to top diameters of-			TOTAL YIELD		INCREMENT CAI		MAI	
Age	No. of Trees	Top Ht. m	Mean Diam cm	Basal Area m²	Form Factor	Mean Vol. per Tree m³	7 cm	18 cm	24 cm	No. of Trees	Mean Diam cm	Mean Vol. per Tree m³	7 cm	18 cm	24 cm	Basal Area m²	Vol. to 7 cm m³	Basal Area m²	Vol. to 7 cm m³	Vol. to 7 cm m³	Age
34	1564	10.5	14.2	24.7	0.43	0.06	98	5	0	0	0.0	0.00	0	0	0	24.7	98	1.62	9.7	2.9	34
39	1557	12.1	16.3	32.4	0.43	0.10	151	20	0	0	0.0	0.00	0	0	0	32.4	151	1.47	11.2	3.9	39
44	1538	13.6	18.1	39.4	0.44	0.14	210	53	3	0	0.0	0.00	0	0	0	39.4	210	1.23	11.6	4.8	44
49	1473	15.0	19.7	44.7	0.44	0.18	268	89	9	0	0.0	0.00	0	0	0	44.7	268	0.94	11.3	5.5	49
54	1399	16.2	21.1	48.9	0.45	0.23	323	156	30	0	0.0	0.00	0	0	0	48.9	323	0.77	10.8	6.0	54
59	1329	17.3	22.4	52.4	0.46	0.28	376	206	48	0	0.0	0.00	0	0	0	52.4	376	0.65	10.3	6.4	59
64	1264	18.4	23.6	55.3	0.46	0.34	425	257	72	0	0.0	0.00	0	0	0	55.3	425	0.55	9.6	6.6	64
69	1208	19.3	24.7	57.9	0.46	0.39	472	310	103	0	0.0	0.00	0	0	0	57.9	472	0.49	8.9	6.8	69
74	1163	20.2	25.7	60.3	0.46	0.44	515	361	140	0	0.0	0.00	0	0	0	60.3	515	0.46	8.2	7.0	74
79	1128	20.9	26.6	62.5	0.46	0.49	553	408	182	0	0.0	0.00	0	0	0	62.5	553	0.42	7.5	7.0	79

APPENDIX III

YIELD MODELS FOR THINNED STANDS

SCOTS PINE YIELD CLASS 10 THINNED

0.9 x 0.9 m spacing

| Age | MAIN CROP After Thinning | | | | | | | | | Yield from THINNINGS | | | | | | TOTAL YIELD | | INCREMENT CAI | | MAI | Age |
	No. of Trees	Top Ht. (m)	Mean Diam (cm)	Basal Area (m²)	Form Factor	Mean Vol. per Tree (m³)	Vol. 7 cm (m³)	Vol. 18 cm (m³)	Vol. 24 cm (m³)	No. of Trees	Mean Diam (cm)	Mean Vol. per Tree (m³)	Vol. 7 cm (m³)	Vol. 18 cm (m³)	Vol. 24 cm (m³)	Basal Area (m²)	Vol. to 7 cm (m³)	Basal Area (m²)	Vol. to 7 cm (m³)	Vol. to 7 cm (m³)	
20	7205	8.2	7.4	31.1	0.30	0.01	66	0	0	0	0.0	0.00	0	0	0	31.1	66	1.21	8.2	3.3	20
25	3436	10.3	8.7	20.2	0.43	0.02	80	0	0	3768	7.8	0.01	35	0	0	38.3	115	1.55	10.8	4.6	25
30	2136	12.2	10.8	19.5	0.48	0.05	105	0	0	1300	9.3	0.03	35	0	0	46.6	175	1.65	12.7	5.8	30
35	1515	14.0	13.4	21.4	0.49	0.09	136	4	0	621	11.4	0.06	35	0	0	54.8	241	1.59	13.7	6.9	35
40	1157	15.7	16.2	23.8	0.50	0.15	172	23	0	358	13.7	0.10	35	1	0	62.5	312	1.49	14.2	7.8	40
45	928	17.2	19.0	26.3	0.49	0.22	209	69	7	230	16.2	0.15	35	5	0	69.7	384	1.38	14.3	8.5	45
50	770	18.6	21.7	28.5	0.49	0.32	245	118	22	158	18.8	0.22	35	9	1	76.3	455	1.27	14.0	9.1	50
55	656	19.9	24.3	30.5	0.49	0.42	279	183	61	114	21.5	0.31	35	17	3	82.4	524	1.16	13.5	9.5	55
60	570	21.0	26.8	32.1	0.48	0.54	309	228	101	86	24.1	0.41	35	23	8	88.0	589	1.04	12.6	9.8	60
65	502	22.1	29.1	33.3	0.48	0.67	337	277	166	67	26.5	0.50	33	25	11	92.9	650	0.93	11.6	10.0	65
70	454	23.0	31.2	34.6	0.48	0.80	362	312	213	48	28.7	0.63	30	24	13	97.2	705	0.82	10.5	10.1	70
75	417	23.8	33.0	35.7	0.47	0.92	385	344	257	37	30.6	0.72	27	23	14	101.0	755	0.71	9.4	10.1	75
80	388	24.6	34.7	36.6	0.47	1.05	406	367	284	29	32.4	0.81	24	21	15	104.4	799	0.62	8.3	10.0	80

1.4 x 1.4 m spacing

| Age | MAIN CROP After Thinning | | | | | | | | | Yield from THINNINGS | | | | | | TOTAL YIELD | | INCREMENT CAI | | MAI | Age |
	No. of Trees	Top Ht. (m)	Mean Diam (cm)	Basal Area (m²)	Form Factor	Mean Vol. per Tree (m³)	Vol. 7 cm (m³)	Vol. 18 cm (m³)	Vol. 24 cm (m³)	No. of Trees	Mean Diam (cm)	Mean Vol. per Tree (m³)	Vol. 7 cm (m³)	Vol. 18 cm (m³)	Vol. 24 cm (m³)	Basal Area (m²)	Vol. to 7 cm (m³)	Basal Area (m²)	Vol. to 7 cm (m³)	Vol. to 7 cm (m³)	
20	4186	8.1	8.8	25.3	0.36	0.02	64	0	0	0	0.0	0.00	0	0	0	25.3	64	1.35	8.1	3.2	20
25	2187	10.2	10.5	18.8	0.45	0.04	77	0	0	1999	9.5	0.02	35	0	0	32.9	112	1.58	10.7	4.5	25
30	1433	12.1	13.1	19.3	0.47	0.07	101	3	0	753	11.4	0.05	35	0	0	41.1	171	1.63	12.5	5.7	30
35	1056	13.9	16.2	21.8	0.47	0.13	132	17	0	377	13.8	0.09	35	1	0	49.2	237	1.57	13.6	6.8	35
40	831	15.6	19.4	24.7	0.47	0.20	167	55	6	225	16.4	0.16	35	5	0	56.8	307	1.47	14.1	7.7	40
45	681	17.1	22.6	27.4	0.46	0.30	204	111	26	150	19.3	0.23	35	12	1	63.9	379	1.36	14.2	8.4	45
50	575	18.5	25.7	29.8	0.46	0.42	240	168	65	106	22.2	0.33	35	19	5	70.4	450	1.25	14.0	9.0	50
55	497	19.8	28.6	31.9	0.46	0.55	273	218	120	79	25.2	0.44	35	25	10	76.5	518	1.15	13.4	9.4	55
60	437	20.9	31.3	33.6	0.45	0.69	304	262	178	60	28.1	0.58	35	28	15	81.9	584	1.03	12.6	9.7	60
65	391	22.0	33.8	35.1	0.45	0.85	331	295	221	46	30.7	0.72	33	28	18	86.8	644	0.92	11.6	9.9	65
70	354	22.7	36.1	36.2	0.45	1.01	356	329	269	37	33.1	0.81	30	27	20	91.1	699	0.81	10.5	10.0	70
75	327	23.7	38.1	37.3	0.45	1.16	379	355	303	27	35.3	0.99	27	24	19	94.8	749	0.70	9.4	10.0	75
80	306	24.5	39.9	38.3	0.45	1.31	400	377	327	21	37.3	1.12	24	22	18	98.1	793	0.63	8.3	9.9	80

1.8 x 1.8 m spacing

	MAIN CROP After Thinning									Yield from THINNINGS						TOTAL YIELD		INCREMENT CAI		MAI	
Age	No. of Trees	Top Mean Ht. (m)	Mean Diam (cm)	Basal Area (m²)	Form Factor	Mean Vol. per Tree (m³)	Vol. to top diam. 7 cm	18 cm	24 cm	No. of Trees	Mean Diam (cm)	Mean Vol. per Tree (m³)	Vol. to top diam. 7 cm	18 cm	24 cm	Basal Area (m²)	Vol. to 7 cm (m³)	Basal Area (m²)	Vol. to 7 cm (m³)	Vol. to 7 cm (m³)	Age
21	2580	8.3	10.3	21.7	0.40	0.03	65	0	0	0	0.0	0.00	0	0	0	21.7	65	1.41	8.2	3.1	21
26	1553	10.4	12.5	19.2	0.43	0.05	78	0	0	1027	11.3	0.03	35	0	0	29.5	113	1.60	10.8	4.4	26
31	1069	12.3	15.6	20.5	0.44	0.10	103	9	0	484	13.5	0.07	35	1	0	37.7	173	1.62	12.6	5.6	31
36	814	14.0	19.1	23.2	0.44	0.16	134	44	4	254	16.2	0.14	35	5	0	45.7	239	1.55	13.6	6.6	36
41	657	15.7	22.5	26.2	0.44	0.26	168	92	21	158	19.1	0.22	35	12	1	53.2	308	1.44	14.0	7.5	41
46	549	17.2	25.9	28.9	0.43	0.37	204	143	55	108	22.1	0.32	35	19	5	60.4	379	1.32	14.1	8.2	46
51	470	18.6	29.1	31.3	0.43	0.51	239	197	117	79	25.2	0.44	35	25	10	66.4	449	1.22	13.7	8.8	51
56	411	19.8	32.2	33.4	0.43	0.66	272	238	171	60	28.4	0.58	35	28	15	72.3	517	1.12	13.1	9.2	56
61	364	21.0	35.0	35.1	0.43	0.83	300	275	219	47	31.4	0.74	35	30	21	77.6	580	1.00	12.3	9.5	61
66	329	22.0	37.6	36.6	0.42	0.99	327	304	255	35	34.2	0.93	33	30	23	82.3	640	0.89	11.3	9.7	66
71	300	22.9	40.0	37.6	0.42	1.17	352	331	288	29	36.7	1.01	29	27	22	86.5	694	0.78	10.2	9.8	71
76	279	23.7	42.1	38.8	0.42	1.34	374	357	323	21	39.0	1.24	26	24	21	90.1	742	0.69	9.1	9.8	76
81	263	24.4	43.9	39.8	0.42	1.50	394	378	345	17	41.0	1.35	23	22	19	93.4	785	0.60	8.1	9.7	81

2.4 x 2.4 m spacing

	MAIN CROP After Thinning									Yield from THINNINGS						TOTAL YIELD		INCREMENT CAI		MAI	
Age	No. of Trees	Top Mean Ht. (m)	Mean Diam (cm)	Basal Area (m²)	Form Factor	Mean Vol. per Tree (m³)	Vol. to top diam. 7 cm	18 cm	24 cm	No. of Trees	Mean Diam (cm)	Mean Vol. per Tree (m³)	Vol. to top diam. 7 cm	18 cm	24 cm	Basal Area (m²)	Vol. to 7 cm (m³)	Basal Area (m²)	Vol. to 7 cm (m³)	Vol. to 7 cm (m³)	Age
24	1485	9.1	13.3	20.5	0.41	0.05	70	2	0	0	0.0	0.00	0	0	0	20.5	70	1.60	9.0	2.9	24
29	990	11.1	16.3	20.7	0.40	0.09	86	11	0	496	14.5	0.07	35	2	0	28.9	121	1.68	11.2	4.2	29
34	728	12.9	20.1	23.0	0.40	0.15	112	46	6	262	17.2	0.13	35	7	0	37.3	182	1.63	12.7	5.4	34
39	579	14.6	24.0	26.1	0.40	0.25	143	86	24	149	20.3	0.23	35	14	2	45.2	248	1.52	13.5	6.4	39
44	481	16.1	27.8	29.1	0.40	0.37	177	136	68	98	23.5	0.36	35	21	6	52.5	317	1.40	13.7	7.2	44
49	411	17.5	31.4	31.9	0.39	0.51	210	181	123	70	26.9	0.50	35	26	12	59.2	385	1.28	13.6	7.9	49
54	358	18.9	34.9	34.1	0.39	0.68	243	219	170	53	30.3	0.66	35	30	19	65.3	453	1.17	13.1	8.4	54
59	317	20.0	38.0	36.0	0.39	0.86	272	255	217	41	33.7	0.85	35	31	23	70.8	517	1.04	12.5	8.8	59
64	283	21.1	41.0	37.4	0.39	1.05	297	283	252	33	36.9	1.06	35	32	26	75.7	577	0.93	11.6	9.0	64
69	258	22.1	43.7	38.7	0.39	1.25	322	308	281	25	39.8	1.23	31	29	25	80.1	632	0.83	10.6	9.2	69
74	240	22.9	46.1	40.0	0.39	1.44	345	333	310	18	42.4	1.52	27	26	24	84.0	683	0.73	9.5	9.2	74
79	225	23.6	48.2	41.1	0.39	1.62	365	355	333	15	44.7	1.61	24	23	21	87.4	728	0.65	8.5	9.2	79

SCOTS PINE   YIELD CLASS 8   THINNED

0.9 x 0.9 m spacing

Age	No. of Trees	Main Crop: Top Ht. (m)	Mean Diam (cm)	Basal Area (m²)	Form Factor	After Thinning: Mean Vol. per Tree (m³)	Vol 7 cm	Vol 18 cm	Vol 24 cm	Thinnings: No. of Trees	Mean Diam (cm)	Mean Vol. per Tree (m³)	Vol 7 cm	Vol 18 cm	Vol 24 cm	Total Basal Area (m²)	Total Vol to 7 cm (m³)	CAI Basal Area (m²)	CAI Vol to 7 cm (m³)	MAI Vol to 7 cm (m³)	Age
19	8440	6.3	6.3	26.3	0.25	0.00	35	0	0	0	0.0	0.00	0	0	0	26.3	35	0.53	4.9	1.8	19
24	7186	8.2	7.4	30.7	0.30	0.01	66	0	0	0	0.0	0.00	0	0	0	30.7	66	1.10	7.3	2.8	24
29	3842	10.1	8.5	21.6	0.41	0.02	80	0	0	3344	7.7	0.01	28	0	0	37.3	108	1.38	9.2	3.7	29
34	2512	11.7	10.2	20.5	0.47	0.04	103	0	0	1330	8.9	0.02	28	0	0	44.5	159	1.43	10.6	4.7	34
39	1834	13.3	12.3	21.8	0.49	0.07	130	1	0	678	10.5	0.04	28	0	0	51.7	214	1.38	11.4	5.5	39
44	1427	14.8	14.5	23.7	0.50	0.11	161	9	0	407	12.3	0.07	28	0	0	58.4	273	1.29	11.7	6.2	44
49	1158	16.1	16.8	25.6	0.50	0.17	192	25	0	269	14.2	0.10	28	2	0	64.5	332	1.19	11.7	6.8	49
54	969	17.3	19.0	27.4	0.50	0.23	222	56	3	189	16.2	0.15	28	4	0	70.3	390	1.10	11.5	7.2	54
59	831	18.4	21.1	29.1	0.50	0.30	250	121	23	139	18.2	0.20	28	7	1	75.6	446	1.01	11.1	7.6	59
64	726	19.5	23.1	30.5	0.49	0.38	276	167	46	105	20.3	0.27	28	12	2	80.4	500	0.93	10.5	7.8	64
69	644	20.4	25.1	31.7	0.49	0.46	299	209	81	82	22.3	0.34	28	15	4	84.8	551	0.83	9.6	8.0	69
74	584	21.2	26.8	32.9	0.49	0.55	320	236	105	60	24.1	0.41	25	16	5	88.7	597	0.71	8.6	8.1	74
79	539	21.9	28.3	33.8	0.48	0.63	339	271	149	45	25.7	0.48	22	15	6	91.9	637	0.59	7.5	8.1	79
84	500	22.5	29.5	34.2	0.49	0.71	355	292	174	38	27.0	0.49	19	14	6	94.5	672	0.49	6.4	8.0	84

1.4 x 1.4 m spacing

Age	No. of Trees	Main Crop: Top Ht. (m)	Mean Diam (cm)	Basal Area (m²)	Form Factor	After Thinning: Mean Vol. per Tree (m³)	Vol 7 cm	Vol 18 cm	Vol 24 cm	Thinnings: No. of Trees	Mean Diam (cm)	Mean Vol. per Tree (m³)	Vol 7 cm	Vol 18 cm	Vol 24 cm	Total Basal Area (m²)	Total Vol to 7 cm (m³)	CAI Basal Area (m²)	CAI Vol to 7 cm (m³)	MAI Vol to 7 cm (m³)	Age
19	4652	6.2	7.3	19.3	0.33	0.01	34	0	0	0	0.0	0.00	0	0	0	19.3	34	0.80	4.8	1.8	19
24	4179	8.1	8.7	25.0	0.36	0.02	64	0	0	0	0.0	0.00	0	0	0	25.0	64	1.25	7.2	2.7	24
29	2407	10.0	10.2	19.7	0.44	0.03	77	0	0	1772	9.3	0.04	28	0	0	31.8	105	1.40	9.1	3.6	29
34	1660	11.6	12.4	20.0	0.47	0.06	99	0	0	747	10.8	0.04	28	0	0	39.0	155	1.42	10.5	4.6	34
39	1258	13.2	14.9	21.9	0.47	0.10	127	7	0	402	12.7	0.07	28	0	0	46.1	211	1.37	11.3	5.4	39
44	1007	14.7	17.5	24.2	0.47	0.16	157	29	0	251	14.8	0.11	28	2	0	52.7	269	1.28	11.7	6.1	44
49	836	16.0	20.1	26.5	0.47	0.22	187	77	11	172	17.0	0.16	28	5	0	58.9	327	1.18	11.6	6.7	49
54	712	17.2	22.6	28.5	0.47	0.30	217	119	27	124	19.3	0.23	28	9	1	64.5	385	1.08	11.4	7.1	54
59	618	18.3	25.0	30.2	0.47	0.40	245	161	53	93	21.6	0.30	28	14	3	69.6	441	0.99	11.0	7.5	59
64	546	19.4	27.2	31.8	0.46	0.50	271	209	104	72	23.9	0.39	28	17	5	74.4	495	0.91	10.4	7.7	64
69	489	20.3	29.4	33.1	0.46	0.60	293	241	144	57	26.1	0.49	28	21	9	78.7	545	0.81	9.6	7.9	69
74	447	21.1	31.3	34.3	0.46	0.70	315	271	185	42	28.1	0.59	25	20	11	82.5	591	0.70	8.6	8.0	74
79	415	21.8	32.9	35.3	0.46	0.80	333	293	210	32	29.8	0.68	22	18	11	85.8	631	0.59	7.5	8.0	79
84	388	22.4	34.3	35.9	0.46	0.90	349	316	244	27	31.3	0.69	19	16	11	88.4	666	0.48	6.4	7.9	84

1.8 x 1.8 m spacing

Age	MAIN CROP (After Thinning) No. of Trees	Top Ht. m	Mean Diam cm	Basal Area m²	Form Factor	Mean Vol per Tree m³	Vol 7 cm	Vol 18 cm	Vol 24 cm	THINNINGS No. of Trees	Mean Diam cm	Mean Vol per Tree m³	Vol 7 cm	Vol 18 cm	Vol 24 cm	TOTAL YIELD Basal Area m²	Vol to 7 cm m³	CAI Basal Area m²	CAI Vol to 7 cm m³	MAI Vol to 7 cm m³	Age
20	2710	6.4	8.5	15.3	0.39	0.01	33	0	0	0	0.0	0.00	0	0	0	15.3	33	0.91	4.7	1.7	20
25	2582	8.3	10.3	21.3	0.40	0.02	64	0	0	0	0.0	0.00	0	0	0	21.3	64	1.29	7.2	2.5	25
30	1693	10.1	12.2	19.7	0.43	0.05	77	0	0	889	11.1	0.03	28	0	0	28.3	105	1.41	9.1	3.5	30
35	1219	11.8	14.7	20.7	0.44	0.08	99	5	0	474	12.8	0.06	28	0	0	35.4	155	1.41	10.5	4.4	35
40	953	13.3	17.5	23.0	0.44	0.13	126	23	0	266	15.0	0.11	28	2	0	42.4	210	1.35	11.3	5.3	40
45	782	14.7	20.4	25.5	0.44	0.20	156	64	9	172	17.2	0.16	28	5	0	48.9	268	1.25	11.5	5.9	45
50	661	16.1	23.2	27.8	0.44	0.28	186	112	31	121	19.6	0.23	28	9	1	54.9	326	1.15	11.5	6.5	50
55	571	17.3	25.8	29.9	0.44	0.38	215	150	58	90	22.0	0.31	28	15	4	60.4	383	1.05	11.2	7.0	55
60	502	18.4	28.3	31.7	0.44	0.48	242	193	106	69	24.5	0.41	28	18	6	65.4	438	0.96	10.8	7.3	60
65	447	19.3	30.7	33.2	0.44	0.60	266	225	144	54	26.9	0.52	28	21	9	70.0	490	0.87	10.2	7.5	65
70	404	20.2	33.0	34.4	0.43	0.71	288	253	182	43	29.2	0.63	27	22	13	74.1	539	0.79	9.4	7.7	70
75	373	21.0	34.9	35.7	0.43	0.83	309	279	216	32	31.4	0.75	24	21	14	77.9	584	0.69	8.4	7.8	75
80	348	21.7	36.6	36.7	0.43	0.94	327	302	247	25	33.2	0.84	21	19	14	81.0	623	0.57	7.3	7.8	80
85	327	22.3	38.1	37.2	0.43	1.05	343	321	274	21	34.8	0.86	18	16	13	83.6	657	0.47	6.2	7.7	85

2.4 x 2.4 m spacing

Age	MAIN CROP (After Thinning) No. of Trees	Top Ht. m	Mean Diam cm	Basal Area m²	Form Factor	Mean Vol per Tree m³	Vol 7 cm	Vol 18 cm	Vol 24 cm	THINNINGS No. of Trees	Mean Diam cm	Mean Vol per Tree m³	Vol 7 cm	Vol 18 cm	Vol 24 cm	TOTAL YIELD Basal Area m²	Vol to 7 cm m³	CAI Basal Area m²	CAI Vol to 7 cm m³	MAI Vol to 7 cm m³	Age
24	1522	7.5	11.1	14.6	0.41	0.03	40	0	0	0	0.0	0.00	0	0	0	14.6	40	1.14	5.4	1.6	24
29	1482	9.3	13.4	21.0	0.41	0.05	73	2	0	0	0.0	0.00	0	0	0	21.0	73	1.38	7.8	2.5	29
34	1070	11.0	16.1	21.8	0.41	0.08	90	12	0	411	14.3	0.07	28	2	0	28.4	118	1.47	9.7	3.5	34
39	824	12.5	19.2	23.8	0.41	0.14	114	37	4	247	16.5	0.11	28	4	0	35.7	170	1.41	10.7	4.3	39
44	672	14.0	22.3	26.3	0.41	0.21	141	77	18	152	18.9	0.18	28	7	1	42.5	225	1.30	11.1	5.1	44
49	567	15.3	25.4	28.7	0.41	0.30	169	118	45	105	21.5	0.27	28	14	3	48.7	281	1.19	11.2	5.7	49
54	490	16.6	28.3	30.9	0.40	0.40	197	157	86	77	24.1	0.36	28	18	6	54.4	337	1.09	11.0	6.2	54
59	431	17.7	31.1	32.8	0.40	0.52	223	192	131	59	26.7	0.47	28	21	9	59.6	391	0.99	10.6	6.6	59
64	384	18.7	33.8	34.4	0.40	0.64	247	220	164	47	29.3	0.60	28	23	14	64.3	443	0.90	10.1	6.9	64
69	346	19.6	36.2	35.7	0.40	0.77	267	247	202	38	31.9	0.74	28	24	16	68.6	491	0.81	9.4	7.1	69
74	318	20.4	38.4	36.9	0.40	0.90	288	269	230	28	34.2	0.88	25	22	17	72.5	536	0.71	8.5	7.2	74
79	297	21.1	40.4	38.1	0.40	1.03	306	290	256	21	36.3	1.03	22	20	16	75.8	576	0.61	7.5	7.3	79
84	281	21.7	42.0	39.0	0.40	1.15	323	308	278	16	38.1	1.16	19	17	15	78.6	611	0.51	6.5	7.3	84

71

SCOTS PINE YIELD CLASS 6 THINNED

0.9 x 0.9 m spacing

	MAIN CROP After Thinning									Yield from THINNINGS						TOTAL YIELD		INCREMENT			
							Volume in cubic metres to top diameters of–						Volume in cubic metres to top diameters of–					CAI	CAI	MAI	
Age	No. of Trees	Top Ht. m	Mean Diam cm	Mean Basal Area m²	Form Factor	Mean Vol. per Tree m³	7 cm	18 cm	24 cm	No. of Trees	Mean Diam cm	Mean Vol. per Tree m³	7 cm	18 cm	24 cm	Basal Area m²	Vol. to 7 cm m³	Basal Area m²	Vol. to 7 cm m³	Vol. to 7 cm m³	Age
23	8572	6.1	6.3	26.6	0.25	0.00	33	0	0	0	0.0	0.00	0	0	0	26.6	33	0.36	4.0	1.4	23
28	7477	7.8	7.1	29.5	0.29	0.01	58	0	0	0	0.0	0.00	0	0	0	29.5	58	0.79	5.7	2.1	28
33	4651	9.4	7.9	22.6	0.37	0.01	69	0	0	2825	7.3	0.01	21	0	0	34.5	90	1.07	7.1	2.7	33
38	3108	10.8	9.1	20.3	0.44	0.03	87	0	0	1543	8.1	0.01	21	0	0	40.2	129	1.17	8.2	3.4	38
43	2321	12.2	10.7	20.9	0.47	0.05	109	0	0	787	9.3	0.03	21	0	0	46.2	172	1.18	8.9	4.0	43
48	1842	13.4	12.5	22.5	0.48	0.07	134	1	0	479	10.6	0.04	21	0	0	52.0	218	1.12	9.2	4.5	48
53	1518	14.6	14.3	24.2	0.49	0.11	160	9	0	324	12.1	0.06	21	0	0	57.4	265	1.04	9.2	5.0	53
58	1285	15.6	16.0	25.8	0.49	0.14	184	16	0	234	13.5	0.09	21	1	0	62.4	310	0.95	9.0	5.4	58
63	1109	16.6	17.7	27.2	0.49	0.19	208	38	0	176	15.0	0.12	21	2	0	66.9	355	0.86	8.7	5.6	63
68	973	17.5	19.3	28.4	0.49	0.24	229	76	8	135	16.5	0.16	21	3	0	71.0	397	0.78	8.2	5.8	68
73	867	18.2	20.8	29.4	0.49	0.29	248	102	15	106	17.9	0.20	21	4	0	74.7	437	0.70	7.5	6.0	73
78	781	18.9	22.2	30.1	0.49	0.34	262	143	33	86	19.3	0.24	21	7	1	77.9	472	0.61	6.7	6.1	78
83	722	19.5	23.4	31.0	0.49	0.38	276	167	46	59	20.5	0.29	17	7	1	80.7	503	0.51	5.8	6.1	83
88	677	20.0	24.4	31.6	0.48	0.43	289	190	63	45	21.6	0.32	14	7	1	83.0	530	0.41	5.0	6.0	88

1.4 x 1.4 m spacing

	MAIN CROP After Thinning									Yield from THINNINGS						TOTAL YIELD		INCREMENT			
							Volume in cubic metres to top diameters of–						Volume in cubic metres to top diameters of–					CAI	CAI	MAI	
Age	No. of Trees	Top Ht. m	Mean Diam cm	Mean Basal Area m²	Form Factor	Mean Vol. per Tree m³	7 cm	18 cm	24 cm	No. of Trees	Mean Diam cm	Mean Vol. per Tree m³	7 cm	18 cm	24 cm	Basal Area m²	Vol. to 7 cm m³	Basal Area m²	Vol. to 7 cm m³	Vol. to 7 cm m³	Age
23	4702	6.0	7.2	19.3	0.33	0.01	32	0	0	0	0.0	0.00	0	0	0	19.3	32	0.75	3.9	1.4	23
28	4289	7.7	8.4	23.7	0.35	0.01	56	0	0	0	0.0	0.01	0	0	0	23.7	56	0.97	5.6	2.0	28
33	2726	9.3	9.5	19.0	0.42	0.02	67	0	0	1562	8.9	0.01	21	0	0	29.0	88	1.12	7.0	2.7	33
38	1941	10.8	11.2	19.0	0.45	0.04	84	0	0	785	10.0	0.03	21	0	0	34.8	126	1.18	8.1	3.3	38
43	1510	12.1	13.2	20.5	0.47	0.07	106	3	0	431	11.4	0.05	21	0	0	40.8	169	1.17	8.8	3.9	43
48	1237	13.3	15.3	22.7	0.47	0.11	130	11	0	274	13.0	0.08	21	1	0	46.5	214	1.11	9.1	4.3	48
53	1045	14.5	17.3	24.7	0.47	0.15	155	29	0	192	14.7	0.11	21	1	0	51.8	260	1.02	9.2	4.9	53
58	902	15.5	19.4	26.6	0.47	0.20	180	60	6	143	16.4	0.15	21	3	0	56.7	306	0.93	9.0	5.3	58
63	791	16.5	21.3	28.2	0.47	0.26	203	98	18	111	18.1	0.19	21	5	0	61.2	350	0.85	8.6	5.6	63
68	703	17.4	23.1	29.5	0.46	0.32	224	135	38	88	19.7	0.24	21	7	1	65.2	392	0.76	8.1	5.8	68
73	632	18.1	24.8	30.6	0.46	0.38	242	159	53	71	21.4	0.30	21	10	2	68.8	431	0.68	7.4	5.9	73
78	574	18.8	26.4	31.4	0.46	0.45	257	189	84	58	22.9	0.36	21	12	3	72.0	467	0.60	6.6	6.0	78
83	534	19.4	27.7	32.3	0.46	0.51	271	209	104	40	24.3	0.42	17	11	4	74.8	498	0.51	5.8	6.0	83
88	504	19.9	28.9	33.0	0.46	0.56	284	227	124	31	25.5	0.46	14	10	4	77.1	525	0.42	5.0	6.0	88

1.8 x 1.8 m spacing

Age	MAIN CROP – After Thinning						Volume to top diameters of-			Yield from THINNINGS			Volume to top diameters of-			TOTAL YIELD		INCREMENT CAI			
	No. of Trees	Top Ht. (m)	Mean Diam (cm)	Basal Area (m²)	Form Factor	Mean Vol. per Tree (m³)	7 cm	18 cm	24 cm	No. of Trees	Mean Diam (cm)	Mean Vol. per Tree (m³)	7 cm	18 cm	24 cm	Basal Area (m²)	Vol. to 7 cm (m³)	Basal Area (m²)	Vol. to 7 cm (m³)	Vol. to 7 cm (m³)	Age
24	2727	6.2	8.4	15.0	0.39	0.01	31	0	0		0.0	0.00	0	0	0	15.0	31	0.81	3.7	1.3	24
29	2615	7.8	9.8	19.7	0.40	0.02	55	0	0		0.0	0.00	0	0	0	19.7	55	1.02	5.5	1.9	29
34	1848	9.4	11.3	18.5	0.42	0.04	65	0	0	767	10.5	0.03	21	0	0	25.1	86	1.13	7.0	2.5	34
39	1374	10.8	13.3	19.1	0.44	0.06	82	2	0	474	11.9	0.04	21	0	0	31.0	124	1.17	8.1	3.2	39
44	1104	12.1	15.6	21.1	0.44	0.09	104	9	0	270	13.5	0.08	21	1	0	36.9	167	1.15	8.7	3.8	44
49	927	13.3	17.9	23.4	0.44	0.14	128	23	0	177	15.3	0.12	21	2	0	42.5	212	1.09	9.0	4.3	49
54	799	14.5	20.3	25.7	0.44	0.19	152	62	9	128	17.1	0.16	21	4	0	47.8	257	1.00	9.1	4.8	54
59	700	15.5	22.4	27.7	0.43	0.25	176	96	22	99	19.0	0.21	21	5	0	52.5	302	0.91	8.8	5.1	59
64	621	16.5	24.5	29.3	0.43	0.32	198	130	43	79	20.8	0.27	21	9	1	56.8	345	0.83	8.4	5.4	64
69	558	17.3	26.5	30.7	0.43	0.39	218	161	71	64	22.6	0.33	21	12	3	60.8	386	0.74	7.9	5.6	69
74	506	18.1	28.3	31.8	0.43	0.47	235	188	103	52	24.3	0.40	21	14	5	64.3	424	0.65	7.2	5.7	74
79	462	18.7	29.9	32.5	0.43	0.54	248	204	122	44	26.0	0.48	21	15	6	67.3	458	0.57	6.4	5.8	79
84	433	19.3	31.4	33.4	0.43	0.61	262	226	154	29	27.4	0.56	16	13	6	70.0	488	0.49	5.6	5.8	84
89	411	19.8	32.6	34.3	0.43	0.67	275	241	173	22	28.7	0.62	14	11	6	72.2	515	0.41	4.9	5.8	89

2.4 x 2.4 m spacing

Age	MAIN CROP – After Thinning						Volume to top diameters of-			Yield from THINNINGS			Volume to top diameters of-			TOTAL YIELD		INCREMENT CAI			
	No. of Trees	Top Ht. (m)	Mean Diam (cm)	Basal Area (m²)	Form Factor	Mean Vol. per Tree (m³)	7 cm	18 cm	24 cm	No. of Trees	Mean Diam (cm)	Mean Vol. per Tree (m³)	7 cm	18 cm	24 cm	Basal Area (m²)	Vol. to 7 cm (m³)	Basal Area (m²)	Vol. to 7 cm (m³)	Vol. to 7 cm (m³)	Age
29	1524	7.3	11.0	14.4	0.41	0.03	38	0	0		0.0	0.00	0	0	0	14.4	38	0.84	4.1	1.3	29
34	1490	8.9	12.9	19.5	0.41	0.04	65	0	0		0.0	0.00	0	0	0	19.5	65	1.09	6.0	1.9	34
39	1123	10.3	15.0	20.0	0.41	0.07	78	7	0	367	13.6	0.06	21	1	0	25.3	99	1.19	7.4	2.5	39
44	897	11.7	17.6	21.8	0.41	0.11	97	18	0	227	15.4	0.09	21	2	0	31.4	139	1.18	8.2	3.1	44
49	753	12.9	20.2	24.2	0.40	0.16	118	48	7	143	17.4	0.15	21	4	0	37.1	181	1.12	8.7	3.7	49
54	652	14.0	22.8	26.6	0.40	0.22	141	77	18	102	19.4	0.21	21	7	1	42.5	225	1.04	8.8	4.2	54
59	574	15.0	25.3	28.7	0.40	0.29	164	115	44	78	21.4	0.27	21	10	2	47.5	269	0.94	8.6	4.6	59
64	512	16.0	27.6	30.5	0.40	0.36	185	143	71	62	23.3	0.34	21	13	4	51.9	311	0.84	8.2	4.9	64
69	461	16.9	29.7	31.9	0.40	0.44	204	168	100	51	25.3	0.41	21	15	6	55.9	351	0.74	7.7	5.1	69
74	418	17.6	31.7	32.9	0.40	0.53	220	190	129	43	27.1	0.49	21	16	8	59.4	388	0.66	7.0	5.2	74
79	382	18.3	33.5	33.6	0.40	0.61	232	207	155	36	28.9	0.58	21	17	9	62.4	421	0.58	6.2	5.3	79
84	359	18.8	35.1	34.7	0.39	0.68	245	224	178	24	30.5	0.68	16	14	9	65.2	450	0.50	5.6	5.4	84
89	341	19.3	36.5	35.6	0.39	0.76	258	238	195	17	31.9	0.80	14	12	8	67.5	477	0.44	5.0	5.4	89

SITKA SPRUCE   YIELD CLASS 16   THINNED

0.9 x 0.9 m spacing

Age	MAIN CROP After Thinning No. of Trees	Top Ht. (m)	Mean Diam (cm)	Basal Area (m²)	Form Factor	Mean Vol. per Tree (m³)	Vol. to 7 cm (m³)	Vol. to 18 cm (m³)	Vol. to 24 cm (m³)	Yield from THINNINGS No. of Trees	Mean Diam (cm)	Mean Vol. per Tree (m³)	Vol. to 7 cm (m³)	Vol. to 18 cm (m³)	Vol. to 24 cm (m³)	TOTAL YIELD Basal Area (m²)	Vol. to 7 cm (m³)	INCREMENT CAI Basal Area (m²)	CAI Vol. to 7 cm (m³)	MAI Vol. to 7 cm (m³)	Age
20	2900	10.0	10.5	24.9	0.45	0.03	91	0	0	3929	8.3	0.01	56	0	0	46.1	147	2.25	18.8	7.4	20
25	1765	13.1	13.5	25.4	0.48	0.08	137	4	0	1146	10.8	0.05	56	0	0	57.1	249	2.15	22.0	10.0	25
30	1229	16.1	17.0	28.0	0.50	0.16	199	37	0	536	13.7	0.10	56	2	0	67.6	367	2.02	24.2	12.2	30
35	935	18.9	20.6	31.1	0.50	0.29	267	110	16	294	16.8	0.19	56	8	0	77.2	491	1.78	24.4	14.0	35
40	743	21.5	23.9	33.3	0.51	0.45	331	200	56	192	19.8	0.29	56	19	2	85.4	611	1.49	22.9	15.3	40
45	610	23.7	26.9	34.7	0.51	0.63	384	283	126	133	22.7	0.42	56	31	7	92.1	720	1.24	20.6	16.0	45
50	523	25.7	29.6	36.0	0.51	0.83	432	356	213	87	25.3	0.57	49	35	13	97.8	817	1.07	18.3	16.3	50
55	465	27.3	32.0	37.5	0.50	1.02	476	418	300	58	27.7	0.73	42	33	16	102.8	903	0.94	16.1	16.4	55
60	424	28.6	34.2	39.0	0.49	1.21	515	466	360	41	29.9	0.90	37	30	18	107.2	979	0.84	13.6	16.3	60

1.4 x 1.4 m spacing

Age	MAIN CROP After Thinning No. of Trees	Top Ht. (m)	Mean Diam (cm)	Basal Area (m²)	Form Factor	Mean Vol. per Tree (m³)	Vol. to 7 cm (m³)	Vol. to 18 cm (m³)	Vol. to 24 cm (m³)	Yield from THINNINGS No. of Trees	Mean Diam (cm)	Mean Vol. per Tree (m³)	Vol. to 7 cm (m³)	Vol. to 18 cm (m³)	Vol. to 24 cm (m³)	TOTAL YIELD Basal Area (m²)	Vol. to 7 cm (m³)	INCREMENT CAI Basal Area (m²)	CAI Vol. to 7 cm (m³)	MAI Vol. to 7 cm (m³)	Age
15	4641	6.7	8.8	28.0	0.45	0.01	63	0	0	0	0.0	0.00	0	0	0	28.0	63	2.36	13.2	4.2	15
20	2236	9.8	11.7	23.9	0.45	0.04	84	0	0	2405	9.2	0.02	56	0	0	40.0	140	2.31	17.7	7.0	20
25	1384	13.0	15.2	25.2	0.45	0.09	128	11	0	851	12.1	0.07	56	0	0	51.1	240	2.18	21.7	9.6	25
30	982	16.0	19.2	28.4	0.47	0.19	189	63	6	403	15.4	0.14	56	5	0	61.8	357	2.03	24.1	11.9	30
35	754	18.8	23.2	31.8	0.47	0.34	257	155	43	228	18.8	0.25	56	14	1	71.5	481	1.78	24.3	13.7	35
40	601	21.4	26.9	34.0	0.48	0.53	321	236	105	153	22.1	0.37	56	31	7	79.6	601	1.49	22.9	15.0	40
45	493	23.6	30.2	35.3	0.48	0.76	374	315	202	108	25.3	0.52	56	39	15	86.3	710	1.24	20.6	15.8	45
50	423	25.5	33.2	36.6	0.48	1.00	421	376	281	71	28.1	0.69	49	39	22	92.0	806	1.06	18.2	16.1	50
55	376	27.1	35.9	38.0	0.48	1.24	465	425	339	47	30.8	0.90	42	36	23	96.9	892	0.92	16.1	16.2	55
60	342	28.5	38.3	39.4	0.48	1.47	503	471	402	34	33.2	1.08	37	33	25	101.2	967	0.79	14.0	16.1	60

1.8 x 1.8 m spacing

Age	MAIN CROP No. of Trees	Top Ht. (m)	Mean Diam (cm)	Basal Area (m²)	Form Factor	After Thinning Mean Vol. per Tree (m³)	Vol. to 7 cm (m³)	Vol. to 18 cm (m³)	Vol. to 24 cm (m³)	Yield from THINNINGS No. of Trees	Mean Diam (cm)	Mean Vol. per Tree (m³)	Vol. to 7 cm (m³)	Vol. to 18 cm (m³)	Vol. to 24 cm (m³)	TOTAL YIELD Basal Area (m²)	Vol. to 7 cm (m³)	INCREMENT CAI Basal Area (m²)	CAI Vol. to 7 cm (m³)	MAI Vol. to 7 cm (m³)	Age
16	2797	7.1	10.7	25.3	0.46	0.02	66	0	0	0	0.0	0.00	0	0	0	25.3	66	2.35	13.3	4.1	16
21	1440	10.3	14.3	23.2	0.43	0.06	88	5	0	1357	11.4	0.04	56	0	0	37.0	144	2.31	18.0	6.9	21
26	947	13.4	18.7	26.0	0.43	0.14	134	34	2	493	14.9	0.11	56	3	0	48.4	246	2.22	22.1	9.5	26
31	704	16.4	23.3	30.0	0.44	0.28	197	118	33	243	18.8	0.23	56	14	1	59.2	365	2.02	24.1	11.8	31
36	559	19.1	27.7	33.7	0.44	0.47	264	203	101	145	22.7	0.39	56	31	7	68.7	488	1.74	24.0	13.5	36
41	457	21.6	31.7	36.0	0.45	0.71	325	280	191	102	26.3	0.55	56	41	18	76.6	605	1.44	22.4	14.8	41
46	382	23.8	35.3	37.3	0.45	0.98	375	343	273	75	29.7	0.75	56	46	28	83.0	711	1.20	20.0	15.5	46
51	334	25.7	38.4	38.7	0.45	1.26	421	395	337	49	32.8	0.98	48	42	30	88.5	805	1.02	17.7	15.8	51
56	301	27.2	41.2	40.1	0.45	1.54	463	441	394	33	35.6	1.25	41	38	30	93.3	888	0.88	15.6	15.9	56
61	277	28.5	43.6	41.4	0.45	1.81	500	480	438	24	38.1	1.50	36	34	29	97.3	961	0.75	13.6	15.8	61

2.4 x 2.4 m spacing

Age	MAIN CROP No. of Trees	Top Ht. (m)	Mean Diam (cm)	Basal Area (m²)	Form Factor	After Thinning Mean Vol. per Tree (m³)	Vol. to 7 cm (m³)	Vol. to 18 cm (m³)	Vol. to 24 cm (m³)	Yield from THINNINGS No. of Trees	Mean Diam (cm)	Mean Vol. per Tree (m³)	Vol. to 7 cm (m³)	Vol. to 18 cm (m³)	Vol. to 24 cm (m³)	TOTAL YIELD Basal Area (m²)	Vol. to 7 cm (m³)	INCREMENT CAI Basal Area (m²)	CAI Vol. to 7 cm (m³)	MAI Vol. to 7 cm (m³)	Age
19	1597	8.6	14.1	24.9	0.47	0.05	86	4	0	0	0.0	0.00	0	0	0	24.9	86	2.42	15.0	4.5	19
24	945	11.7	18.6	25.5	0.44	0.12	118	30	2	652	14.9	0.09	56	3	0	36.8	174	2.34	19.8	7.2	24
29	658	14.8	23.6	28.8	0.44	0.26	172	104	29	286	19.1	0.20	56	19	2	48.3	284	2.16	23.1	9.8	29
34	509	17.6	28.5	32.5	0.44	0.46	237	189	104	149	23.4	0.38	56	34	10	58.5	405	1.88	24.0	11.9	34
39	414	20.3	33.0	35.5	0.44	0.72	300	268	200	95	27.6	0.59	56	43	22	67.1	524	1.57	23.0	13.4	39
44	346	22.6	37.3	37.3	0.45	1.02	355	330	276	68	31.4	0.82	56	48	33	74.1	635	1.28	20.8	14.4	44
49	295	24.5	40.6	38.2	0.45	1.34	397	376	331	51	34.9	1.10	56	51	39	79.9	733	1.06	18.4	14.9	49
54	264	26.2	43.6	39.5	0.44	1.66	439	421	384	31	38.0	1.41	44	41	34	84.7	819	0.90	16.2	15.2	54
59	242	27.6	46.3	40.8	0.44	1.97	477	461	429	22	40.8	1.72	38	36	32	88.9	894	0.76	14.2	15.2	59
64	225	28.8	48.7	41.9	0.44	2.27	510	495	465	16	43.3	2.08	33	32	29	92.4	961	0.65	12.4	15.0	64

SITKA SPRUCE YIELD CLASS 12 THINNED

0.9 x 0.9 m spacing

Age	MAIN CROP No. of Trees	Top Ht. m	Mean Diam cm	Basal Area m²	Form Factor	After Thinning Mean Vol per Tree m³	Vol to 7 cm m³	Vol to 18 cm m³	Vol to 24 cm m³	Yield from Thinnings No. of Trees	Mean Diam cm	Mean Vol per Tree m³	Vol to 7 cm m³	Vol to 18 cm m³	Vol to 24 cm m³	Total Yield Basal Area m²	Vol to 7 cm m³	CAI Basal Area m²	CAI Vol to 7 cm m³	MAI Vol to 7 cm m³	Age
22	4138	8.8	9.2	27.5	0.38	0.02	73	0	0	3440	7.3	0.01	42	0	0	42.0	115	1.91	14.5	5.2	22
27	2574	11.4	11.6	27.0	0.43	0.04	110	0	0	1547	9.2	0.03	42	0	0	51.7	194	1.86	16.9	7.2	27
32	1789	14.0	14.1	28.1	0.46	0.09	157	9	0	786	11.2	0.05	42	0	0	60.6	283	1.70	18.3	8.8	32
37	1337	16.3	16.9	29.8	0.49	0.16	209	28	0	452	13.5	0.09	42	1	0	68.8	377	1.53	18.7	10.2	37
42	1055	18.4	19.5	31.4	0.50	0.25	260	86	9	282	15.7	0.15	42	4	0	75.9	470	1.31	18.0	11.2	42
47	857	20.4	22.0	32.4	0.51	0.36	305	148	28	198	17.9	0.21	42	8	0	81.8	557	1.10	16.6	11.9	47
52	725	22.0	24.2	33.3	0.52	0.48	346	227	75	132	19.9	0.29	38	13	1	86.8	636	0.93	14.8	12.2	52
57	638	23.5	26.2	34.4	0.52	0.60	383	283	126	88	21.8	0.36	32	16	3	91.2	705	0.80	12.9	12.4	57
62	576	24.6	28.0	35.4	0.52	0.72	415	320	160	61	23.4	0.46	28	17	5	94.8	765	0.68	11.1	12.3	62

1.4 x 1.4 m spacing

Age	MAIN CROP No. of Trees	Top Ht. m	Mean Diam cm	Basal Area m²	Form Factor	After Thinning Mean Vol per Tree m³	Vol to 7 cm m³	Vol to 18 cm m³	Vol to 24 cm m³	Yield from Thinnings No. of Trees	Mean Diam cm	Mean Vol per Tree m³	Vol to 7 cm m³	Vol to 18 cm m³	Vol to 24 cm m³	Total Yield Basal Area m²	Vol to 7 cm m³	CAI Basal Area m²	CAI Vol to 7 cm m³	MAI Vol to 7 cm m³	Age
18	4675	6.5	8.6	26.9	0.44	0.01	57	0	0		0.0	0.00	0	0	0	26.9	57	2.18	11.7	3.2	18
23	2595	9.2	11.1	24.9	0.43	0.03	81	0	0	2080	8.8	0.02	42	0	0	37.6	123	2.06	14.5	5.3	23
28	1741	11.8	14.0	26.6	0.44	0.07	119	3	0	853	11.1	0.05	42	0	0	47.5	203	1.89	17.0	7.2	28
33	1278	14.3	17.0	28.9	0.46	0.13	167	22	0	464	13.5	0.09	42	1	0	56.5	293	1.71	18.4	8.9	33
38	995	16.6	20.0	31.3	0.47	0.22	219	90	13	283	16.1	0.15	42	6	0	64.5	387	1.50	18.6	10.2	38
43	808	18.7	22.9	33.1	0.48	0.33	269	147	34	187	18.5	0.22	42	11	1	71.4	479	1.27	17.7	11.1	43
48	672	20.6	25.5	34.3	0.48	0.46	312	219	84	136	20.9	0.31	42	17	3	77.2	564	1.06	16.2	11.8	48
53	581	22.2	27.8	35.5	0.49	0.61	352	272	135	91	23.0	0.40	37	22	6	82.1	641	0.90	14.4	12.1	53
58	519	23.6	29.9	36.4	0.49	0.75	388	319	191	62	25.0	0.50	31	21	7	86.2	708	0.76	12.5	12.2	58
63	475	24.7	31.7	37.4	0.49	0.88	418	361	246	44	26.7	0.62	27	20	9	89.7	765	0.65	10.7	12.1	63

1.8 x 1.8m spacing

Age	MAIN CROP After Thinning									Yield from Thinnings						TOTAL YIELD		INCREMENT			Age
	No. of Trees	Top Ht. (m)	Mean Diam (cm)	Basal Area (m²)	Form Factor	Mean Vol per Tree (m³)	Vol to 7 cm (m³)	Vol to 18 cm (m³)	Vol to 24 cm (m³)	No. of Trees	Mean Diam (cm)	Mean Vol per Tree (m³)	Vol 7 cm (m³)	Vol 18 cm (m³)	Vol 24 cm (m³)	Basal Area (m²)	Vol to 7 cm (m³)	CAI Basal Area (m²)	CAI Vol to 7 cm (m³)	MAI Vol to 7 cm (m³)	
20	2781	7.4	10.9	25.9	0.46	0.03	71	0	0	0	0.0	0.00	0	0	0	25.9	71	2.16	12.0	3.5	20
25	1620	10.1	14.0	25.1	0.45	0.06	97	5	0	1162	11.2	0.04	42	0	0	36.4	139	2.03	15.1	5.5	25
30	1144	12.7	17.5	27.5	0.45	0.12	138	25	0	476	14.0	0.09	42	1	0	46.2	222	1.86	17.4	7.4	30
35	876	15.1	21.0	30.4	0.45	0.21	187	90	17	269	16.9	0.16	42	6	0	55.1	313	1.66	18.4	8.9	35
40	706	17.3	24.4	32.9	0.46	0.34	238	156	52	170	19.8	0.25	42	14	2	62.8	406	1.43	18.2	10.2	40
45	588	19.3	27.5	34.8	0.46	0.49	286	220	110	118	22.5	0.36	42	23	5	69.4	496	1.20	17.1	11.0	45
50	502	21.1	30.2	36.0	0.46	0.65	327	276	177	86	25.1	0.47	40	28	11	74.8	577	0.99	15.4	11.5	50
55	445	22.6	32.6	37.1	0.47	0.82	365	321	230	57	27.3	0.60	34	26	13	79.3	650	0.83	13.5	11.8	55
60	405	23.9	34.7	38.3	0.47	0.98	399	361	279	40	29.3	0.73	29	24	14	83.2	712	0.71	11.6	11.9	60
65	375	24.9	36.5	39.3	0.47	1.14	427	394	323	30	31.1	0.86	26	22	15	86.4	766	0.61	10.1	11.8	65

2.4 x 2.4m spacing

Age	MAIN CROP After Thinning									Yield from Thinnings						TOTAL YIELD		INCREMENT			Age
	No. of Trees	Top Ht. (m)	Mean Diam (cm)	Basal Area (m²)	Form Factor	Mean Vol per Tree (m³)	Vol to 7 cm (m³)	Vol to 18 cm (m³)	Vol to 24 cm (m³)	No. of Trees	Mean Diam (cm)	Mean Vol per Tree (m³)	Vol 7 cm (m³)	Vol 18 cm (m³)	Vol 24 cm (m³)	Basal Area (m²)	Vol to 7 cm (m³)	CAI Basal Area (m²)	CAI Vol to 7 cm (m³)	MAI Vol to 7 cm (m³)	
23	1597	8.6	14.1	24.8	0.47	0.05	85	4	0	0	0.0	0.00	0	0	0	24.8	85	2.11	12.6	3.7	23
28	1066	11.2	17.8	26.6	0.44	0.11	116	21	0	531	14.3	0.08	42	2	0	35.1	158	1.99	15.9	5.6	28
33	785	13.7	21.8	29.4	0.44	0.20	161	77	14	281	17.6	0.15	42	8	0	44.7	245	1.81	17.8	7.4	33
38	621	16.0	25.7	32.2	0.44	0.34	210	147	57	164	20.9	0.26	42	17	3	53.1	336	1.56	18.2	8.8	38
43	515	18.1	29.2	34.5	0.44	0.50	259	213	127	106	24.1	0.40	42	28	9	60.3	427	1.31	17.5	9.9	43
48	436	20.0	32.4	35.9	0.45	0.69	301	264	190	79	27.0	0.53	42	31	14	66.3	511	1.09	16.0	10.6	48
53	384	21.6	35.1	37.3	0.45	0.89	340	311	248	53	29.6	0.69	37	30	18	71.2	587	0.89	14.1	11.1	53
58	347	23.0	37.5	38.3	0.45	1.08	374	348	291	36	31.8	0.87	31	27	18	75.1	652	0.74	12.1	11.2	58
63	321	24.1	39.5	39.3	0.45	1.26	403	380	330	27	33.8	1.01	27	24	18	78.6	708	0.64	10.5	11.2	63
68	301	25.0	41.3	40.3	0.45	1.42	428	408	364	20	35.6	1.21	24	22	18	81.5	757	0.55	9.5	11.1	68

F

SITKA SPRUCE   YIELD CLASS 8   THINNED

0.9 x 0.9 m spacing

	MAIN CROP — After Thinning									Yield from THINNINGS						TOTAL YIELD		INCREMENT			
	No. of Trees	Top Ht.	Mean Diam	Basal Area	Form Factor	Mean Vol. per Tree	Vol 7cm	Vol 18cm	Vol 24cm	No. of Trees	Mean Diam	Mean Vol. per Tree	Vol 7cm	Vol 18cm	Vol 24cm	Basal Area	Vol to 7cm	CAI Basal Area	CAI Vol to 7cm	MAI Vol to 7cm	
Age		m	cm	m²		m³	cm	cm	cm		cm	m³	cm	cm	cm	m²	m³	m²	m³	m³	Age
26	5367	8.0	8.3	29.4	0.37	0.01	65	0	0	2725	6.7	0.01	28	0	0	38.9	93	1.48	10.2	3.6	26
31	3589	10.0	10.0	28.0	0.41	0.03	93	0	0	1778	7.9	0.02	28	0	0	46.3	149	1.46	11.8	4.8	31
36	2634	12.0	11.8	28.7	0.44	0.05	127	0	0	955	9.3	0.03	28	0	0	53.5	211	1.39	12.8	5.9	36
41	2043	13.8	13.7	29.9	0.47	0.08	165	5	0	591	10.9	0.05	28	0	0	60.2	277	1.26	13.1	6.8	41
46	1640	15.4	15.5	30.9	0.48	0.12	202	18	0	404	12.4	0.07	28	0	0	66.0	342	1.06	12.5	7.4	46
51	1354	16.9	17.2	31.4	0.50	0.17	235	43	0	286	13.8	0.10	28	1	0	70.8	403	0.88	11.5	7.9	51
56	1166	18.2	18.7	32.1	0.51	0.23	265	67	4	188	15.1	0.13	25	2	0	74.8	458	0.74	10.4	8.2	56
61	1035	19.3	20.1	32.8	0.51	0.28	293	120	18	131	16.3	0.16	21	3	0	78.3	506	0.64	9.1	8.3	61
66	941	20.2	21.3	33.5	0.52	0.34	316	153	29	95	17.3	0.20	19	3	0	81.2	548	0.52	7.7	8.3	66
71	866	20.9	22.3	33.8	0.52	0.39	334	183	43	75	18.2	0.23	17	4	0	83.5	584	0.43	6.7	8.2	71

1.4 x 1.4 m spacing

	MAIN CROP — After Thinning									Yield from THINNINGS						TOTAL YIELD		INCREMENT			
	No. of Trees	Top Ht.	Mean Diam	Basal Area	Form Factor	Mean Vol. per Tree	Vol 7cm	Vol 18cm	Vol 24cm	No. of Trees	Mean Diam	Mean Vol. per Tree	Vol 7cm	Vol 18cm	Vol 24cm	Basal Area	Vol to 7cm	CAI Basal Area	CAI Vol to 7cm	MAI Vol to 7cm	
Age		m	cm	m²		m³	cm	cm	cm		cm	m³	cm	cm	cm	m²	m³	m²	m³	m³	Age
23	4681	6.5	8.7	27.8	0.45	0.01	60	0	0	0	0.0	0.00	0	0	0	27.8	60	1.56	8.5	2.6	23
28	2913	8.7	10.6	25.8	0.45	0.03	80	0	0	1768	8.4	0.02	28	0	0	35.6	108	1.54	10.6	3.9	28
33	2131	10.7	12.7	27.1	0.45	0.05	110	0	0	781	10.1	0.04	28	0	0	43.2	166	1.49	12.1	5.0	33
38	1666	12.6	14.9	29.2	0.46	0.09	146	8	0	466	11.9	0.06	28	0	0	50.5	230	1.38	12.9	6.0	38
43	1351	14.3	17.1	31.1	0.47	0.14	183	34	0	315	13.7	0.09	28	1	0	57.0	295	1.20	12.9	6.9	43
48	1123	15.9	19.2	32.3	0.48	0.19	219	72	8	228	15.4	0.12	28	3	0	62.4	359	1.00	12.1	7.5	48
53	955	17.3	21.0	33.0	0.48	0.26	249	102	15	168	16.9	0.17	28	4	0	66.9	417	0.83	11.1	7.9	53
58	846	18.5	22.6	33.9	0.49	0.33	278	152	35	109	18.4	0.21	23	6	0	70.7	469	0.70	9.8	8.1	58
63	768	19.5	24.0	34.8	0.49	0.40	304	199	66	79	19.6	0.25	20	7	1	74.0	515	0.59	8.5	8.2	63
68	708	20.4	25.3	35.5	0.49	0.46	325	227	88	59	20.7	0.31	18	7	1	76.6	554	0.48	7.3	8.1	68
73	659	21.1	26.3	35.8	0.49	0.52	342	252	112	49	21.7	0.34	17	8	2	78.7	588	0.41	6.5	8.1	73

1.8 x 1.8 m spacing

	MAIN CROP — After Thinning									Yield from THINNINGS						TOTAL YIELD		INCREMENT			
							Volume in cubic metres to top diameters of-						Volume in cubic metres to top diameters of-					CAI		MAI	
Age	No. of Trees	Top Ht. m	Mean Diam cm	Basal Area m²	Form Factor	Mean Vol. per Tree m³	7 cm m³	18 cm m³	24 cm m³	No. of Trees	Mean Diam cm	Mean Vol. per Tree m³	7 cm m³	18 cm m³	24 cm m³	Basal Area m²	Vol. to 7 cm m³	Basal Area m²	Vol. to 7 cm m³	Vol. to 7 cm m³	Age
25	2794	7.2	10.8	25.4	0.47	0.02	68	0	0	0	0.0	0.00	0	0	0	25.4	68	1.60	8.6	2.7	25
30	1929	9.3	13.1	26.0	0.44	0.05	89	2	0	865	10.4	0.03	28	0	0	33.3	117	1.56	10.8	3.9	30
35	1470	11.3	15.6	28.1	0.43	0.08	120	10	0	459	12.4	0.06	28	0	0	41.0	176	1.49	12.3	5.0	35
40	1188	13.1	18.1	30.7	0.44	0.13	156	39	2	282	14.5	0.10	28	2	0	48.2	240	1.35	12.9	6.0	40
45	988	14.8	20.5	32.7	0.44	0.19	192	79	11	200	16.5	0.14	28	4	0	54.5	304	1.15	12.6	6.8	45
50	838	16.3	22.7	34.0	0.45	0.27	225	123	29	150	18.3	0.19	28	7	1	59.7	365	0.94	11.7	7.3	50
55	734	17.6	24.6	35.0	0.45	0.35	256	168	55	104	20.0	0.24	25	8	1	64.0	421	0.78	10.5	7.7	55
60	662	18.8	26.3	35.9	0.46	0.43	283	209	93	72	21.5	0.30	22	11	2	67.5	470	0.66	9.2	7.8	60
65	609	19.7	27.7	36.8	0.46	0.50	307	237	118	53	22.8	0.36	19	10	2	70.5	513	0.55	7.9	7.9	65
70	567	20.5	29.0	37.4	0.46	0.58	326	261	143	42	23.9	0.41	17	10	3	73.0	550	0.46	6.9	7.9	70
75	532	21.2	30.1	37.8	0.46	0.64	343	289	186	36	24.9	0.45	16	11	4	75.1	582	0.38	6.1	7.8	75

2.4 x 2.4 m spacing

	MAIN CROP — After Thinning									Yield from THINNINGS						TOTAL YIELD		INCREMENT			
							Volume in cubic metres to top diameters of-						Volume in cubic metres to top diameters of-					CAI		MAI	
Age	No. of Trees	Top Ht. m	Mean Diam cm	Basal Area m²	Form Factor	Mean Vol. per Tree m³	7 cm m³	18 cm m³	24 cm m³	No. of Trees	Mean Diam cm	Mean Vol. per Tree m³	7 cm m³	18 cm m³	24 cm m³	Basal Area m²	Vol. to 7 cm m³	Basal Area m²	Vol. to 7 cm m³	Vol. to 7 cm m³	Age
29	1598	8.5	13.9	24.1	0.47	0.05	83	2	0	0	0.0	0.00	0	0	0	24.1	83	1.64	9.0	2.9	29
34	1199	10.5	16.8	26.5	0.43	0.09	107	14	0	399	13.4	0.07	28	1	0	32.1	135	1.55	11.3	4.0	34
39	950	12.3	19.8	29.1	0.43	0.15	140	46	5	249	15.9	0.11	28	3	1	39.6	196	1.43	12.5	5.0	39
44	788	14.0	22.6	31.7	0.43	0.22	176	96	22	163	18.3	0.17	28	7	1	46.5	260	1.25	12.5	5.9	44
49	669	15.6	25.2	33.4	0.44	0.31	209	146	56	119	20.5	0.24	28	12	2	52.1	321	1.02	11.8	6.6	49
54	579	16.9	27.5	34.4	0.44	0.41	238	183	91	90	22.5	0.31	28	15	4	56.7	378	0.83	10.6	7.0	54
59	523	18.1	29.4	35.5	0.44	0.51	265	218	130	56	24.2	0.40	22	15	5	60.4	427	0.68	9.3	7.2	59
64	481	19.1	31.1	36.4	0.44	0.60	288	249	169	42	25.7	0.47	20	14	5	63.5	470	0.57	8.1	7.3	64
69	449	19.9	32.5	37.2	0.44	0.69	308	271	194	32	27.0	0.55	18	14	7	66.1	508	0.49	7.1	7.4	69
74	423	20.6	33.7	37.8	0.44	0.77	325	290	217	27	28.2	0.61	17	13	7	68.4	541	0.41	6.3	7.3	74

0.9 x 0.9m spacing

	MAIN CROP – After Thinning									Yield from Thinnings						TOTAL YIELD		INCREMENT CAI		MAI	
Age	No. of Trees	Top Ht. (m)	Mean Diam (cm)	Basal Area (m²)	Form Factor	Mean Vol. per Tree (m³)	Vol. 7cm	Vol. 18cm	Vol. 24cm	No. of Trees	Mean Diam (cm)	Mean Vol. per Tree (m³)	Vol. 7cm	Vol. 18cm	Vol. 24cm	Basal Area (m²)	Vol. to 7cm (m³)	Basal Area (m²)	Vol. to 7cm (m³)	Vol. to 7cm (m³)	Age
17	7982	7.8	6.6	27.6	0.35	0.01	55	0	0	0	0.0	0.00	0	0	0	27.6	55	2.89	12.8	3.2	17
22	3290	10.6	9.5	23.5	0.40	0.02	80	0	0	4692	7.0	0.01	56	0	0	41.5	136	2.65	18.6	6.2	22
27	1984	13.4	12.9	25.9	0.44	0.06	129	1	0	1306	9.9	0.04	56	0	0	54.0	241	2.36	21.9	8.9	27
32	1362	16.0	16.4	28.7	0.47	0.14	188	25	0	622	13.1	0.09	56	2	0	65.2	356	2.10	23.3	11.1	32
37	1013	18.3	19.8	31.3	0.49	0.25	249	83	9	349	16.3	0.16	56	8	0	75.0	473	1.87	23.3	12.8	37
42	805	20.4	23.1	33.8	0.50	0.38	309	186	52	208	19.6	0.27	56	19	2	83.9	589	1.68	22.6	14.0	42
47	655	22.3	26.3	35.7	0.50	0.56	364	268	119	149	22.8	0.38	56	31	7	91.8	700	1.53	21.7	14.9	47
52	552	24.0	29.4	37.5	0.50	0.75	413	340	203	103	26.0	0.54	56	39	15	99.1	805	1.40	20.5	15.5	52
57	475	25.5	32.4	39.1	0.50	0.96	456	401	288	77	29.1	0.73	56	46	28	105.8	904	1.29	19.1	15.9	57
62	419	26.9	35.1	40.6	0.49	1.18	496	453	361	57	32.1	0.92	53	46	33	112.0	996	1.18	17.7	16.1	62
67	378	28.1	37.7	42.3	0.48	1.41	534	497	416	41	35.0	1.13	47	42	33	117.6	1081	1.07	16.4	16.1	67
72	346	29.2	40.2	43.8	0.48	1.65	571	541	477	32	37.7	1.32	42	39	33	122.7	1160	0.99	15.3	16.1	72

1.4 x 1.4 m spacing

	MAIN CROP – After Thinning									Yield from Thinnings						TOTAL YIELD		INCREMENT CAI		MAI	
Age	No. of Trees	Top Ht. (m)	Mean Diam (cm)	Basal Area (m²)	Form Factor	Mean Vol. per Tree (m³)	Vol. 7cm	Vol. 18cm	Vol. 24cm	No. of Trees	Mean Diam (cm)	Mean Vol. per Tree (m³)	Vol. 7cm	Vol. 18cm	Vol. 24cm	Basal Area (m²)	Vol. to 7cm (m³)	Basal Area (m²)	Vol. to 7cm (m³)	Vol. to 7cm (m³)	Age
18	4321	8.3	8.7	25.4	0.39	0.02	65	0	0	0	0.0	0.00	0	0	0	25.4	65	2.90	14.5	3.6	18
23	1980	11.2	12.4	23.9	0.42	0.05	96	0	0	2341	9.2	0.02	56	0	0	39.4	152	2.66	19.4	6.6	23
28	1314	13.9	16.5	28.0	0.43	0.11	147	19	0	666	12.8	0.08	56	0	0	52.0	259	2.36	22.4	9.3	28
33	955	16.4	20.4	31.3	0.45	0.22	207	85	12	360	16.4	0.16	56	8	0	62.9	375	2.06	23.3	11.4	33
38	739	18.7	24.3	34.1	0.46	0.36	268	176	58	216	20.1	0.26	56	23	3	72.6	492	1.83	23.2	13.0	38
43	604	20.7	27.9	36.8	0.47	0.54	327	252	126	135	23.7	0.41	56	34	10	81.2	607	1.64	22.4	14.1	43
48	501	22.6	31.3	38.6	0.47	0.76	381	328	224	103	27.2	0.54	56	43	22	89.0	717	1.49	21.4	14.9	48
53	429	24.3	34.6	40.4	0.47	1.00	429	388	300	72	30.7	0.78	56	47	30	96.1	821	1.36	20.2	15.5	53
58	374	25.8	37.8	41.9	0.47	1.26	470	438	366	55	34.1	1.02	56	51	39	102.6	918	1.24	18.8	15.8	58
63	334	27.1	40.7	43.5	0.46	1.52	509	483	426	40	37.3	1.28	51	48	40	108.5	1008	1.14	17.4	16.0	63
68	304	28.3	43.4	45.0	0.46	1.80	548	525	479	30	40.3	1.52	46	43	38	114.0	1092	1.04	16.2	16.1	68
73	281	29.4	46.0	46.6	0.45	2.08	584	564	522	23	43.2	1.81	42	40	37	118.9	1170	0.95	15.1	16.0	73

1.8 x 1.8 m spacing

	NAIN CROP After Thinning						Volume in cubic metres to top of-			Yield from THINNINGS			volume in cubic metres to top diameters of-			TOTAL YIELD		INCREMENT CAI		MAI	
Age	No. of Trees	Top Ht. m	Mean Diam cm	Basal Area m²	Form Factor	Mean Vol per Tree m³	7 cm	18 cm	24 cm	No. of Trees	Mean Diam cm	Mean Vol per Tree m³	7 cm	18 cm	24 cm	Basal Area m²	Vol to 7 cm m³	Basal Area m²	Vol to 7 cm m³	Vol to 7 cm m³	Age
19	2700	8.8	10.5	23.5	0.42	0.03	72	0	0	0	0.0	0.00	0	0	0	23.5	72	2.72	14.8	3.8	19
24	1266	11.6	15.1	22.6	0.45	0.08	103	9	0	1435	11.2	0.04	56	0	0	36.8	159	2.58	19.6	6.6	24
29	890	14.3	20.0	27.9	0.44	0.18	156	52	5	376	15.6	0.15	56	5	0	49.3	268	2.34	22.5	9.2	29
34	675	16.8	24.6	32.2	0.44	0.32	216	142	47	215	19.9	0.26	56	19	2	60.3	384	2.04	23.2	11.3	34
39	539	19.0	29.0	35.5	0.45	0.51	277	221	121	136	24.1	0.41	56	37	12	69.8	501	1.80	23.0	12.8	39
44	446	21.0	33.0	38.2	0.45	0.75	334	298	223	93	28.2	0.60	56	45	25	78.3	614	1.61	22.2	13.9	44
49	379	22.8	36.9	40.4	0.45	1.02	386	357	292	66	32.1	0.85	56	49	35	85.9	722	1.46	21.1	14.7	49
54	329	24.5	40.5	42.3	0.45	1.32	433	410	362	50	36.0	1.12	56	51	41	92.9	825	1.33	19.8	15.3	54
59	290	25.9	43.9	43.9	0.44	1.63	473	453	413	39	39.7	1.44	56	53	46	99.2	921	1.20	18.5	15.6	59
64	261	27.2	47.1	45.4	0.44	1.96	512	496	464	28	43.2	1.78	50	48	44	104.8	1009	1.09	17.1	15.8	64
69	240	28.4	50.0	47.1	0.43	2.29	549	535	504	21	46.5	2.12	45	43	40	110.1	1092	1.01	15.9	15.8	69
74	223	29.5	52.7	48.7	0.43	2.63	585	572	543	17	49.6	2.41	41	40	38	115.0	1169	0.93	14.8	15.8	74

2.4 x 2.4 m spacing

	NAIN CROP After Thinning						Volume in cubic metres to top of-			Yield from THINNINGS			volume in cubic metres to top diameters of-			TOTAL YIELD		INCREMENT CAI		MAI	
Age	No. of Trees	Top Ht. m	Mean Diam cm	Basal Area m²	Form Factor	Mean Vol per Tree m³	7 cm	18 cm	24 cm	No. of Trees	Mean Diam cm	Mean Vol per Tree m³	7 cm	18 cm	24 cm	Basal Area m²	Vol to 7 cm m³	Basal Area m²	Vol to 7 cm m³	Vol to 7 cm m³	Age
22	1571	10.3	13.7	23.3	0.43	0.06	89	2	0	0	0.0	0.00	0	0	0	23.3	89	2.82	17.0	4.1	22
27	876	13.0	19.1	25.2	0.44	0.15	131	43	4	695	14.6	0.08	56	3	0	36.8	187	2.57	21.0	6.9	27
32	649	15.6	24.5	30.5	0.43	0.29	188	123	41	228	19.4	0.25	56	19	2	49.0	300	2.24	22.9	9.4	32
37	511	17.9	29.3	34.5	0.43	0.48	247	203	121	138	24.1	0.41	56	37	12	59.2	415	1.92	22.9	11.2	37
42	422	20.0	33.8	37.8	0.43	0.72	305	272	203	89	28.4	0.63	56	45	25	68.2	529	1.68	22.4	12.6	42
47	356	21.9	37.9	40.2	0.43	1.01	359	334	279	66	32.7	0.85	56	49	35	76.1	639	1.50	21.4	13.6	47
52	308	23.6	41.8	42.2	0.43	1.32	407	387	346	48	36.7	1.17	56	52	42	83.2	743	1.35	20.2	14.3	52
57	271	25.1	45.4	43.8	0.43	1.66	449	433	401	37	40.6	1.51	56	53	47	89.6	841	1.22	18.9	14.8	57
62	243	26.5	48.7	45.3	0.43	2.01	488	473	445	28	44.3	1.88	53	51	47	95.4	932	1.09	17.6	15.0	62
67	222	27.7	51.8	46.8	0.42	2.37	526	513	486	20	47.8	2.32	47	45	42	100.5	1017	1.02	16.3	15.2	67
72	207	28.9	54.7	48.6	0.42	2.72	562	550	525	16	51.1	2.64	42	41	39	105.6	1095	0.95	15.3	15.2	72
77	194	29.9	57.3	50.0	0.42	3.07	596	585	561	13	54.2	3.05	40	39	37	110.0	1169	0.86	13.9	15.2	77

NORWAY SPRUCE   YIELD CLASS 12   THINNED

0.9 x 0.9 m spacing

Age	MAIN CROP After Thinning — No. of Trees	Top Ht. m	Mean Diam cm	Basal Area m²	Form Factor	Mean Vol. per Tree m³	After Thin Vol to 7 cm	Vol to 18 cm	Vol to 24 cm	Thinnings No. of Trees	Mean Diam cm	Mean Vol. per Tree m³	Thin Vol to 7 cm	Vol to 18 cm	Vol to 24 cm	Total Yield Basal Area m²	Total Yield Vol to 7 cm m³	CAI Basal Area m²	CAI Vol to 7 cm m³	MAI Vol to 7 cm m³	Age
20	8033	7.7	6.6	27.2	0.34	0.01	53	0	0	0	0.0	0.00	0	0	0	27.2	53	2.53	11.2	2.6	20
25	3918	10.2	9.1	25.3	0.38	0.02	78	0	0	4115	6.6	0.01	42	0	0	39.2	120	2.26	14.9	4.8	25
30	2518	12.5	11.7	27.2	0.42	0.05	118	0	0	1400	8.9	0.03	42	0	0	49.8	202	1.97	16.9	6.7	30
35	1790	14.6	14.4	29.1	0.45	0.09	163	9	0	728	11.3	0.06	42	0	0	58.9	289	1.73	17.6	8.3	35
40	1356	16.4	17.0	30.8	0.47	0.15	210	39	0	434	13.7	0.10	42	1	0	67.0	378	1.54	17.6	9.4	40
45	1079	18.2	19.6	32.5	0.49	0.24	255	85	9	277	16.1	0.15	42	6	0	74.3	465	1.39	17.2	10.3	45
50	894	19.7	22.0	34.1	0.49	0.33	298	163	38	185	18.5	0.23	42	11	1	80.9	550	1.26	16.6	11.0	50
55	755	21.2	24.4	35.4	0.50	0.45	337	221	73	140	20.9	0.30	42	17	3	87.0	631	1.14	15.8	11.5	55
60	653	22.4	26.7	36.5	0.50	0.57	372	274	122	102	23.1	0.41	42	25	7	92.4	708	1.04	14.8	11.8	60
65	579	23.6	28.8	37.7	0.50	0.70	404	323	177	74	25.3	0.52	39	27	10	97.3	779	0.95	13.8	12.0	65
70	525	24.6	30.8	39.2	0.50	0.83	438	369	237	53	27.4	0.64	34	26	13	101.9	846	0.90	13.1	12.1	70
75	484	25.6	32.7	40.7	0.49	0.97	470	413	297	42	29.5	0.74	31	26	15	106.3	909	0.82	12.0	12.1	75

1.4 x 1.4 m spacing

Age	MAIN CROP After Thinning — No. of Trees	Top Ht. m	Mean Diam cm	Basal Area m²	Form Factor	Mean Vol. per Tree m³	After Thin Vol to 7 cm	Vol to 18 cm	Vol to 24 cm	Thinnings No. of Trees	Mean Diam cm	Mean Vol. per Tree m³	Thin Vol to 7 cm	Vol to 18 cm	Vol to 24 cm	Total Yield Basal Area m²	Total Yield Vol to 7 cm m³	CAI Basal Area m²	CAI Vol to 7 cm m³	MAI Vol to 7 cm m³	Age
21	4326	8.1	8.5	24.7	0.39	0.01	61	0	0	0	0.0	0.00	0	0	0	24.7	61	2.52	12.1	2.9	21
26	2209	10.6	11.8	24.2	0.42	0.04	90	0	0	2117	8.7	0.02	42	0	0	36.6	132	2.25	15.4	5.1	26
31	1561	12.8	15.1	28.0	0.42	0.08	131	11	0	648	11.5	0.06	42	0	0	47.2	215	1.96	17.1	6.9	31
36	1179	14.9	18.3	30.8	0.44	0.15	177	45	3	383	14.4	0.11	42	2	0	56.2	303	1.70	17.6	8.4	36
41	932	16.7	21.3	33.1	0.45	0.24	223	107	20	247	17.2	0.17	42	8	0	64.2	391	1.52	17.5	9.5	41
46	766	18.4	24.2	35.1	0.46	0.35	267	175	58	166	19.9	0.25	42	14	2	71.4	477	1.36	17.1	10.4	46
51	650	20.0	26.9	36.9	0.46	0.48	310	228	101	116	22.6	0.36	42	23	5	77.9	562	1.23	16.4	11.0	51
56	558	21.4	29.5	38.2	0.46	0.62	348	287	171	92	25.3	0.46	42	29	11	83.7	642	1.11	15.5	11.5	56
61	489	22.6	32.0	39.2	0.47	0.78	381	329	224	69	27.8	0.61	42	32	16	89.0	717	1.02	14.5	11.8	61
66	440	23.8	34.3	40.6	0.46	0.94	414	374	289	50	30.2	0.75	38	32	20	93.9	787	0.95	13.6	11.9	66
71	404	24.8	36.4	42.1	0.46	1.11	447	413	338	36	32.5	0.92	33	29	21	98.4	853	0.88	12.9	12.0	71
76	375	25.7	38.5	43.6	0.46	1.28	479	448	383	29	34.7	1.06	31	28	22	102.7	916	0.80	11.7	12.1	76

1.8 x 1.8 m spacing

Age	|	M A I N	C R O P				After Thinning				Yield from	T H I N N I N G S					T O T A L	Y I E L D	I N C R E M E N T			Age
		No. of Trees	Top Ht. (m)	Mean Diam (cm)	Basal Area (m²)	Form Factor	Mean Vol. per Tree (m³)	\multicolumn{3}{c}{Volume in cubic metres to top diameters of-}			No. of Trees	Mean Diam (cm)	Mean Vol. per Tree (m³)	\multicolumn{3}{c}{Volume in cubic metres to top diameters of-}			Basal Area (m²)	Vol. to 7 cm (m³)	CAI Basal Area (m²)	CAI Vol. to 7 cm (m³)	MAI Vol. to 7 cm (m³)	
								7 cm	18 cm	24 cm				7 cm	18 cm	24 cm						

Age	No. of Trees	Top Ht.	Mean Diam	Basal Area	Form Factor	Mean Vol./Tree	Vol 7cm	Vol 18cm	Vol 24cm	No. of Trees	Mean Diam	Mean Vol./Tree	Vol 7cm	Vol 18cm	Vol 24cm	Total BA	Total Vol 7cm	CAI BA	CAI Vol 7cm	MAI Vol 7cm	Age
22	2718	8.5	10.3	22.4	0.42	0.02	66	0	0	0	0.0	0.00	0	0	0	22.4	66	2.35	12.0	3.0	22
27	1438	11.0	14.2	22.7	0.44	0.07	94	5	0	1281	10.5	0.03	42	0	0	33.7	136	2.14	15.2	5.0	27
32	1059	13.2	18.1	27.2	0.42	0.13	134	34	2	378	13.8	0.11	42	1	0	43.9	218	1.92	17.0	6.8	32
37	832	15.2	21.8	31.0	0.43	0.22	179	87	16	228	17.2	0.18	42	8	0	52.9	305	1.70	17.5	8.3	37
42	677	17.0	25.2	33.8	0.43	0.33	225	157	61	154	20.4	0.27	42	17	3	60.8	393	1.50	17.4	9.4	42
47	569	18.6	28.5	36.2	0.43	0.47	269	215	118	108	23.6	0.39	42	25	7	68.0	479	1.35	16.9	10.2	47
52	491	20.2	31.5	38.3	0.44	0.63	310	268	182	78	26.6	0.54	42	31	14	74.4	562	1.21	16.2	10.8	52
57	427	21.5	34.4	39.7	0.44	0.81	347	314	243	64	29.5	0.66	42	35	21	80.1	641	1.10	15.3	11.3	57
62	379	22.8	37.1	40.9	0.44	1.00	379	353	295	49	32.3	0.86	42	37	27	85.4	715	1.00	14.3	11.5	62
67	344	23.9	39.6	42.3	0.44	1.20	412	388	337	35	34.9	1.05	37	33	26	90.2	784	0.93	13.4	11.7	67
72	319	24.9	41.9	44.1	0.43	1.39	444	423	378	26	37.4	1.25	33	30	25	94.7	849	0.87	12.7	11.8	72
77	298	25.8	44.1	45.6	0.43	1.60	475	457	421	21	39.8	1.46	31	29	25	98.9	911	0.78	11.5	11.8	77

2.4 x 2.4 m spacing

Age	No. of Trees	Top Ht.	Mean Diam	Basal Area	Form Factor	Mean Vol./Tree	Vol 7cm	Vol 18cm	Vol 24cm	No. of Trees	Mean Diam	Mean Vol./Tree	Vol 7cm	Vol 18cm	Vol 24cm	Total BA	Total Vol 7cm	CAI BA	CAI Vol 7cm	MAI Vol 7cm	Age
26	1572	10.3	13.7	23.2	0.43	0.06	89	2	0	0	0.0	0.00	0	0	0	23.2	89	2.27	13.6	3.4	26
31	978	12.5	18.2	25.3	0.43	0.13	123	31	2	593	13.8	0.07	42	1	0	34.1	165	2.07	16.2	5.3	31
36	759	14.6	22.4	29.9	0.42	0.22	167	91	21	219	17.5	0.19	42	8	0	44.0	251	1.83	17.2	7.0	36
41	616	16.4	26.2	33.3	0.42	0.34	212	156	69	143	21.1	0.29	42	20	4	52.4	338	1.59	17.2	8.2	41
46	517	18.1	29.8	36.0	0.42	0.49	255	210	125	100	24.5	0.42	42	28	9	59.8	423	1.40	16.9	9.2	46
51	445	19.6	33.1	38.3	0.42	0.67	297	265	198	72	27.7	0.58	42	32	16	66.4	507	1.24	16.3	9.9	51
56	388	21.0	36.2	39.9	0.42	0.86	334	308	252	57	30.9	0.74	42	35	23	72.3	586	1.11	15.4	10.5	56
61	344	22.3	39.0	41.1	0.42	1.07	366	345	300	44	33.8	0.95	42	38	28	77.5	660	0.99	14.3	10.8	61
66	312	23.4	41.6	42.5	0.42	1.28	398	379	338	32	36.5	1.18	38	35	28	82.2	729	0.91	13.4	11.1	66
71	289	24.4	44.1	44.1	0.42	1.49	430	414	380	23	39.1	1.44	33	31	27	86.6	795	0.85	12.8	11.2	71
76	270	25.4	46.4	45.6	0.42	1.71	462	447	416	19	41.7	1.62	31	29	26	90.7	858	0.78	12.0	11.3	76
81	254	26.3	48.4	46.8	0.42	1.93	489	475	446	17	43.9	1.75	30	29	26	94.4	914	0.72	10.7	11.3	81

NORWAY SPRUCE YIELD CLASS 8 THINNED

0.9 x 0.9 m spacing

Age	MAIN CROP No. of Trees	Top Ht. (m)	Mean Diam (cm)	Basal Area (m²)	Form Factor	After Thinning Mean Vol. per Tree (m³)	Vol. 7 cm	Vol. 18 cm	Vol. 24 cm	Yield from THINNINGS No. of Trees	Mean Diam (cm)	Mean Vol. per Tree (m³)	Vol. 7 cm	Vol. 18 cm	Vol. 24 cm	TOTAL YIELD Basal Area (m²)	Vol. to 7 cm (m³)	INCREMENT CAI MAI Basal Area (m²)	Vol. to 7 cm (m³)	Vol. to 7 cm (m³)	Age
30	4488	9.6	9.0	28.6	0.35	0.02	74	0	0	2423	6.5	0.01	28	0	0	36.5	102	1.75	10.7	3.4	30
35	3165	11.3	11.0	29.9	0.37	0.03	102	0	0	1323	8.1	0.02	28	0	0	44.6	158	1.52	11.6	4.5	35
40	2391	12.8	12.9	31.1	0.40	0.06	134	1	0	774	9.8	0.04	28	0	0	51.7	218	1.34	12.1	5.4	40
45	1883	14.3	14.7	32.1	0.42	0.09	167	9	0	508	11.5	0.06	28	0	0	58.0	279	1.19	12.1	6.2	45
50	1533	15.6	16.6	33.0	0.44	0.13	199	26	0	350	13.2	0.08	28	1	0	63.7	339	1.08	11.8	6.8	50
55	1285	16.8	18.3	33.9	0.46	0.18	229	58	4	248	14.8	0.11	28	2	0	68.8	397	0.98	11.4	7.2	55
60	1102	17.9	20.0	34.7	0.47	0.23	257	105	15	183	16.4	0.15	28	4	0	73.4	453	0.88	10.9	7.6	60
65	982	18.9	21.5	35.8	0.48	0.29	287	139	26	120	17.9	0.19	23	4	0	77.6	506	0.79	10.3	7.8	65
70	893	19.9	23.0	37.0	0.48	0.35	317	173	40	89	19.3	0.23	21	7	1	81.4	557	0.73	9.8	8.0	70
75	826	20.7	24.3	38.3	0.48	0.42	345	226	75	67	20.6	0.30	20	8	1	84.9	604	0.69	9.2	8.1	75
80	758	21.5	25.6	39.0	0.49	0.49	370	259	100	68	21.9	0.29	20	10	2	88.2	649	0.64	8.6	8.1	80

1.4 x 1.4 m spacing

Age	MAIN CROP No. of Trees	Top Ht. (m)	Mean Diam (cm)	Basal Area (m²)	Form Factor	After Thinning Mean Vol. per Tree (m³)	Vol. 7 cm	Vol. 18 cm	Vol. 24 cm	Yield from THINNINGS No. of Trees	Mean Diam (cm)	Mean Vol. per Tree (m³)	Vol. 7 cm	Vol. 18 cm	Vol. 24 cm	TOTAL YIELD Basal Area (m²)	Vol. to 7 cm (m³)	INCREMENT CAI MAI Basal Area (m²)	Vol. to 7 cm (m³)	Vol. to 7 cm (m³)	Age
26	4349	8.0	8.4	24.3	0.39	0.01	59	0	0	0	0.0	0.00	0	0	0	24.3	59	1.87	9.0	2.3	26
31	2738	9.9	10.9	25.5	0.39	0.03	81	0	0	1611	7.8	0.02	28	0	0	33.3	109	1.71	10.6	3.5	31
36	2065	11.5	13.2	28.4	0.39	0.05	110	3	0	673	9.9	0.04	28	0	0	41.4	166	1.52	11.7	4.6	36
41	1632	13.1	15.5	30.8	0.41	0.09	142	12	0	433	11.8	0.06	28	0	0	48.5	226	1.33	12.1	5.5	41
46	1328	14.5	17.6	32.4	0.42	0.13	174	32	0	304	13.8	0.09	28	1	0	54.7	286	1.18	12.1	6.2	46
51	1109	15.8	19.7	33.8	0.43	0.19	206	68	7	219	15.7	0.13	28	3	0	60.2	346	1.06	11.7	6.8	51
56	948	17.0	21.7	34.9	0.44	0.25	236	114	21	161	17.5	0.17	28	5	0	65.3	404	0.96	11.3	7.2	56
61	825	18.1	23.5	35.9	0.45	0.32	263	159	44	123	19.3	0.23	28	9	1	69.9	459	0.87	10.8	7.5	61
66	745	19.1	25.2	37.2	0.45	0.39	293	205	79	81	21.0	0.28	23	9	1	74.0	512	0.78	10.2	7.8	66
71	684	20.0	26.8	38.5	0.46	0.47	322	237	105	61	22.5	0.34	21	11	3	77.7	561	0.72	9.6	7.9	71
76	638	20.8	28.2	39.9	0.46	0.55	349	279	153	47	24.0	0.42	20	12	3	81.2	608	0.68	9.1	8.0	76
81	590	21.5	29.7	40.7	0.46	0.63	374	308	184	48	25.4	0.41	20	14	5	84.5	652	0.63	8.4	8.1	81

1.8 x 1.8m spacing

Columns grouped as: **MAIN CROP After Thinning** (Age → Vol to 24 cm) · **Yield from THINNINGS** (No. of Trees → Vol to 24 cm) · **TOTAL YIELD** (Basal Area, Vol to 7 cm) · **INCREMENT CAI** (Basal Area, Vol to 7 cm) · **MAI** (Vol to 7 cm) · Age

Age	No. of Trees	Top Ht. (m)	Mean Diam (cm)	Basal Area (m²)	Form Factor	Mean Vol. per Tree (m³)	Vol to 7 cm (m³)	Vol to 18 cm (m³)	Vol to 24 cm (m³)	No. of Trees	Mean Diam (cm)	Mean Vol. per Tree (m³)	Vol to 7 cm (m³)	Vol to 18 cm (m³)	Vol to 24 cm (m³)	Total Basal Area (m²)	Total Vol to 7 cm (m³)	CAI Basal Area (m²)	CAI Vol to 7 cm (m³)	MAI Vol to 7 cm (m³)	Age
27	2735	8.3	10.0	21.5	0.42	0.02	61	0	0	.	0.0	0.00	0	0	0	21.5	61	1.73	8.6	2.3	27
32	1784	10.1	12.9	23.4	0.41	0.05	81	0	0	951	9.4	0.03	28	0	0	29.9	109	1.62	10.3	3.4	32
37	1394	11.7	15.7	26.9	0.40	0.08	109	9	0	390	11.7	0.07	28	0	0	37.6	165	1.49	11.5	4.4	37
42	1143	13.3	18.3	30.1	0.40	0.12	141	35	2	250	14.1	0.11	28	2	0	44.8	225	1.34	12.0	5.3	42
47	958	14.7	20.8	32.6	0.40	0.18	173	71	10	186	16.3	0.15	28	4	0	51.1	285	1.18	11.9	6.1	47
52	818	16.0	23.1	34.3	0.41	0.25	204	123	34	140	18.5	0.20	28	7	1	56.6	344	1.06	11.6	6.6	52
57	712	17.1	25.3	35.9	0.42	0.33	233	163	63	107	20.6	0.26	28	12	2	61.7	401	0.96	11.1	7.0	57
62	628	18.2	27.4	37.0	0.42	0.41	259	200	100	84	22.5	0.33	28	15	4	66.2	455	0.86	10.7	7.3	62
67	574	19.2	29.3	38.6	0.43	0.50	289	238	142	54	24.4	0.41	22	15	5	70.3	507	0.77	10.0	7.6	67
72	533	20.1	30.9	40.0	0.43	0.59	317	267	172	41	26.1	0.50	21	15	7	73.9	556	0.71	9.4	7.7	72
77	501	20.8	32.5	41.6	0.43	0.69	343	302	216	32	27.7	0.62	20	15	8	77.4	602	0.65	8.8	7.8	77
82	465	21.6	34.0	42.2	0.43	0.79	366	331	256	35	29.2	0.56	20	16	10	80.4	644	0.59	8.2	7.9	82

2.4 x 2.4m spacing

Age	No. of Trees	Top Ht. (m)	Mean Diam (cm)	Basal Area (m²)	Form Factor	Mean Vol. per Tree (m³)	Vol to 7 cm (m³)	Vol to 18 cm (m³)	Vol to 24 cm (m³)	No. of Trees	Mean Diam (cm)	Mean Vol. per Tree (m³)	Vol to 7 cm (m³)	Vol to 18 cm (m³)	Vol to 24 cm (m³)	Total Basal Area (m²)	Total Vol to 7 cm (m³)	CAI Basal Area (m²)	CAI Vol to 7 cm (m³)	MAI Vol to 7 cm (m³)	Age
34	1564	10.5	14.2	24.7	0.43	0.06	98	5	0		0.0	0.00	0	0	0	24.7	98	1.62	9.7	2.9	34
39	1121	12.1	17.4	26.5	0.43	0.11	124	23	0	443	13.1	0.06	28	1	0	32.5	152	1.51	11.4	3.9	39
44	925	13.6	20.3	30.1	0.42	0.17	156	64	9	196	15.7	0.14	28	3	0	39.8	212	1.36	11.5	4.8	44
49	782	15.0	23.0	32.6	0.42	0.24	187	112	31	143	18.2	0.20	28	7	1	46.0	271	1.18	11.7	5.5	49
54	675	16.2	25.6	34.6	0.42	0.32	216	151	58	107	20.5	0.26	28	12	2	51.6	328	1.05	11.3	6.1	54
59	593	17.3	27.9	36.2	0.42	0.41	244	188	94	82	22.7	0.34	28	15	4	56.5	384	0.93	10.9	6.5	59
64	527	18.4	30.1	37.4	0.42	0.51	269	227	145	66	24.8	0.42	28	18	6	60.9	437	0.83	10.3	6.8	64
69	487	19.3	32.0	39.1	0.42	0.61	297	256	175	41	26.7	0.52	21	16	7	64.8	487	0.75	9.8	7.1	69
74	455	20.2	33.7	40.6	0.42	0.71	325	290	217	32	28.5	0.63	20	16	9	68.4	534	0.68	9.1	7.2	74
79	429	20.9	35.3	42.0	0.42	0.81	349	319	254	26	30.1	0.76	20	17	11	71.6	578	0.60	8.5	7.3	79

JAPANESE LARCH   YIELD CLASS 10   THINNED

1.2 x 1.2 m spacing

	MAIN CROP — After Thinning									Yield from THINNINGS						TOTAL YIELD		INCREMENT			
							Volume in cubic metres to top diameters of-						Volume in cubic metres to top diameters of-						CAI	MAI	
Age	No. of Trees	Top Ht. (m)	Mean Diam (cm)	Basal Area (m²)	Form Factor	Mean Vol. per Tree (m³)	7 cm	18 cm	24 cm	No. of Trees	Mean Diam (cm)	Mean Vol. per Tree (m³)	7 cm	18 cm	24 cm	Basal Area (m²)	Vol. to 7 cm (m³)	Basal Area (m²)	Vol. to 7 cm (m³)	Vol. to 7 cm (m³)	Age
12	4967	7.3	7.3	20.8	0.30	0.01	40	0	0	0	0.0	0.00	0	0	0	20.8	40	1.96	9.3	3.3	12
17	2468	10.2	9.6	17.7	0.38	0.03	63	0	0	2498	8.0	0.01	35	0	0	30.3	98	1.80	12.7	5.7	17
22	1481	12.8	12.2	17.3	0.47	0.07	97	0	0	988	10.7	0.04	35	0	0	38.8	167	1.55	14.1	7.6	22
27	1054	15.1	14.9	18.4	0.51	0.13	133	7	0	427	13.4	0.08	35	1	0	45.8	238	1.28	13.9	8.8	27
32	809	17.1	17.4	19.3	0.53	0.20	166	30	0	245	16.0	0.14	35	3	0	51.6	306	1.05	12.9	9.6	32
37	649	18.7	19.7	19.8	0.54	0.30	192	64	7	160	18.3	0.22	35	9	1	56.4	367	0.88	11.6	9.9	37
42	545	20.2	21.8	20.4	0.55	0.40	216	104	20	104	20.5	0.30	32	13	2	60.4	422	0.75	10.4	10.1	42
47	475	21.4	23.8	21.1	0.55	0.50	237	143	40	70	22.5	0.40	28	15	4	63.9	472	0.66	9.4	10.0	47
52	424	22.5	25.6	21.8	0.55	0.61	257	180	69	51	24.4	0.49	25	16	5	67.0	516	0.58	8.6	9.9	52
57	384	23.4	27.3	22.5	0.54	0.72	275	212	106	40	26.1	0.58	23	17	8	69.8	558	0.52	7.9	9.8	57
62	351	24.3	28.9	22.9	0.54	0.83	292	233	128	32	27.7	0.68	22	17	8	72.2	596	0.47	7.4	9.6	62

86

1.8 x 1.8 m spacing

	MAIN CROP After Thinning									Yield from THINNINGS						TOTAL YIELD		INCREMENT CAI MAI			
							Volume in cubic metres to top diameters of-						Volume in cubic metres to top diameters of-						CAI	MAI	
Age	No. of Trees	Top Ht. m	Mean Diam cm	Basal Area m²	Form Factor	Mean Vol. per Tree m³	7 cm	18 cm	24 cm	No. of Trees	Mean Diam cm	Mean Vol. per Tree m³	7 cm	18 cm	24 cm	Basal Area m²	Vol. to 7 cm m³	Basal Area m²	Vol. to 7 cm m³	Vol. to 7 cm m³	Age
12	2700	7.3	9.1	17.4	0.35	0.01	39	0	0	0	0.0	0.00	0	0	0	17.4	39	1.94	9.1	3.2	12
17	1302	10.2	12.2	15.3	0.42	0.05	60	0	0	1398	10.2	0.03	35	0	0	26.8	95	1.78	12.5	5.6	17
22	862	12.8	15.8	17.0	0.46	0.11	93	8	0	440	13.8	0.08	35	1	0	35.1	163	1.54	14.0	7.4	22
27	650	15.1	19.3	19.0	0.48	0.20	129	43	4	213	17.3	0.16	35	7	0	42.1	234	1.27	13.9	8.7	27
32	517	17.0	22.4	20.3	0.49	0.31	162	88	20	132	20.5	0.27	35	14	2	47.8	302	1.04	12.9	9.4	32
37	426	18.7	25.1	21.1	0.50	0.44	188	132	51	92	23.3	0.38	35	21	6	52.5	363	0.86	11.6	9.8	37
42	364	20.1	27.6	21.8	0.50	0.58	211	163	81	61	25.9	0.52	32	22	9	56.4	418	0.73	10.4	10.0	42
47	322	21.4	29.8	22.5	0.50	0.72	233	192	114	42	28.2	0.66	28	22	12	59.8	467	0.64	9.4	9.9	47
52	291	22.4	31.9	23.3	0.50	0.87	253	218	149	31	30.4	0.80	25	21	13	62.8	512	0.58	8.6	9.8	52
57	267	23.4	33.8	24.0	0.50	1.02	271	242	181	25	32.4	0.92	23	20	15	65.5	553	0.51	7.9	9.7	57
62	246	24.3	35.6	24.5	0.50	1.17	288	263	209	20	34.2	1.08	22	20	15	67.8	591	0.45	7.4	9.5	62

2.4 x 2.4 m spacing

	MAIN CROP After Thinning									Yield from THINNINGS						TOTAL YIELD		INCREMENT CAI MAI			
							Volume in cubic metres to top diameters of-						Volume in cubic metres to top diameters of-						CAI	MAI	
Age	No. of Trees	Top Ht. m	Mean Diam cm	Basal Area m²	Form Factor	Mean Vol. per Tree m³	7 cm	18 cm	24 cm	No. of Trees	Mean Diam cm	Mean Vol. per Tree m³	7 cm	18 cm	24 cm	Basal Area m²	Vol. to 7 cm m³	Basal Area m²	Vol. to 7 cm m³	Vol. to 7 cm m³	Age
14	1516	8.3	12.0	17.1	0.40	0.03	51	0	0	0	0.0	0.00	0	0	0	17.1	51	1.79	10.0	3.6	14
19	912	11.1	15.6	17.5	0.41	0.08	75	6	0	605	13.3	0.06	35	1	0	25.9	110	1.66	12.8	5.8	19
24	652	13.6	19.4	19.3	0.44	0.17	109	36	4	260	17.2	0.13	35	7	0	33.8	179	1.45	13.9	7.5	24
29	511	15.8	22.9	21.1	0.46	0.28	144	78	18	141	20.8	0.25	35	14	2	40.3	249	1.18	13.5	8.6	29
34	417	17.6	26.0	22.2	0.47	0.42	174	128	57	94	23.9	0.37	35	21	6	45.6	314	0.96	12.3	9.2	34
39	349	19.2	28.8	22.7	0.47	0.56	197	157	86	68	26.8	0.51	35	26	12	49.9	372	0.80	11.1	9.5	39
44	305	20.5	31.2	23.3	0.48	0.72	220	189	129	44	29.4	0.68	30	25	15	53.6	424	0.68	10.0	9.6	44
49	274	21.7	33.4	24.1	0.48	0.88	241	215	160	31	31.7	0.85	26	23	15	56.7	472	0.61	9.0	9.6	49
54	251	22.7	35.5	24.8	0.48	1.03	260	237	189	24	33.8	1.00	24	22	16	59.6	515	0.53	8.3	9.5	54
59	231	23.6	37.3	25.3	0.48	1.20	277	258	216	19	35.8	1.18	22	21	16	62.0	555	0.47	7.7	9.4	59
64	215	24.5	39.1	25.8	0.48	1.36	293	276	239	16	37.6	1.33	21	20	17	64.3	591	0.43	7.1	9.2	64

JAPANESE LARCH   YIELD CLASS 8   THINNED

1.2 x 1.2m spacing

Age	MAIN CROP After Thinning No. of Trees	Top Ht. (m)	Mean Diam (cm)	Basal Area (m²)	Form Factor	Mean Vol. per Tree (m³)	Vol. 7 cm	Vol. 18 cm	Vol. 24 cm	Yield from THINNINGS No. of Trees	Mean Diam (cm)	Mean Vol. per Tree (m³)	Vol. 7 cm	Vol. 18 cm	Vol. 24 cm	TOTAL YIELD Basal Area (m²)	Vol. to 7 cm (m³)	INCREMENT CAI Basal Area (m²)	CAI Vol. to 7 cm (m³)	MAI Vol. to 7 cm (m³)	Age
14	4992	7.2	7.2	20.6	0.23	0.01	39	0	0	0	0.0	0.00	0	0	0	20.6	39	1.69	7.8	2.8	14
19	2888	9.7	9.2	19.2	0.29	0.02	59	0	0	2104	7.6	0.01	28	0	0	28.8	87	1.58	10.6	4.6	19
24	1763	12.0	11.4	18.1	0.38	0.05	89	0	0	1125	9.9	0.02	28	0	0	36.3	145	1.39	11.7	6.1	24
29	1280	14.0	13.7	18.8	0.43	0.09	121	3	0	484	12.2	0.06	28	0	0	42.7	205	1.15	11.5	7.1	29
34	999	15.7	15.8	19.5	0.46	0.15	148	13	0	281	14.3	0.10	28	2	0	47.8	260	0.93	10.5	7.7	34
39	812	17.2	17.6	19.8	0.48	0.21	170	31	0	187	16.2	0.15	28	4	0	52.0	310	0.76	9.4	8.0	39
44	678	18.4	19.3	19.9	0.49	0.27	186	62	6	134	17.9	0.21	28	5	0	55.4	354	0.64	8.4	8.0	44
49	598	19.4	20.9	20.4	0.49	0.34	204	84	12	81	19.5	0.27	22	7	1	58.4	394	0.56	7.6	8.0	49
54	539	20.4	22.3	21.0	0.50	0.41	222	121	28	59	20.9	0.32	19	8	1	61.0	430	0.50	6.9	8.0	54
59	493	21.2	23.6	21.5	0.50	0.48	238	143	40	46	22.3	0.37	17	9	2	63.3	463	0.43	6.3	7.9	59
64	456	21.9	24.8	21.9	0.50	0.55	251	165	55	37	23.5	0.44	16	10	3	65.3	493	0.38	5.7	7.7	64

1.8 x 1.8m spacing

Age	MAIN CROP After Thinning: No. of Trees	Top Ht. (m)	Mean Diam (cm)	Basal Area (m²)	Form Factor	Mean Vol. per Tree (m³)	Vol. to 7 cm (m³)	Vol. to 18 cm (m³)	Vol. to 24 cm (m³)	Yield from THINNINGS: No. of Trees	Mean Diam (cm)	Mean Vol. per Tree (m³)	Vol. to 7 cm (m³)	Vol. to 18 cm (m³)	Vol. to 24 cm (m³)	TOTAL YIELD: Basal Area (m²)	Vol. to 7 cm (m³)	INCREMENT CAI: Basal Area (m²)	CAI Vol. to 7 cm (m³)	MAI Vol. to 7 cm (m³)	Age
14	2707	7.1	9.0	17.1	0.34	0.01	37	0	0	0	0.0	0.00	0	0	0	17.1	37	1.67	7.6	2.7	14
19	1443	9.7	11.8	15.8	0.40	0.04	57	0	0	1264	9.8	0.02	28	0	0	25.3	85	1.56	10.4	4.4	19
24	984	12.0	14.9	17.2	0.45	0.09	86	4	0	458	12.9	0.06	28	0	0	32.7	142	1.37	11.6	5.9	24
29	758	14.0	17.9	19.0	0.47	0.15	117	21	0	226	15.9	0.12	28	3	0	39.0	201	1.14	11.5	6.9	29
34	615	15.7	20.5	20.3	0.48	0.23	144	59	8	143	18.5	0.20	28	7	1	44.1	256	0.92	10.5	7.5	34
39	513	17.1	22.7	20.8	0.49	0.32	166	91	21	102	20.9	0.27	28	12	2	48.1	306	0.74	9.4	7.8	39
44	437	18.4	24.8	21.4	0.49	0.42	182	119	39	76	22.9	0.37	28	15	4	51.5	350	0.62	8.4	8.0	44
49	391	19.4	26.6	21.7	0.50	0.51	200	147	65	46	24.8	0.47	22	14	5	54.4	390	0.54	7.6	8.0	49
54	357	20.3	28.3	22.4	0.50	0.61	218	174	95	34	26.5	0.56	19	14	6	56.9	426	0.49	6.9	7.9	54
59	331	21.2	29.8	23.0	0.50	0.71	233	192	115	27	28.1	0.64	17	14	8	59.3	459	0.42	6.3	7.8	59
64	308	21.9	31.1	23.4	0.50	0.80	247	213	145	22	29.5	0.74	16	13	8	61.1	489	0.36	5.7	7.6	64

2.4 x 2.4m spacing

Age	MAIN CROP After Thinning: No. of Trees	Top Ht. (m)	Mean Diam (cm)	Basal Area (m²)	Form Factor	Mean Vol. per Tree (m³)	Vol. to 7 cm (m³)	Vol. to 18 cm (m³)	Vol. to 24 cm (m³)	Yield from THINNINGS: No. of Trees	Mean Diam (cm)	Mean Vol. per Tree (m³)	Vol. to 7 cm (m³)	Vol. to 18 cm (m³)	Vol. to 24 cm (m³)	TOTAL YIELD: Basal Area (m²)	Vol. to 7 cm (m³)	INCREMENT CAI: Basal Area (m²)	CAI Vol. to 7 cm (m³)	MAI Vol. to 7 cm (m³)	Age
16	1519	8.1	11.7	16.4	0.39	0.03	47	0	0	0	0.0	0.00	0	0	0	16.4	47	1.55	8.3	2.9	16
21	979	10.6	15.0	17.3	0.40	0.07	68	3	0	539	12.6	0.05	28	0	0	24.0	96	1.45	10.6	4.6	21
26	719	12.7	18.3	19.0	0.43	0.13	97	24	1	260	16.0	0.11	28	4	0	30.9	153	1.29	11.5	5.9	26
31	577	14.6	21.4	20.8	0.44	0.22	127	61	11	142	19.2	0.20	28	9	1	36.9	211	1.07	11.1	6.8	31
36	480	16.2	24.1	21.9	0.45	0.32	152	99	33	97	21.9	0.29	28	14	3	41.6	264	0.85	10.0	7.3	36
41	408	17.5	26.4	22.3	0.46	0.42	171	126	56	72	24.3	0.39	28	18	6	45.4	311	0.69	8.9	7.6	41
46	361	18.7	28.4	22.9	0.46	0.52	189	151	83	47	26.4	0.50	24	17	8	48.5	353	0.59	8.0	7.7	46
51	328	19.7	30.2	23.5	0.47	0.63	207	174	112	33	28.3	0.62	20	16	9	51.2	391	0.51	7.3	7.7	51
56	303	20.6	31.9	24.2	0.47	0.74	224	193	131	25	30.0	0.73	18	15	9	53.7	426	0.44	6.7	7.6	56
61	282	21.4	33.4	24.6	0.47	0.85	239	213	159	20	31.5	0.83	17	14	10	55.7	457	0.39	6.0	7.5	61
66	265	22.1	34.7	25.0	0.47	0.95	251	227	176	18	32.9	0.88	16	14	10	57.6	486	0.35	5.4	7.4	66

JAPANESE LARCH YIELD CLASS 6 THINNED

1.2 x 1.2 m spacing

	MAIN CROP					After Thinning				Yield from THINNINGS						TOTAL YIELD		INCREMENT			
							Volume in cubic metres to top diameters of–						Volume in cubic metres to top diameters of–					CAI		MAI	
Age	No. of Trees	Top Ht. (m)	Mean Diam (cm)	Basal Area (m²)	Form Factor	Mean Vol. per Tree (m³)	7 cm	18 cm	24 cm	No. of Trees	Mean Diam (cm)	Mean Vol. per Tree (m³)	7 cm	18 cm	24 cm	Basal Area (m²)	Vol. to 7 cm (m³)	Basal Area (m²)	Vol. to 7 cm (m³)	Vol. to 7 cm (m³)	Age
17	4992	7.2	7.2	20.1	0.30	0.01	38	0	0	0	0.0	0.00	0	0	0	20.1	38	1.50	6.7	2.2	17
22	3466	9.3	8.8	21.1	0.32	0.02	57	0	0	1526	7.2	0.01	21	0	0	27.4	78	1.38	8.7	3.6	22
27	2188	11.3	10.6	19.4	0.41	0.04	83	0	0	1279	9.1	0.02	21	0	0	33.9	125	1.20	9.3	4.6	27
32	1624	12.9	12.4	19.6	0.46	0.07	108	0	0	564	10.8	0.04	21	0	0	39.3	171	0.97	8.9	5.3	32
37	1289	14.3	14.0	19.8	0.49	0.10	130	4	0	334	12.5	0.06	21	0	0	43.6	214	0.76	8.0	5.8	37
42	1063	15.5	15.4	19.7	0.51	0.14	146	13	0	226	13.9	0.09	21	1	0	46.9	251	0.61	7.0	6.0	42
47	916	16.5	16.6	19.8	0.52	0.18	161	21	0	148	15.1	0.12	18	2	0	49.7	284	0.53	6.3	6.0	47
52	820	17.3	17.8	20.3	0.53	0.21	176	32	0	96	16.3	0.16	15	2	0	52.2	314	0.47	5.8	6.0	52
57	751	18.1	18.8	20.9	0.53	0.25	191	48	3	68	17.4	0.19	13	2	0	54.4	342	0.41	5.3	6.0	57
62	697	18.7	19.8	21.4	0.54	0.29	204	68	7	54	18.4	0.21	12	3	0	56.3	367	0.35	4.6	5.9	62
67	652	19.3	20.6	21.6	0.54	0.33	215	88	13	45	19.2	0.24	11	4	0	57.9	388	0.30	4.1	5.8	67

90

1.8 × 1.8m spacing

	MAIN CROP After Thinning						Volume in cubic metres to top of diameters of-			Yield from THINNINGS			Volume in cubic metres to top of diameters of-			TOTAL YIELD		INCREMENT CAI MAI			
Age	No. of Trees	Top Ht. (m)	Mean Diam (cm)	Basal Area (m²)	Form Factor	Mean Vol. per Tree (m³)	7 cm	18 cm	24 cm	No. of Trees	Mean Diam (cm)	Mean Vol. per Tree (m³)	7 cm	18 cm	24 cm	Basal Area (m²)	Vol. to 7 cm (m³)	Basal Area (m²)	Vol. to 7 cm (m³)	Vol. to 7 cm (m³)	Age
17	2707	7.1	8.9	16.7	0.35	0.01	36	0	0	0	0.0	0.00	0	0	0	16.7	36	1.48	6.5	2.1	17
22	1627	9.3	11.4	16.5	0.39	0.03	55	0	0	1080	9.3	0.02	21	0	0	23.9	76	1.36	8.5	3.4	22
27	1161	11.2	13.9	17.7	0.43	0.07	79	2	0	466	11.9	0.05	21	0	0	30.3	121	1.18	9.2	4.5	27
32	918	12.9	16.3	19.2	0.45	0.11	105	14	0	243	14.3	0.09	21	1	0	35.7	168	0.96	8.8	5.2	32
37	758	14.3	18.4	20.1	0.47	0.17	126	32	2	159	16.4	0.13	21	3	0	39.9	210	0.75	8.0	5.7	37
42	642	15.4	20.1	20.4	0.48	0.22	142	58	8	116	18.1	0.18	21	5	0	43.2	247	0.60	7.0	5.9	42
47	564	16.4	21.6	20.7	0.49	0.28	157	75	14	78	19.7	0.24	18	6	1	45.9	280	0.51	6.3	6.0	47
52	513	17.3	23.0	21.4	0.49	0.33	172	103	29	51	21.1	0.29	15	7	1	48.3	310	0.46	5.8	6.0	52
57	477	18.0	24.3	22.1	0.49	0.39	187	122	40	37	22.4	0.35	13	7	2	50.6	338	0.41	5.3	5.9	57
62	448	18.7	25.4	22.7	0.49	0.45	200	140	54	29	23.6	0.40	12	7	2	52.4	363	0.34	4.6	5.9	62
67	422	19.3	26.4	23.0	0.50	0.50	211	155	69	26	24.6	0.42	11	7	2	54.0	384	0.29	4.1	5.7	67

2.4 × 2.4m spacing

	MAIN CROP After Thinning						Volume in cubic metres to top of diameters of-			Yield from THINNINGS			Volume in cubic metres to top of diameters of-			TOTAL YIELD		INCREMENT CAI MAI			
Age	No. of Trees	Top Ht. (m)	Mean Diam (cm)	Basal Area (m²)	Form Factor	Mean Vol. per Tree (m³)	7 cm	18 cm	24 cm	No. of Trees	Mean Diam (cm)	Mean Vol. per Tree (m³)	7 cm	18 cm	24 cm	Basal Area (m²)	Vol. to 7 cm (m³)	Basal Area (m²)	Vol. to 7 cm (m³)	Vol. to 7 cm (m³)	Age
20	1516	8.4	12.0	17.1	0.40	0.03	51	0	0	0	0.0	0.00	0	0	0	17.1	51	1.33	7.3	2.6	20
25	1088	10.4	14.7	18.4	0.40	0.07	71	4	0	428	12.3	0.05	21	0	0	23.5	92	1.21	8.6	3.7	25
30	837	12.1	17.3	19.7	0.43	0.11	95	17	0	251	15.0	0.08	21	1	0	29.2	137	1.05	8.9	4.6	30
35	688	13.6	19.7	20.9	0.44	0.17	118	39	4	149	17.4	0.14	21	4	0	34.0	181	0.85	8.3	5.2	35
40	583	14.9	21.7	21.5	0.45	0.23	136	65	12	106	19.5	0.20	21	7	1	37.7	220	0.67	7.3	5.5	40
45	507	15.9	23.4	21.8	0.45	0.30	150	90	25	76	21.2	0.26	20	10	2	40.7	254	0.55	6.5	5.6	45
50	458	16.9	24.9	22.3	0.46	0.36	165	108	36	49	22.8	0.33	16	9	2	43.2	285	0.48	5.9	5.7	50
55	425	17.6	26.3	23.1	0.46	0.42	180	133	59	33	24.2	0.41	13	9	3	45.5	313	0.43	5.5	5.7	55
60	399	18.3	27.6	23.8	0.47	0.49	194	150	74	26	25.5	0.45	12	8	3	47.5	339	0.37	4.9	5.7	60
65	377	19.0	28.6	24.2	0.47	0.55	206	165	90	22	26.6	0.50	11	8	4	49.2	362	0.31	4.3	5.6	65
70	358	19.5	29.5	24.5	0.47	0.60	216	177	106	20	27.6	0.53	11	8	4	50.7	382	0.27	3.8	5.5	70

Printed in England for Her Majesty's Stationery Office by Swindon Press Ltd., Swindon, Wilts.

Dd. 505268 K26 7/74.